# Deleuze and Law

## Deleuze Connections

'It is not the elements or the sets which define the multiplicity. What defines it is the AND, as something which has its place between the elements or between the sets. AND, AND, AND – stammering.'

Gilles Deleuze and Claire Parnet, *Dialogues*

**General Editor**
Ian Buchanan

**Editorial Advisory Board**

Keith Ansell-Pearson
Rosi Braidotti
Claire Colebrook
Tom Conley

Gregg Lambert
Adrian Parr
Paul Patton
Patricia Pisters

**Titles Available in the Series**
Ian Buchanan and Claire Colebrook (eds), *Deleuze and Feminist Theory*
Ian Buchanan and John Marks (eds), *Deleuze and Literature*
Mark Bonta and John Protevi (eds), *Deleuze and Geophilosophy*
Ian Buchanan and Marcel Swiboda (eds), *Deleuze and Music*
Ian Buchanan and Gregg Lambert (eds), *Deleuze and Space*
Martin Fuglsang and Bent Meier Sørensen (eds), *Deleuze and the Social*
Ian Buchanan and Adrian Parr (eds), *Deleuze and the Contemporary World*
Constantin V. Boundas (ed.), *Deleuze and Philosophy*
Ian Buchanan and Nicholas Thoburn (eds), *Deleuze and Politics*
Chrysanthi Nigianni and Merl Storr (eds), *Deleuze and Queer Theory*
Jeffrey A. Bell and Claire Colebrook (eds), *Deleuze and History*
Laura Cull (ed.), *Deleuze and Performance*
Mark Poster and David Savat (eds), *Deleuze and New Technology*
Simone Bignall and Paul Patton (eds), *Deleuze and the Postcolonial*
Stephen Zepke and Simon O'Sullivan (eds), *Deleuze and Contemporary Art*
Laura Guillaume and Joe Hughes (eds), *Deleuze and the Body*
Daniel W. Smith and Nathan Jun (eds), *Deleuze and Ethics*
Frida Beckman (ed.), *Deleuze and Sex*
David Martin-Jones and William Brown (eds), *Deleuze and Film*
Laurent de Sutter and Kyle McGee (eds), *Deleuze and Law*

**Forthcoming Titles in the Series**
Rebecca Coleman and Jessica Ringrose (eds), *Deleuze and Research Methodologies*
Inna Semetsky and Diana Masny (eds), *Deleuze and Education*

Visit the Deleuze Connections website at
www.euppublishing.com/series/delco

# Deleuze and Law

Edited by Laurent de Sutter
and Kyle McGee

EDINBURGH
University Press

© editorial matter and organisation Laurent de Sutter and Kyle McGee, 2012
© the chapters their several authors

Edinburgh University Press Ltd
22 George Square, Edinburgh EH8 9LF

www.euppublishing.com

Typeset in 10.5/13 Adobe Sabon
by Servis Filmsetting Ltd, Stockport, Cheshire,
and printed and bound in Great Britain by
CPI Group (UK) Ltd, Croydon CR0 4YY

A CIP record for this book is available from the British Library

ISBN 978 0 7486 4414 8 (hardback)
ISBN 978 0 7486 4413 1 (paperback)
ISBN 978 0 7486 6454 2 (webready PDF)
ISBN 978 0 7486 5539 7 (epub)
ISBN 978 0 7486 5538 0 (Amazon ebook)

The right of the contributors
to be identified as author of this work
has been asserted in accordance with
the Copyright, Designs and Patents Act 1988.

# Contents

|    | Introduction<br>Laurent de Sutter and Kyle McGee | 1 |
|----|---|---|
| 1  | Immanence, Transcendence, and the Creation of Rights<br>Paul Patton | 15 |
| 2  | The Poetry of Black Letters: Deleuze and *lex amicitia*<br>Peter Goodrich | 32 |
| 3  | Human Rights in Deleuze and Bergson's Later Philosophy<br>Alexandre Lefebvre | 48 |
| 4  | On 'Cruelty': Law, Literature, and Difference<br>Penelope Pether | 69 |
| 5  | Law, Space, Bodies: The Emergence of Spatial Justice<br>Andreas Philippopoulos-Mihalopoulos | 90 |
| 6  | Institutions and Interactions: On the Problem of the Molecular and Molar<br>Marc Schuilenburg | 111 |
| 7  | The Perception of the Middle<br>Nathan Moore | 132 |
| 8  | Rhizomatics, the Becoming of Law, and Legal Institutions<br>James MacLean | 151 |
| 9  | Deleuze and Camus: Strange Encounters<br>Lissa Lincoln | 169 |
| 10 | Cases Against Transcendence: Gilles Deleuze and Bruno Latour in Defence of Law<br>David Saunders | 185 |

Postscript: A Brief Reflection on the Universality of
Jurisprudence 204
    Laurent de Sutter and Kyle McGee

Notes on Contributors 213
Index 216

# Introduction

*Laurent de Sutter and Kyle McGee*

During his long conversation with Claire Parnet, filmed by the late Pierre-André Boutang and published after his death, Gilles Deleuze made a strange revelation: 'If I hadn't become a philosopher', he said, 'I would have studied law' (Deleuze 1994a: '*G comme Gauche*'). Before intellectual biographer François Dosse summoned it to discuss Deleuze's academic history and to describe his course of study (Dosse 2007: 141), this declaration provoked hardly a comment in the Francophone world,[1] as though it was not surprising in the least that Deleuze, inventor of the rhizome, philosopher of pure immanence, and sometime revolutionary, had dreamt of studying law, that arboreal science of reactionary transcendence. This utterance sits uneasily with Deleuze's well-known antipathy towards the representational economy of generality and particularity as well as the logic of profit and loss that forms the heart of modern instrumentalist legality. More, the image of a philosopher hostile towards the very idea of judgment – Deleuze's ethics, as we know, constitutes a war machine bent on undermining the diabolical apparatus of judgment and the logic of infinite debt – does not dovetail neatly with this expression of interest in law as an alternative to philosophy. We may hear Deleuze's remark as giving voice to an irretrievable moment in his past, a reflection on and a reference to 'lost time', to the adolescence of one who was not yet present, or who was, in a word, yet to 'strike out on his own'. But the more useful 'audition' of this puzzling claim is to give it our full attention and to acknowledge that it does not merely sit uneasily with his mature work, but actively deterritorialises it. It is time now that we problematised all these tensions, contradictions and aberrant lines by making Deleuze's work as a whole pass through this opening.

That is, in short, the object of this book. Our job is only to provide the window-dressing, this Introduction and the concluding Postscript – a humble enough but, in fact, a very demanding job. We are tasked with saying something, but not too much; with 'laying a foundation' but leaving it bare, sacrificing control over what happens next; with attracting your interest, but refraining from alienating you (what's the *point*, we hear Kafka saying). We would like, therefore, to introduce in this text merely a handful of notions, intuitions and semi-formed concepts that may be valuable from the perspective of the reader about to plunge into *Deleuze and Law* for the first time. (As will become evident, we love our contributors passionately and fully expect that you will too, and so you will return to read this book again.)

Let's return for just a moment to the connection Deleuze draws between law and philosophy by situating himself as its vertex. Reflecting on the hesitation that he felt when the time came to choose an academic curriculum, Deleuze added that he continued to be interested in law despite choosing philosophy. Instead of some kind of intellectual teenage fling, law never ceased to haunt his philosophical work. The science of the case practised in law courts on a daily basis was for him such an object of admiration that one may hazard the thesis that philosophy was never an exclusive pursuit for the young Gilles or even the mature Professor Deleuze, that his perspective on philosophy was always informed by law to a substantial degree. We know that he came to the subject of his thesis, David Hume, through the concept of law, we know that he counted himself a casuist by the 1960s, and we know that his literary studies are shot through with elements that can only be called legal. Sacher-Masoch, Kafka, Melville's Bartleby, the Proustian law of love, and others again: these are the objects of a deeply jurisprudential philosophical engagement with literature. There was something like regret in his voice when he spoke to Parnet about law: the regret that philosophy, at least as it was practised in mid-century Europe, was not enough. And when one reads Deleuze's work while keeping that hint of regret in mind – the regret concerning the importance, the exemplarity of law – one cannot resist the conclusions that form the taproot of this collaboration. From *Empirisme et subjectivité* to *Critique et clinique*, all of his books in one way or another testify to his persistent interest in, even passion for, law. Often, even most of the time, such testimony only concerns one or two sentences: fragments of analysis, lapidary theses, mere illustration, spectres of thought. But whether they materialise in the form of analysis, thesis, or illustration, each of these elements allows us to assert the hypothesis that, contrary to appearances, there was and is a real Deleuzian philosophy of law that remains to be unfolded. And perhaps even further: this philosophy is not fragmentary in any pejorative sense but is a conceptually articulated system of sometimes inarticulate propositions, a virtual system that is perfectly differentiated lying beneath his actual metaphysics, as though it were its shadow.

Can we reconstruct that system? Assuredly not, not here: in addition to the fact that such a project calls for precisely the kind of sustained treatment that we must deny ourselves here, we run the risk of looking like despots overcoding the territory that the chapters that follow this text will actually trace out in detail. Therefore we want only to entice you. We want only to mark some of the coordinates, indicate potential properties of the system. Is it a system? We don't know. But we think it might be, so we will accept the hypothesis provisionally, run an initial experiment, and see where it takes us. If things look promising, read on to the next chapter.

Two main theses constitute this system. The first thesis is voiced by Deleuze in his *Présentation de Sacher-Masoch*: 'Irony and humour are the essential forms through which we apprehend the law' (Deleuze 1967: 75; Deleuze 1989: 82). And the second, in an interview with François Ewald and Raymond Bellour, later published in *Pourparlers*: 'Jurisprudence is the philosophy of law, and deals with singularities, it advances by working out from [or prolonging] singularities' (Deleuze 1990: 209–10; Deleuze 1995: 153). All the clues spread across Deleuze's work are mere commentaries, developments, or illustrations of these two theses. Here is the basis of our experiment. Those which flow from the first one form the 'critical' part of his system of philosophy of law, devoted to the critique of law and judgment. On the other hand, those which relate by a more or less lengthy chain of *rationes* back to the second thesis form the 'clinical' part of the system, devoted to the description of the practice of law and jurisprudence. The aim of the entire system is to displace and substitute for the critical economy of law understood as *loi* a kind of clinical economy of law understood as *droit*, removed from the classical philosophical frameworks within which, since at least Cicero, law has been imprisoned. Critique is not to be despised, but neither is it to be valorised for itself. It is a part of a more expansive programme – and cannot be allowed to dominate. The totalising spirit is strong with critical practice and represents a real obstacle to the functioning of the constructive system. We can say that *critique*, then, grasped as a component rather than a whole, is nothing but a movement towards *clinique*. Law's grandeur, praised by Deleuze throughout his entire oeuvre, comes precisely from its cultivated distance towards philosophy, or at least a certain (critical) philosophical attitude. The long history of the relationship between philosophy and law has consisted in an attempt to *submit* law to the transcendent categories of judgment created by the Greek master-philosophers and developed in the thought of Roman Stoicism. To this manoeuvre, law has always responded with the strictly immanent pertinence of the science of the case, considered as the sole horizon of practice. As is shown by (among other jurispolitical currents) the widespread invocation and arguable success of the contemporary universalising ideology of human rights, which relies upon and entrenches the capitalist *socius* and its semiotic of reactionary archaisms, this defence continues to work on the sidelines, to foster resistance to the imperial locutions of transcendent Law – the dumbest philosophy (using Deleuze's own words), the most insensitive and ham-handed philosophy, has triumphed, or offers itself as triumphant, imposing upon law another horizon and form of organisation, artificial, pretentious and expropriative.

Deleuze's thinking on law is an appraisal of law's grandeur – and a critique of the kind of philosophy which tends to diminish it. But because it is an appraisal formulated by a philosopher who has never renounced his own conceptual practice, it presents a very peculiar twist. As Alain Badiou claims in his widely misread book, Deleuze is a 'classical' philosopher, who belongs to the – very French – tradition of René Descartes and Nicolas Malebranche (Badiou 1997: 29; 2000: 45). He is a philosopher whose work takes aim at one single goal: the perfection of philosophy itself. Because we mean this 'perfection' to register in the great classical tenor of G.W. Leibniz, whose eclecticism never derogated from but always augmented his univocal constructive adventure in pure thought, it is clear that to sing law's grandeur is part of an enterprise that remains altogether philosophical. What Deleuze wants is to proclaim philosophically law's specificity so that it becomes an example *for philosophy*. As an immanent practice of the case, law (*droit*) is the incarnation of what philosophy has to achieve for herself in order to be able to leave the world of law (*loi*), judgment and debt, whose fascinated observation has caused her stagnation. In that sense, to take an interest in and to learn from law to the extent that it becomes possible to present the latter as a model for philosophy has always meant, for Deleuze, to remain faithful to the discipline to which he devoted his life. His purpose was to put an end to the conflict of faculties opposing the teachers and disciplines of law and philosophy until the fall of theology by the end of the eighteenth century, one more favourable to the latter than to the former. By singing the grandeur of the practice of law, he wanted to sing the grandeur of a philosophical practice able to perceive law's grandeur by its own means and in its own way, rather than that of the practices that tried to diminish law, and, in that way, to sadden and diminish themselves. Pursuing his interest in law, Deleuze nevertheless remained completely faithful to his metaphysical commitments and his theoretical programme: to have done with judgment, and to announce the arrival of a practical philosophy, a new philosophical pragmatism, focusing on the singular case rather than on law (*loi*). Philosophising law had proven to be a conceptual failure (although an historical, imperial, bourgeois success): it was time to inject philosophy with a dose of law.

If Deleuze's interest and humour-riddled attitude towards law helped him to implement his programmatic reversal of all philosophical values, it also produced a similar reversal in the realm of law itself. Since Cicero, jurisprudes and legal theorists have devoted themselves to the problems posed by the philosophy of law and judgment: the foundation of the legal order, the rationality of judgment, the principled justification of court decisions, the legitimacy of rules and norms, and so on. From Deleuze's point of view, these problems could be divided into four categories: legalism (justification of *droit* by *loi*), naturalism (foundation of *droit* in *loi*), conventionalism (guarantee of *droit* by *loi*), and institutionalism (limitation of *droit* by *loi*). For him, all the questions belonging to these four categories belonged to the realm of what he called, following Bergson, 'false problems' (Deleuze 1966: 3; Deleuze 1991: 15–21; see also Deleuze 1994b: 168ff.), that is, problems requiring of thought nothing more than the already-known. The most important critique addressed by Deleuze to the philosophy of law and judgment is precisely that it always asked questions to which it already had all the answers prepared. Only the opposite, the unrecognised which exceeds the categories of law and judgment, can be interesting from a properly juristic perspective, Deleuze suggests. A problem is worth examining only if it can generate or cause the emergence of new questions, questions to which it is impossible to respond with mere confirmation and dogmatic classification, but which can only be handled through the invention of an unthought, unrecognisable consequence. By focusing on the *clinique* of the practice of law, he tried later to formulate the problems specific to law (*droit*), without any regard for those imposed on them by law (*loi*) and overcoded by judgment. For the justifications of legalism, he substituted strategies of practical intervention; for the foundation of naturalism, the transformations of *droit*; for the guarantees of conventionalism, the *bricolage* of new *rapports*; and for the limitations of institutionalism, the creativity proper to legal invention. For a perverse, negative vision of law – as a tool for maintaining the status quo or as an instrument of repression, which are perversions because *law is only passage* – he tried to substitute an integrally affirmative vision, focusing on its own productivity.

Deleuze's take on law produced not only a deep restatement of philosophy, then, but also of law. How far does this rearticulation reach? What are its concrete consequences, effects, resonances? These are the two general questions the present book wants to explore. If the primary objects of the programme formulated by Deleuze have here begun to be probed (that is: the passage from the *critique* of law to its *clinique*), the crucial details as well as the way concrete legal practices are affected by them have not. But if one is to take seriously the clinical thesis, stating that 'jurisprudence [of the case] is the philosophy of law', it seems that one has first to accept that, in the first instance, only those phenomena belonging to the realm of adjudication can be considered 'concrete legal practices' concerned by it. For Deleuze, legislation belongs to another practice than that of law, even though it is a practice that cuts across the latter and frequently enters into composition with it. This other practice is politics. By adjudication, one has then to broaden the usual definition and understand by this the whole ensemble of operations through which a case individuates and becomes an occasion for law to exercise, to practice its inherent creativity. To grasp the concrete consequences engineered in this transformation of the understanding of law requires us to try to map all these operations. But to draw such a map can only be done by way of the cases submitted to our attention through world-historical processes characterising and shaping our present milieu, directly or indirectly: the crises of contemporary law and legal rationalities, the emergence of biological regulation and genomic law, the problem of human rights, the role of illegalisms and the expansion of antisocial regulatory efforts, the classical and modern images of law (Plato, Leibniz, Kant), the classical and modern critiques of law (Socrates, Sade, Sacher-Masoch, Kafka, Melville), the exemplarity of Roman law and the neoarchaistic appropriation of its concepts and models of reasoning, the conceptual personae of the advocate and the judge, the place of law in the axiomatics of capital, and so on. Throughout his oeuvre, Deleuze multiplies entries into the realm of legal practice, and we can no longer marginalise their importance for his thought, for philosophy, and for law.

The critical part of the system consists partly in re-reading the history of thinking (philosophical as well as literary) as the progressive self-destruction of law. To the classical image of law created by Plato can be opposed the critique of this very image by Socrates, a critique that ruins both its foundational pretences (the Good to which law must be referred) and its projected redemptive or soteriological power (the Good expected

Introduction 7

from its exercise). Similarly, to the modern image of law developed by Kant can be opposed its critique by Sade, Sacher-Masoch, Kafka and Melville. This critique, explains Deleuze, takes the form of a skewed comical gloss put on Kant's straight-laced image of law. For Sade, this perspective consists in ironically perverting law by referring it not to its intrinsic Good (the form of law), but to its intrinsic Evil, as expressed by an outside (the Sadian institution). For Sacher-Masoch, it consists in humorously subverting law by making it produce, while maintaining its form, consequences contrary to those necessarily expected from it (the Masochist contract). For Kafka, it consists in nonsensically inverting law by explaining how the universality of the assumed purity of the form of law is haunted by the singularity of the impure desire which is its motor. And, for Melville, it consists in converting law through slapstick by showing how its success is always also its failure (Captain Vere's or Bartleby's pact). Following this history of the image of law, and of its critique, jurists are put in a curious situation. What if the comical operators of law were the lawyers themselves? What if they were those who incarnate the comical dimension of law, better than any philosopher or any writer – simply because law (*loi*) is not their problem? What if the critical operations of the modern image of law were the very operations of law (*droit*), those that lawyers practise every day without even noticing?

The same goes with the clinical part of the system. Exactly as there is a critical history of law (*loi*), there is a clinical history of the practice of law (*droit*). The latter is composed of several important steps. The two most important ones are named 'topical' and 'axiomatic' by Deleuze and Guattari, borrowing the distinction from Paul Veyne's classic *Le pain et le cirque*. The axiomatic practice of law is the practice of jurisprudence – of case law – as manipulated and framed by the philosophical apparatus of capture. It is immanently within the framework of this practice that the four categories of false problems engendered by the philosophy of law and judgment (legalism, naturalism, conventionalism, institutionalism) are challenged and resisted through the exercise of four regimes of legal practice (intervention, subvention, convention, invention). But precisely because it still has to fight against the modern image of law, the axiomatic practice of law remains too tightly bound to it. Contrarily, the topical practice of law, corresponding to Roman law before Cicero's attempt to introduce Greek philosophy into it, doesn't have to face the same difficulty. It is only in such a practice that one can discover the last active remnants of the Leibnizian dream of a 'Universal Jurisprudence', a dream shared by Deleuze. That is: the project of a casuistic practice of law proceeding directly to the *creation* of principle and legal concepts rather than to their application. To free law from Law, then, requires that law become devoted to the 'free and savage' creation of non-decomposable, non-transposable principles extracted from singular cases, remaining always within the strict limits of the case or singularity. The philosophy of law (*loi*) and judgment tried to define a sort of a programme posing the principles at a transcendent height broodingly inaccessible to law (*droit*). The topical practice of law replies by displacing principles from the government of its action to its end, understood as the ultimate moment of its process of creation and invention.

To draw the map of the operations of legal practice implies an investigation of the entire history of the *critique* of law, as well as of the *clinique* of law. The different moments of this history, as has been too briefly shown, are articulated by an extreme technical coherence, corresponding to very precise developments of either the philosophy of law, or of its practice. Together, they form a closed system, as complexly folded, rich and intricate as Deleuze's philosophical system in general, if we continue to accept, with Badiou, that this system can be called 'classical' – if only because it wrenches thought beyond the critical. The different essays gathered in this volume are but short investigations into one or the other of the moments of this double history, or into one of its multiple articulations, contemporaneities, compossibilities, or futures. These investigations each enact the idea that it is always necessary to begin with a case in order to retrace the creation of a given principle. This is why they all must be considered case studies, as limited to their case as are such transcendental-empirical principles. Nevertheless, as they all take, generally and for the most part, a systematic view of law, it will not be surprising to observe that they all, in the end, contribute to constructing or reconstructing the global architectonic of law envisioned and initiated by Deleuze across the course of his life. This doesn't mean, however, that these essays must be seen as mere illustrations of this architectonic. On the contrary, reading these essays, one must accept that these interventions literally extend the compass of that system, following one of Deleuze's dearest theoretical commitments – that a system never exceeds the cases which concur towards its composition. And yet the wish of the editors and the contributors is that theorists and thinkers inclining towards a philosophico-legal alchemy may find in these texts resources for the better discernment and the multiplication of singular cases so that new folds can be developed within this metajuridical framework in an endless process of legal creation and jurisprudential hybridisation. The invention of new clinical-juridical folds might even end in a new theory of law that seizes a potentiality circulating in Deleuze's architectonic – a *speculative* theory of law at once supremely indifferent to the calls addressed to it by either philosophy, politics, anthropology, or anything else seeking its intellectual subordination, and swiftly responsive to the elements and problems constituting the case, be they philosophical, political, anthropological, or of some other nature. A few of the essays collected here gesture in this direction, while others unrelentingly fix their attention on molecular legal processes coursing through the body of the system, and yet others forge connections between law and its *semblables*. All, however, unite in taking us one or several steps closer to the revaluation of legality that would advance the movement from *critique* to *clinique*.

Paul Patton undertakes this project by offering up a conception of *becoming-right* that responds to the question of whether Deleuze's philosophy offers any ground for 'resistance to the present'. As such, Patton's is a welcome contribution not only to the nascent conjunction of Deleuze and law but to an ongoing discourse in the literature on whether radical immanence implies and embodies a reactionary political posture modelled on the free market. Patton proceeds by asking how 'right' can be understood in a Deleuzian framework and rejects candidates drawn from the domains of positive law and morality. Instead of these wellsprings of transcendence, he argues, we need to maintain 'immanentism' by rethinking the emergence of new capacities for action in concrete social and political environments. To seek refuge under rights as ordinarily conceived is precisely to annul the problematic milieu that had given rise to the need for a new capacity. The way forward is to model the becoming of rights both within and beyond the confines of law (*loi*). Patton explores the establishment of emergent capacities to act through specific examples and the conceptual arsenal offered by Deleuze and Guattari and argues that, through micropolitical processes, counter-actualisation of and thus resistance to the present become both possible and intelligible.

In an essay that is as nimble and humorous as it is precise and trenchant, Peter Goodrich unearths the *lex amicitia*, the law of amity, buried in our legal and philosophical traditions. Through a delightfully crooked path that takes us from Vico to Derrida and from Cicero to Félix G., Goodrich summons the figure of the friend in its company with affect, image and concept to explore the peculiarly Deleuzian image of thought. The philosopher is also the foolosopher, what Deleuze affectionately called 'the idiot', encountering what resists recognition, hands probing in the dark, and inventing a way to see. Epiphany. It is a question of interpretation, of encountering the opacity of the black letter and the legacies and agencies of the fathers and the gods that preceded us, a question, thus, also of black holes. Goodrich undoes and recouples along the way a series of invisible abstract lines tethering law to poetry, text to image, word to enigma.

Alexandre Lefebvre returns us from the liminal to the laminar world of politics and positive rights, asking how we can make sense of Deleuze's noted antipathy to rights and human rights in particular while justifying a progressive vision of politics and humanitarianism. Lefebvre turns to the important final text on the immanence of 'a life' to recover, or invent, a defensible ground for human rights quite apart from the hazy abstractions and oppressive transcendences invoked by the contemporary discourse on human rights. But this gets us only an outline, a provisional structure in which to think human rights. To carry the task forward Lefebvre plumbs Bergson's late *Two Sources* book and discovers a new vitalistic foundation for human rights in the dyadic order of openness and closure, unity and multiplicity, and the two species of love that they engender. Lefebvre redraws the kinship relation of Bergson and Deleuze along the lines of love, love not for this or that object but for all, any, you or we, perhaps, in so far as we express *a* life.

Penelope Pether fruitfully reimagines the conjugation of law and literature by plugging the fabled, or fabling, interdiscipline into the schizoanalytical machine. Traversing discrete but deeply connected territories, from legal pedagogy to neoliberalism and from legal-literary narratology to Guantánamo Bay, Pether poignantly confronts the slumbering interdiscipline with its own conceits and challenges it to reorient itself, praxiologically and pedagogically, and to find a new footing from which it can help 'make law do justice'. Minor literatures are not enough, we cannot expect idly that they will produce the changes that law-and-lit wants to effect – we must prolong the text, insert it into the extratextual flows passing through our very different worlds, to make it act. An essentially cruel exercise, then, that provokes and unsettles, making facile and clichéd gestures about 'thinking like a lawyer' difficult, because it causes legal discourse itself to stutter and, perhaps, to seize the molecular current running through the molar apparatus of the law school classroom.

Andreas Philippopoulos-Mihalopoulos also wants to intermingle the legal and the literary, but through the essential mediation of spatiality. A dazzling reading of Michel Tournier's *Friday* yields up an intensive cartography of possible worlds glistening in the desert island's sunlight. We begin as Tournier's Robinson did: with a code of law and a map.

Introduction 11

But we move towards their displacement, their redundancies or ironic twins, an embodied legality and a constructive diagram. Robinson takes the structuration of the Other with him to the island without Others, but gradually, progressively frees himself from himself, that Other, to constitute a new nonhuman territoriality populated by percepts and affects (and Friday). It is a process, not a given: the interiority of the twofold legality of *logos* and *nomos*, depth and surface, striation and smoothness, inseparable yet incommensurable, tilts, favouring now the free distribution of singularities which earlier had to remain tucked neatly inside the depths. A second island emerges from within the first. *Logos* and *nomos* converge towards but simultaneously withdraw from that 'second island', a disjunctive synthesis that would, perhaps, give rise to that enigmatic creature: justice, emerging sometimes, unpredictably and incalculably, from the interplay of the modes of legality.

Drawing an important connection between Deleuze's work on Hume and the later *Capitalisme et schizophrénie* project, Marc Schuilenburg asks how social science and theory may best approach the disjunction between 'law' and 'institutions'. Institution, at least in that early work, is a category Deleuze finds susceptible to leverage against the domineering tutelage of the 'law' that condemns and judges rather than creating. Schuilenburg explains that the later conception of the molar and the molecular can be helpful in making sense of the alternative jurisprudence Deleuze seems to have in mind in the Hume book. However, he argues that a detour through the sociologies of Gabriel Tarde and Emile Durkheim is necessary to implement the molar/molecular divide in social research. Having demonstrated the importance of both the molarity of Durkheimian 'social facts' and the molecularity of passional Tardean 'interactions' like imitation, Schuilenburg contends that a sociological perspectivism premised on this insight is essential. The 'law' and 'jurisprudence' distinction that Deleuze draws later is profitably understood on this basis.

Finding inspiration in the figure of the artisan, Nathan Moore hammers out an alternative to the classical 'constitutional' question of the grounds of law, arguing that indeed this question is merely a dull repetition of the even more classical ontological distinction between materiality and ideality. Instead of the theology of the absent foundation, he tempts us, dares us, to plunge headlong into the reality of the image. In his artisanal hands the image becomes not a representation of the thing, nor the 'thing itself', but that which distributes representation and thing, ideality and materiality, the point at which they meet and form an assemblage. Duration, affect, power, hesitation: these are the province, if there is a province, of the image. They converge on the function of the artisan, which is precisely that which political theory – political theology – has attributed, gratuitously and unjustifiably, to the sovereign, that is, to decide. It is the artisan and not the sovereign that actualises potentials and brings them into proximity with one another, weaving a new politico-legal texture 'on the fly'. The threat to which the artisan may be made to respond is that of the 'society of control' which operates through the contract and the manufacture of liabilities and responsibilities, the paradox of enforced freedom.

James MacLean takes issue with the powerful 'institutional theory of law', which derives from postpositivist legal philosophy, for serving us obscurity under the sign of clarity and precision. Revisiting canonical legal-theoretical problems such as the nature of legal reasoning and the relationships between rule and fact as well as justification and application, MacLean pokes a hole in the construct of the legal institution, taken as a hierarchical rule-system, in order to create a pathway into the latencies and the instabilities lurking beneath the finely-knit fabric of the institutional discourse. In fact, he stresses, it is considerably more accurate to say that the way law 'works' is to constantly run fact into rule, to conjoin unrelated elements, to compose heterogeneous assemblages, and cutting straight through established boundaries and normative barriers. Legal institutions are rhizomes, and legal reasoning is rhizomatic extension, pulsation, fulguration – it is a damaging error to act, in legal theory, as though law was a stable entity, a creature of pre-givenness, necessity, apodicticity.

Lissa Lincoln retrieves an unexpected link somewhere between law, literature and philosophy that serves to connect Deleuze to the despised moralist Albert Camus. Camus is a victim of injustice; we have mistaken him. Lincoln stages the encounter that never happened, deploying elements of the theory of minor literatures to present a compelling argument for reconsidering the *cas Camus*. All the scorn heaped upon romanticism and irrationalism have diminished Camus' philosophical and literary value, ossifying his corpus to the point that it has become impossible to *encounter* it. To peel away the several layers of opacity that now cover it, to render Camus meaningful and consequential once more, we can read him as Deleuze and Guattari read Kafka: the form of expression is complicit, uncontroversial, utterly ordinary, but the content is a dynamo, a dismantling machine. On the far side of the text we find subtle vacillations or drastic undoings that are dimly indexed on the near side. Camus becomes a user's guide to the apparatus of power that is the system of judgment.

David Saunders addresses the much more plausible, but no less interesting relation between Deleuze and Bruno Latour, two philosophers who have spilled litres of ink unsettling conventions in a panoply of fields but who, curiously, both defend law, legal practice and casuistry. To develop an account of this convergence, Saunders extols the virtues of *la pratique topique du droit* as against *la pensée de la loi*. Cutting skilfully through several historical cases of jurisprudential invention, Saunders delivers on his promise to advance our understanding of this defence of law as clinical practice: for both Deleuze and Latour, law is the extension of singularities, the flicker upon the surface, and never the imposition of 'impossible virtues' that philosophy has – indulging its self-conception – so graciously charged law with managing.

To say that we have been impressed by the calibre of the contributions to *Deleuze and Law* would be an egregious understatement. The book is rife with contrasting perspectives on the meaning of the 'and' in the title and is thus embedded in an exceedingly broad range of intellectual trajectories. This is to be expected, perhaps, because of law's own polyvalence, or its essential relation of dependence on a multitude of non-legal practices, its heteronomy. Or perhaps it is expected because of law's singularity, its uniqueness, its irreducibility to that on which it nevertheless depends. The chapters that follow are provocations to thought, exercises in *critique* as well as *clinique*, mapping the distances and proximities of problems that happen to pass through *la pratique du droit*. We try in the Postscript to return to some of the themes sketched in this Introduction, though our text is not the equal of the several chapters.

## References

Badiou, A. (1997), *Deleuze: La clameur de l'Etre*, Paris: Hachette.
Badiou, A. (2000), *Deleuze: The Clamor of Being*, trans. Louise Burchill, Minneapolis: University of Minnesota Press.
Deleuze, G. (1966), *Le Bergsonisme*, Paris: PUF.
Deleuze, G. (1967), *Présentation de Sacher-Masoch*, Paris: Minuit.
Deleuze, G. (1989), *Masochism: Coldness and Cruelty*, trans. Jean McNeil, New York: Zone.
Deleuze, G. (1990), *Pourparlers: 1972–1990*, Paris: Minuit.
Deleuze, G. (1991), *Bergsonism*, trans. Hugh Tomlinson and Barbara Habberjam, New York: Zone.
Deleuze, G. (1994a), *L'Abécédaire de Gilles Deleuze, avec Claire Parnet*, Paris: DVD Editions Montparnasse.
Deleuze, G. (1994b), *Difference and Repetition*, trans. Paul Patton, New York: Columbia University Press.
Deleuze, G. (1995), *Negotiations 1972–1990*, trans. Martin Joughin, New York: Columbia University Press.

Dosse, F. (2007), *Gilles Deleuze et Félix Guattari: Biographie croisée*, Paris: La Découverte.

## Note

1. The *International Journal for the Semiotics of Law* published a special edition in 2007 (vol. 20, no. 1) dedicated to unpacking this alternative history.

Chapter 1

# Immanence, Transcendence, and the Creation of Rights

*Paul Patton*\*

Deleuze's critical comments about human rights and his praise of jurisprudence pose several problems for the further elaboration of a Deleuzian approach to law and politics. He criticises conceptions of human rights that imply new forms of transcendence, thereby raising the question: what would a non-transcendent, immanent conception of rights be like? At the same time, he advocates a practice of jurisprudence understood as the creation of new rights, thereby raising the question: what would it mean to create new rights? In this chapter, I will outline answers to these questions, drawing on the work of Deleuze and Guattari but also others who have defended a conception of rights as immanent to existing regimes of power, affect and belief. These answers raise a further question: supposing that we can understand rights as entirely immanent to the social fields in which they operate, can a Deleuzian political philosophy sustain a concept of 'becoming-right' that, like 'becoming-democratic', would help to counter-actualise some forms of resistance to the present in societies governed by law?

The refusal of transcendence is one of the constant motifs of Deleuze's philosophy. His thought renounces all forms of appeal to transcendent values, concepts of history, or human nature in favour of a radical immanentism. At the same time, it purports to be an untimely philosophy in Nietzsche's sense of the term, opposed to the present in the name of a time and a people to come. This raises a problem: if Deleuzian political philosophy is denied recourse to any kind of transcendence, how does it attain the necessary distance that enables it to be critical of the present? The answer relies on the distinction between virtuality

---

\* I am grateful to Moira Gatens and Alexandre Lefebvre for their helpful comments on an earlier draft.

and actuality that runs throughout Deleuze and Guattari's political philosophy. In *A Thousand Plateaus*, they contrast the plane of organisation or actuality, on which we encounter real things, real people and various kinds of becoming (becoming-woman, becoming-animal, and so on), with the plane of immanence or virtuality, on which we encounter abstract machines, pure events and becomings-imperceptible. The plane of organisation is where history unfolds through processes of relative deterritorialisation and transformation or metamorphosis of existing institutions, forms of life and subjectivity, along with processes of reterritorialisation, capture, or blockage of such transformative processes. Deleuzian philosophy is properly described as a philosophy of immanence because the planes of immanence and organisation are mutually implicated in one another and because the plane of immanence is the more profound inner realm of reality.

With reference to this dual-aspect ontology, Deleuze and Guattari suggest that every process or event simultaneously inhabits both the historical world of actuality and the ahistorical world of the virtual events or processes. Pure events or becomings are never exhausted by the historical events in which they are actualised. Rather, they constitute 'a shadowy or secret part that is continually subtracted from or added to its actualization' (Deleuze and Guattari 1991: 147; 1994: 156). Deleuzian criticism of the present then takes the form of identifying those social, intellectual and artistic or other movements in which pure eventness or becoming is expressed. These are the lines of flight along which change happens. They are the processes of relative deterritorialisation by means of which existing assemblages are transformed into something else. Such criticism is always situational or site-specific. There is no master plan and no general recipe for effecting change in a particular direction. That is why Deleuze prefers the multiple forms of becoming-revolutionary over any unitarian concept of the revolution, or the varieties of becoming-minority over the position of the majority. The majoritarian subject of modern Western political societies is always an abstract figure that corresponds to no particular individual or to nobody, whereas minorities understood as expressions of becoming-minor are 'seeds, crystals of becoming whose value is to trigger uncontrollable movements and deterritorializations of the mean or majority' (Deleuze and Guattari 1980: 134; 1987: 106).

This preference for particular and local forms of resistance to the present explains why, towards the end of his life, Deleuze criticised the increasingly popular recourse to human rights as a basis for criticism. In conversation with Antoine Dulaure and Claire Parnet in 1985, he complained of the recourse to abstraction and reluctance to embrace movement in contemporary thought and politics:

> In philosophy we're coming back to eternal values, to the idea of the intellectual as custodian of eternal values. We're back to Benda complaining that Bergson was a traitor to his own class, the clerical class, in trying to think motion. These days it's the rights of man that provide our eternal values. It's the constitutional state (*état de droit*) and other notions that everyone recognizes as very abstract. And it's in the name of all this that thinking is fettered and that any analysis in terms of movements is blocked. (Deleuze and Guattari 1990: 166; 1995: 121–2)

*What is Philosophy?* is equally critical of the uses made of rights talk in the contemporary world. Deleuze and Guattari argue that human rights have come to function as axioms within the immanent axiomatic of global capital. As such, the basic civil and political rights regarded as human rights coexist alongside other axioms, such as those designed to ensure the security of property. The result is that when economic conditions demand the tightening of credit or the withdrawal of employment, the rights of the poor to basic social goods are effectively suspended. Human rights are widely proclaimed but, in the absence of any effective institutional mechanism for their enforcement, it is left to individual states and non-state organisations to decide when and where their infringement is so serious as to require action. In addition to these familiar criticisms of the operation of human rights, Deleuze and Guattari are critical of the very concept of *human* rights in so far as these are supposed to be grounded in universal features of human nature such as human freedom, rationality, or the capacity to communicate. Such universal rights 'say nothing about the immanent modes of existence of people provided with rights' (Deleuze and Guattari 1991: 103; 1994: 107). Since they presuppose a universal and abstract subject of rights, irreducible to any singular, existent figures, they are eternal, abstract and transcendent rights belonging to everyone and no one in particular. This may well appear from the perspective of contemporary conceptions of human rights to be an outdated understanding. Nevertheless, it goes some way towards explaining Deleuze's response, when asked by Raymond Bellour and Francois Ewald in 1988 why, unlike Foucault, he took no part in the human rights movement or debates about the constitutional state: 'If you are talking about establishing new forms of transcendence, new universals, restoring a reflective subject as the bearer of rights, or setting up a communicative intersubjectivity, then it's not much of a philosophical advance' (Deleuze 1990: 208; 1995: 152).[1]

Deleuze elaborates on the emptiness of abstract human rights in his *Abécédaire* interviews with Claire Parnet, with reference to the problems facing an Armenian population that had been subjected to a massacre by Turks and, after having fled to the then Armenian Soviet Socialist Republic, to a massive earthquake.[2] He objects that, when people make declarations about human rights in such situations,

> these declarations are never made as a function of the people who are directly concerned, the Armenian society, the Armenian communities, etc. Their problem is not 'the rights of man' ... I would say that it's not a question of 'the rights of man', it's not a question of justice, rather it's a question of territory, of jurisprudence. (Deleuze 1996: 'G comme Gauche')

In this passage, Deleuze contrasts the outdated, abstract and empty concept of human rights with the rights required in order for this Armenian enclave within the former USSR to survive. These rights, he suggests, must be considered in the context of a quite specific territorial and political assemblage, just as he had earlier explained in relation to desire: desire is never simply desire for someone or something but always desire for and from within a particular aggregate or assemblage (Deleuze 1996: 'D comme Désir'). The specific needs and context of the Armenian people concerned call for the creation of new rights, or the modification of existing rights, rather than the simple application of universal principles to this particular case. Human rights grounded in a particular rights-bearing feature of human nature are useless because they are fixed and ahistorical, unable to evolve in accordance with the requirements of a particular case. Situations such as this call for a creative response that Deleuze calls jurisprudence: 'This Armenian problem is typically what can be called an extraordinarily complex problem of jurisprudence' (Deleuze 1996: 'G comme Gauche').

## Jurisprudence

Throughout the period in which he was critical of the recourse to human rights as a transcendent ground of moral and political criticism, Deleuze defended a conception of jurisprudence as the creation of law or right (*droit*). In the *Abécédaire* interviews with Claire Parnet, he famously identified being on the left with the creation of rights and confessed that

> I have always been fascinated by jurisprudence, by law ... If I hadn't studied philosophy, I would have studied law, but precisely not 'the rights of man', rather I'd have studied jurisprudence. That's what life is. There

are no 'rights of man', only rights of life, and so, life unfolds case by case. (Deleuze 1996: '*G comme Gauche*')

Deleuze's comments here draw no significant difference between rights and human rights. My own interest in what follows lies in the concept of rights and the creation of rights rather than specifically human rights: what does it mean exactly for Deleuze to defend jurisprudence as the creation of *droit*? The word can be translated either as law or as right and different translators have opted for one or the other term in English.[3] Does he mean simply that jurisprudence is the creation of law, or does he mean that it is the creation of rights?

A system of law does many things, but among its fundamental functions is the protection of the rights of citizens, by providing legal remedies for their infringement. It is clear that Deleuze recognises that we live in constitutional states in which our rights are, by and large, protected by law. Within such states, the very concept of a right implies that certain kinds of action on the part of citizens will be protected from interference by the state or by other citizens. Conversely, so long as we are talking about effective rights and not simply the mere assertion of a moral principle, the existence of rights implies the enforcement of limits to the degree to which the state or citizens can interfere with the actions of others. While there are philosophers and jurists who believe that the only rights are those enshrined in positive law, there is no reason to restrict the concept of a right to this degree. Non-state territorial societies also have rights and even in societies governed by law it is common to criticise laws and other institutions for not recognising rights, or for recognising rights that they should not. The fact that there are cases in which we would agree that the rights of individuals or groups have not been respected, even though they were treated in accordance with the law, is taken to imply that rights exist independently of their institutional expression. In this way, the criticism of laws and constitutions for their denial of civil rights to minority groups is taken as evidence that these rights exist in some sense outside of or apart from their legal enactment.[4] This implies that there is a difference between the rights that are protected and the laws by means of which they are protected. It follows that a more general concept of rights will be one that does not differentiate between legal, political or customary rights. So considered, rights may be defined as 'established ways of acting *or* established ways of being acted toward, ways of being treated' (Martin 1993: 41). There is more to be said about what is meant by saying that a particular way of acting is 'established', but the important point here is that this definition gives us a concept of rights as immanent to the social relations and practices of a given community. It does not rely on any transcendent conception of human nature or of the moral ground of rights. All forms of right will involve some kind of protection of certain ways of behaving, but the different institutional expressions of rights are all downstream from this definition. Different kinds of right, whether customary, political or legal, will protect different behaviours or call for different institutional provisions to ensure the rights of individuals.

The context of Deleuze's definition of jurisprudence in conversation with Negri makes it clear that he understands the relation between law and rights in this manner. What interests him, he points out, is not the law or laws (*ni la loi ni les lois*), nor is it right or rights (*le droit ou les droits*): '*C'est la jurisprudence qui est vraiment créatrice de droit*' (Deleuze 1990: 230; 1995: 169). Deleuze is not a legal positivist and his thesis that jurisprudence creates *droit* can be taken to mean, certainly that it involves the creation of law but, more profoundly, that it also involves the creation of the right or rights that are expressed by law. The example that Deleuze goes on to invoke supports this reading. He refers to the project of establishing law/right in relation to modern biology, where this implies the rights of individuals in relation to the new technologies made possible by modern biology. The new situations to which modern biology gives rise, the new events that it makes possible, are all matters for jurisprudence. Moreover, Deleuze suggests, these matters ought not be left to ethics committees or to judges but should involve those directly concerned: 'it is jurisprudence that truly creates law/right: this should not be left to judges' (Deleuze 1990: 230; 1995: 169). So we might suppose, for example, that decisions about rights of access to genetic material should involve the users of fertility treatments, or decisions about access to genetic information should involve the users of genetic screening techniques. At this point, he comments, we move from law to politics.

In effect, for Deleuze, jurisprudence was always a matter of politics, in the broad sense in which he understood the term, and not merely confined to the legal institution. Jurisprudence involves the creation of new laws but also the creation of the rights that are expressed in these laws. In his 1988 conversation with Raymond Bellour and François Ewald, he identified jurisprudence as the field or process through which peoples organised into constitutional states (*états de droit*) enter into becomings. In the case of peoples governed by means of such states 'it is not established and codified rights that count, but everything that currently creates problems for the law and that threatens to call what is established into question' (Deleuze 1990: 209; 1995: 153, translation modified). Whether we consider the Civil or the Penal code, Deleuze suggests, there is no shortage of such problems confronting the law. In this context, where he is clearly referring to rights codified in law, he advances the thesis that 'It is not codes or declarations that create law (*droit*) but jurisprudence. Jurisprudence is the philosophy of law and proceeds by singularities, by working out from singularities' (Deleuze 1990: 209–10; 1995: 153, translation modified).

The suggestion that jurisprudence is the philosophy of law is open to misinterpretation, particularly in the English-speaking context where a primary sense of 'jurisprudence' is that of philosophical reflection on law and legal concepts. This is not what Deleuze means by 'philosophy of law'. Rather, he means to suggest that jurisprudence should be understood in relation to law in the way that philosophy, as he understands it, relates to concepts. For Deleuze, philosophy creates concepts and, as he says here, jurisprudence creates law, where law must be understood as involving, among other things, a system of rights (Deleuze 1990: 230; 1995: 169). In addition, in so far as jurisprudence is also a matter of politics, it involves the processes through which new ways of acting or being acted towards become established (or old ways disestablished).

## Creating Rights

Up to this point, I have argued that rights are not reducible to laws and that Deleuze's conception of jurisprudence refers to the creation of rights as well as new laws. This raises the question: what is a right? And what is it to create new rights? Deleuze nowhere offers an answer to these questions. The challenge is to provide answers that are compatible with his opposition to transcendence and his commitment to immanence. Nietzsche and other historically minded political philosophers show that this is not an impossible task. We must begin by setting aside the widespread view that rights, in so far as they exist independently of their recognition and protection in law, can only be moral rights. Many philosophers believe that individuals possess certain rights by virtue of some rights-bearing feature of human nature, such as rationality, sentience or the capacity to act in pursuit of chosen ends. In concert with a universalist understanding of morality, this leads to the implausible idea that if a particular right exists then it has always existed, whether or not it has been recognised. There may be historical changes in the beliefs that people hold about rights and rights bearers (who qualifies) but there is no change in what rights there are. According to this view, it makes no sense to say that new rights have come into existence or that old ones have disappeared. As such, it is a concept of rights that is clearly incompatible with Deleuze's concept of jurisprudence.

Nietzsche provides an account of the origins of rights and duties that is more congenial to Deleuze's understanding of social relations as mobile relations of power and desire.[5] It also satisfies the requirement of allowing that rights may exist independently of their embodiment in law, without being committed to ahistorical or transcendent conceptions of moral rights. In *Daybreak* 112, *On the natural history of rights and duties*, he defines rights as recognised and guaranteed degrees of power. My rights, he argues, 'are that part of my power which others have not merely conceded me, but which they wish me to preserve' (Nietzsche 1982: 67). He goes on to canvass reasons why others might wish me to preserve a part of my power to act, offering different reasons according to the nature of the power-relation involved. In this passage, he does not explicitly consider the situation in which reciprocal rights and duties might arise between parties of approximately equal power. However, he does canvass this situation in *Human, All Too Human* 92, where he suggests that the idea of justice arises from a perceived equality of power between the parties involved.[6] Nietzsche's definition of rights and duties is cast in the terms of his conception of the parties involved as subjects of power, which means not only as bodies endowed with certain capacities for action but also as bodies endowed with a feeling of power that is acutely sensible to changes in the relations of power that obtain between itself and other such bodies. That is one of the reasons that rights may come to exist where they did not before, or go out of existence where they had previously existed.

Nietzsche does not consider the situation of modern democratic societies governed by means of laws, where it is assumed that all citizens are equal before the law and in their capacity to influence the formulation of new law. In particular, he does not consider the situation of democratic government where it is assumed that there must be some form of public justification for the ways in which citizens collectively exercise coercive power over one another. Modern theorists of constitutional democracy such as Rawls or Habermas do approach basic civil and political rights in these terms. Such rights define the kinds of action by citizens and the kinds of action towards others that all would allow for themselves and for their co-citizens. In Nietzsche's terms, these would be the 'degrees of power' that all citizens would be willing to leave to themselves and to one another.

Habermas and Rawls agree that some system of basic rights is required to establish the framework within which democratic decision making and a rule of law could operate. Habermas supposes that basic legal and political rights may be derived from the requirements of living together as equal citizens and regulating social relations by means of law (Habermas 1998). Rawls supposes that much the same system of rights will follow from the first principle of justice that would be agreed to by individual citizens or their representatives behind a veil of ignorance with regard to their own social circumstances and their own fundamental moral, religious and other beliefs (Rawls 2005). Both agree, however, that basic rights are political rather than moral in the sense that there can be agreement on the basic requirements of legitimate government even if there is disagreement on fundamental moral principles (Finlayson and Freyenhagen 2010). Moreover, according to Rawls, in the ideal case of a society that is effectively democratic and self-governing, the rights guaranteed for all citizens would not be the result of a simple *modus vivendi* but would derive from publicly endorsed opinions about what is right and just. These opinions ultimately would be based on what he refers to as the 'settled' or 'considered' convictions of the people concerned (Rawls 2005: 8). It would be up to the members of a particular society whether or not they chose to enshrine those rights in a constitution or other founding legal document. It would even be open to citizens to reconsider the basic rights themselves in the light of changes to the collective view of what was fair or just.[7]

Upon such bases and within the resulting institutional framework, it is clear what procedures would allow for the creation of new law. Properly constituted legislative assemblies could decide on legislation that gave new rights to citizens. Duly appointed judges in higher courts could develop the law in particular ways, in response to changing circumstances, whether these involved new economic or technological developments or the emergence of new attitudes and beliefs among a sufficient number of citizens. Consider Deleuze's example from his *Abécédaire* interviews with Claire Parnet. He explains his understanding of a jurisprudence that proceeds case by case with reference to French legal decisions relating to the banning of smoking in taxis. A first decision refused to allow such a ban on the grounds that the occupant was considered to be in the position of a tenant renting an apartment. A subsequent decision upheld the ban on the grounds that a taxi was considered to be a public service and the occupant in a public rather than a private space.

While this is a good example of the modification of law in response to a particular situation, it is not a particularly good example of the creation of a right. In the first place, these cases involve a conflict between the rights of citizens to smoke and the rights of the state or the owners of taxis to prevent them from smoking while in a taxi. There is no new right created here – unless we suppose that this was an early stage in the emergence of the right to a smoke-free work environment – but rather the re-drawing of the boundaries between the right to smoke and the right to prohibit smoking in certain places. What we see in this example, as Alex Lefebvre points out, 'is a differential distribution or evolution of rights according to the construction of a juridical problem' (Lefebvre 2008: 58). The difference between the two decisions turns on the legal characterisation of the taxi: in the latter case, it is considered public space whereas in the former it was considered private. A second reason why this is not a particularly strong example of the creation of a new right is that Deleuze's discussion is limited to the legal characterisation of the situation and the decisions that followed from the different constructions. There is no consideration of the larger shifts in the weight of medical evidence and public opinion with regard to the dangers of passive smoking. These are the more important changes that have made possible the ever more stringent restrictions on the freedom of citizens to smoke in recent years. In the terms of the relational and historical conceptions of rights alluded to above, it is these changes that have allowed for the increased restriction of the right to smoke.

William Connolly's conception of micropolitics and its relation to the rights of individuals and groups offers a more comprehensive picture of what is involved in the emergence of new rights. Connolly views democracy as a unique form of cultural and political practice that 'enables participation in collective decisions while enabling contestation of sedimented settlements from the past' (Connolly 1995: 103). On this view, a distinctive feature of democratic politics is that even the most strongly held convictions expressed in its laws and institutions are open to change. For example, homosexual relations were illegal in many Western countries until the 1970s when cultural and political movements sought to challenge established norms of sexual behaviour:

> A political movement was necessary in this case to place a new right on the register of individual rights. The evil it remedies was (and is) palpable and painful for a large number of people, but the new right itself is not simply derivable from a fixed set of principles. It is a political invention, requiring . . . a whole lot of micropolitical preparation. (Connolly 1999: 140)

Connolly illustrates the micropolitical preparation behind the emergence of a new right by reference to the 'right to die'. This is a right still in the course of becoming established throughout many Western democracies that continue to afford institutional protection to Christian moral beliefs. The strict laws against euthanasia in those countries reflect the fundamentally Christian belief that suicide or assisted death is morally wrong. Connolly points to the kinds of experience that might lead citizens to reconsider this particular belief such as watching a loved family member endure a prolonged and agonising period of suffering in the course of a terminal illness, reading a novel, seeing a film or hearing reports of such experiences from friends. The internal conflict that such experiences might initiate between moral beliefs and concern for the suffering of the dying could then be further exacerbated by being exposed to a better understanding of the complexity of human death or more information about the available means to ensure that it is relatively painless, and so on. Such experiences can lead to changes in the beliefs, attitudes and affective responses of individuals towards active involvement in one's own death or the death of others, often as a result of prolonged movement backwards and forwards between these different 'registers of subjectivity'. In the course of this process, Connolly points out, we become aware 'how judgment occurs on several registers, and how much more there is to thinking than argument' (Connolly 1999: 148). Once this kind of intra-subjective experience has become sufficiently widespread and individuals have begun to share their newly revised attitudes and beliefs, it may become the basis for the establishment of a right to die:

> If the right to die becomes installed as a fervent demand by a significant constellation, they will work to encase it in institutional practices such as court decisions, medical practices, legislative enactments, living wills, family obligations and insurance policies. The political project will now be to devise procedural protections against the misuse of this institutionally entrenched right rather than to prohibit it to guard a contestable conception or nature of God from performative assault by those who do not endorse it. (Connolly 1999: 149)

Connolly provides an entirely immanentist account of the sorts of movement in the sensibilities and beliefs of individuals and populations that are required in order for new behaviours, or ways of being treated, to become established, first in a range of social attitudes and practices and then in law. This account follows the general coordinates of Deleuze and Guattari's theory of micropolitics.[8] These are the kind of subterranean political processes that Deleuze has in mind when he remarks that, in moving beyond judges and moral experts to consider new rights in relation to modern biology, we move from law to politics. While these are below the threshold of public political reason and its institutional mechanisms, there is no privileged site for the emergence of new rights. Sometimes this may begin with changes in the affective constitution of people and their relations to one another as in the case of homosexual rights or the right to die. At other times, it may begin with a legal decision that is in advance of the beliefs and desires of even a majority of the people, but that creates the conditions under which new beliefs, affects and interpersonal relations become possible. The Australian High Court's 1992 decision in favour of Aboriginal or Native title to land was an example of the latter kind. This judgment created a right which was entirely new in Australian property law and which attracted violent condemnation from many in a community accustomed to the idea that Indigenous people had no rights to the land. The creation of rights that is called for by Deleuzian jurisprudence inevitably involves both micro and macro politics, along with legislative and judicial decision. However the precise order and relationship between these elements may vary from one situation to another.

## Becoming-right

The task of philosophy, according to Deleuze and Guattari, is the creation of concepts or the modification of old ones that give expression to the abstract machines and pure events on the plane of immanence. Indeed, because the concepts that philosophy creates are supposed to express pure events, it follows that philosophy shapes many of the mundane events in terms of which we understand and respond to the history that unfolds around us. For this reason, and because the task of philosophy as they conceive of it is to create new concepts, philosophy is an inherently political activity. Philosophy has provided the concepts in terms of which we describe political life and its processes: the social contract, revolution, republican and democratic government have all been reinterpreted many times in the course of modern political history. The social contract has been differently defined by Hobbes, Locke, Rousseau and Rawls. The concept of revolution has pursued 'its immanent path' from the English through the French, American and then Soviet revolutions, each with their different ideals and aims (Deleuze and Guattari 1994: 100). The concept of democracy contains at its core an idea of the equality of all who are governed that is only partially or temporarily expressed in the idea of a well-ordered society governed in accordance with a particular historical conception of justice.

The philosophical expression of pure events in concepts enables the redescription and evaluation of actual historical processes and states of affairs, an activity which Deleuze and Guattari call 'countereffectuation' and which serves to restore the connection of the actual to the virtual, thereby loosening the hold that existing ways of thinking about the present have over our actions and opening up space for the emergence of new ways of thinking and being (Patton 2010: 58). The critical function of the concept is ensured by the fact that, qua expression of a pure event, it is never exhausted by its empirical manifestations, but also by the fact that it relates to the milieu in which it is deployed. Philosophical concepts, they argue, are always created in response to particular problems. As a result, as Deleuze insists in the *Abécédaire*, 'there are no philosophical concepts that do not refer to non-philosophical co-ordinates' (Deleuze 1996: '*D comme Désir*').

Deleuze and Guattari's own contribution to political philosophy, understood in the narrow sense of those concepts that relate specifically to the political institutions and structure of modern societies, has been to propose concepts of open-ended transformative processes, such as becoming-minoritarian, becoming-revolutionary and becoming-democratic, as well as concepts of the processes of capture that constrain the actualisation of these transformative processes in the present, such as the capitalist axiomatic or the 'control-society'. Thus, while the philosophical concept of democracy gives expression to a pure event of democratisation that is both incarnated within and betrayed by actually existing democracies, the concept of becoming-democratic reminds us that this pure event is also expressed in ongoing efforts to give institutional expression to its core egalitarian ideals, whether in relation to decision making, social status or the distribution of the material benefits of social cooperation (Patton 2010: 154–9, 191–3). The difference between the pure event or process of democracy and its current historical forms allows Deleuze and Guattari both to undertake the criticism of actually existing democracies and to call for resistance to the present in the name of a 'becoming-democratic that is not the same as existing forms of constitutional state' (Deleuze and Guattari 1994: 113).

Deleuze and Guattari do not explicitly consider the concept of right as a philosophical concept of the same order as revolution or democracy, even though they invoke this concept from time to time (Deleuze and Guattari 1994: 102–4).[9] However, there is no reason why they could not regard the concept of right as a philosophical concept that, like revolution, has pursued its own immanent path from ancient Greece up to the present. In these terms, another way to construe Deleuze's support for jurisprudence and his call for the creation of new rights would be to propose a concept of 'becoming-right' alongside the concepts of 'becoming-revolutionary' and 'becoming-democratic' that together define the normative orientation of Deleuze's later political philosophy (Patton 2010: 154). His and Guattari's commitment to democracy already provides reasons to think that they are committed to the existence of the basic civil and political rights that are, in Habermas's phrase, 'co-originally constituted' with one another and with the requirements of a modern constitutional democracy (Habermas 1998: 122). Within the political and legal framework established by such basic rights, it is open to citizens and their various representatives to forge new rights. Ultimately, this can only refer to the 'establishment', through changes in custom, public opinion and eventually law, of certain ways of behaving and being treated. The preceding discussion of the micropolitics of embracing a right to die provides one example of the 'becoming-right' of certain behaviours in relation to wilfully chosen death.

Since it does imply the emergence of a majority view in favour of the right concerned, the concept of becoming-right appears to conflict with Deleuze and Guattari's principle that 'all becoming is a becoming-minoritarian' (Deleuze and Guattari 1980: 356; 1987: 291). A footnote to this page in *A Thousand Plateaus* refers to the paradoxes of collective decision making as evidence of the difficulty of determining the majority view within a given political community. However, more recent theories of deliberative democracy take these paradoxes to show the inappropriateness of understanding democratic decision simply as the aggregation of preferences rather than as objections to the very idea of a majority view. In whatever way the process is understood, the formation and reformation of majoritarian opinions occurs at all levels of the political organisation of society, from day to day opinions on matters of public concern to the relatively settled opinions on fundamental questions of justice and right. The reformation of such opinions is implied by the idea that deterritorialised assemblages of desires, affect and opinion become reterritorialised into new more or less settled assemblages that in turn affect the public political institutions of the society. Deleuze and Guattari acknowledge the importance of such reterritorialisation when they suggest that lines of flight or molecular escapes would be pointless if they did not react back on the molar structure of social and political life to reshuffle its distribution of rights, status and access to social goods (Deleuze and Guattari 1980: 264; 1987: 216–17).

The concept of becoming-right helps to make sense of Deleuze's criticism of human rights alongside his praise of jurisprudence. His remarks make it clear that he is not opposed to rights as such. His preference for jurisprudence over a transcendent list of human rights implies opposition to the idea that there exists a definitive set of human rights grounded in some rights-bearing feature of human nature. He opposes the idea that rights are ahistorical or acontextual. Just as philosophical concepts must refer to the milieu in which they are developed or modified, if they are to be politically effective and to realise the political vocation of philosophy, so too must rights refer to the 'immanent modes of existence' of the people concerned. In this sense, rights like concepts are situational or site-specific. The establishment and protection of particular ways of behaving or being treated is part of the ongoing struggle to maintain human freedom: 'To act for freedom, becoming revolutionary, is to operate in jurisprudence when one turns to the justice system . . . that's what the invention of right is ...' (Deleuze 1996: 'G comme Gauche').

Finally, Deleuze's preference for jurisprudence over declarations of human rights or their enshrinement in legal codes is a preference for the ongoing and open-ended micro and macro political processes that lead to the invention of new rights and the modification of existing laws. Just as philosophy responds to problems by the creation of concepts, so when we respond to particular situations by legal means we are involved in jurisprudence, meaning the creative modification of existing legal principles or the invention of new ones to fit particular cases. That is why Deleuze argues that situations such as the Armenian events he refers to must be considered as *cases* to be decided rather than 'elements of abstract law'. In other words, the judicial response to such cases must be properly creative and not simply the rote application of universal human rights. In law as in thought, this case-by-case approach is a means to introduce movement into abstractions and thereby to approach more closely the conditions of life:

> That's what life is; there are no 'rights of man,' only rights of life, and so, life unfolds case by case. (Deleuze 1996: 'G comme Gauche')

## References

Connolly, W. E. (1995), *The Ethos of Pluralization*, Minneapolis and London: University of Minnesota Press.
Connolly, W. E. (1999), *Why I Am Not a Secularist*, Minneapolis and London: University of Minnesota Press.
Deleuze, G. (1990), *Pourparlers*, Paris: Minuit.
Deleuze, G. (1995), *Negotiations 1972–1990*, trans. Martin Joughin, New York: Columbia University Press.
Deleuze, G. (1996), *L'Abécédaire de Gilles Deleuze avec Claire Parnet*, available on video cassette and DVD (2004) from Vidéo Editions Montaparnasse.
Deleuze, G., and F. Guattari (1980), *Mille plateaux*, Paris: Minuit.

Deleuze, G., and F. Guattari (1987), *A Thousand Plateaus: Capitalism and Schizophrenia*, trans. Brian Massumi, Minneapolis: University of Minnesota Press.
Deleuze, G., and F. Guattari (1991), *Qu'est-ce que la philosophie?*, Paris: Minuit.
Deleuze, G., and F. Guattari (1994), *What Is Philosophy?*, trans. Hugh Tomlinson and Graham Burchell, New York: Columbia University Press.
Deleuze, G., and C. Parnet (1996), *Dialogues* (avec Claire Parnet), Paris: Flammarion; new edition, Collection Champs.
Deleuze, G., and C. Parnet (2002), *Dialogues II*, trans. Hugh Tomlinson and Barbara Habberjam, 'The Actual and the Virtual', trans. Eliot Ross Albert, London: Athlone Press.
Finlayson, J. G. and F. Freyenhagen (eds) (2010), *Habermas and Rawls: Disputing the Political*, London: Routledge.
Foucault, M. (2000), 'Confronting Governments: Human Rights', in *Essential Works of Foucault 1954–1984, Volume 3, Power*, ed. James D. Faubion, trans. Robert Hurley and others, New York: The New Press, 474–5.
Habermas, J. (1998), *Between Facts and Norms: Contributions to a Discourse Theory of Law and Democracy*, trans. William Rehg, Cambridge, MA: MIT Press.
Lefebvre, A. (2008), *The Image of Law: Deleuze, Bergson, Spinoza*, Stanford: Stanford University Press.
Martin, R. (1993), *A System of Rights*, Oxford: Clarendon Press.
Nietzsche, F. (1982), *Daybreak: Thoughts on the Prejudices of Morality*, trans. R. Hollingdale, Cambridge: Cambridge University Press.
Nietzsche, F. (1986), *Human, All Too Human: A Book for Free Spirits*, trans. R. Hollingdale, Cambridge: Cambridge University Press.
Patton, P. (2004), 'Power and Right in Nietzsche and Foucault', *International Studies in Philosophy*, 36 (3): 43–61.
Patton, P. (2005), 'Foucault, Critique and Rights', *Critical Horizons*, 6:1, December: 267–87.
Patton, P. (2008), 'Nietzsche on Rights, Power and the Feeling of Power', in Herman W. Siemens and Vasti Roodt (eds), *Nietzsche, Power, and Politics: Rethinking Nietzsche's Legacy for Political Thought*, Berlin: Walter de Gruyter, 471–90.
Patton, P. (2010), *Deleuzian Concepts: Philosophy, Colonization, Politics*, Stanford: Stanford University Press.
Rawls, J. (2005), *Political Liberalism: Expanded Edition*, New York: Columbia University Press.
Smith, D. W. (2003), 'Deleuze and the Liberal Tradition: Normativity, Freedom and Judgment', *Economy and Society*, 32 (2): 312–17.
Sumner, L. W. (1987), *The Moral Foundation of Rights*, Oxford: Clarendon Press.
Whyte, J. (2012), 'Human Rights: Confronting Governments?: Michel Foucault and the Right to Intervene', in M. Stone, I. Wall and C. Douzinas (eds), *New Critical Legal Thinking: Law and the Political*, London: Routledge.

## Notes

1. Foucault 2000. For discussion of this text see Patton 2005. For more detail on Foucault's engagement with human rights, see Whyte 2012.
2. Deleuze is referring to the earthquake that struck on 7 December 1988. Daniel Smith comments on this discussion and on these passages from *L'Abécédaire* (Smith 2003). Alexandre Lefebvre also comments on these passages in discussing Deleuze's concept of jurisprudence (Lefebvre 2008: 53–9).

3. Lefebvre provides a helpful discussion of the meanings of 'jurisprudence'. He also tends to prefer 'right' rather than 'law' in translating Deleuze's remarks about jurisprudence (Lefebvre 2008: 54–8).
4. It is widely assumed that rights in so far as they exist independently of law must be moral rights: 'We say that black South Africans have the moral right to full representation even though this right has not been accorded legal recognition, and in saying this we mean to point to the right as a moral reason for changing the legal system so as to accord it recognition' (Sumner 1987: 13).
5. For further discussion of Nietzsche's approach to an immanent historical understanding of the origin of rights, see Patton 2004: 43–61; 2005: 270–1; 2008.
6. 'Justice originates between parties of approximately equal power . . . where there is no clearly recognizable superiority of force and a contest would result in mutual injury producing no decisive outcome the idea arises of coming to an understanding and negotiating over one another's demands: the characteristic of *exchange* is the original characteristic of justice. Each satisfies the other, inasmuch as each acquires what he values more than the other does. One gives to the other what he wants to have, to be henceforth his own, and in return receives what one oneself desires. Justice is thus requital and exchange under the presupposition of an approximately equal power position: revenge therefore belongs originally within the domain of justice, it is an exchange. Gratitude likewise . . .' (Nietzsche 1986: 49).
7. For further discussion of the historicity of Rawlsian justice, see Patton 2010: 205–9.
8. In Plateau 9, '1933 Micropolitics and Segmentarity', they suggest that 'Political decision making necessarily descends into a world of microdeterminations, attractions and desires, which it must sound out or evaluate in a different fashion. Beneath linear conceptions and segmentary decisions, an evaluation of flows and their quanta' (Deleuze and Guattari 1980: 270–1; 1987: 221).
9. Deleuze and Parnet summed up the variety of social movements and lines of flight in relation to linguistic, ethnic, regional, sexual, youth and other minorities that challenged the capitalist economy and nation state assemblages in the 1970s as expressions of a '*right to desire*' (Deleuze and Parnet 1996: 176; 2002: 147).

# Chapter 2
# The Poetry of Black Letters: Deleuze and *lex amicitia*

*Peter Goodrich* \*

> Perhaps the most painful aspects of remembering a dead friend are the gestures and glances that still reach us, that still come to us long after he is gone.

An initial clue. A curious verbal concatenation from the great philologist and follower of Varro, Giambattista Vico. Well into the *New Science*, discussing the 'first and most proper' form of jurisprudence, Vico elaborates upon the etymology of interpretation. It derives, he claims, from the forgotten or traduced Latin root of *interpatrari* meaning 'to enter into the fathers' (Vico 1984: 343). This could be given a humanist gloss, meaning that the dead send on their amity and other elaborations by means of texts, by dint of the plenitude of sense and longevity of speech that the history of books entails. For Vico, however, the proper sense of this patristic root of juristic construction engages with three less obvious connotations. The first is theogonic. Jurisprudence engages with a mystery, an invisible prior and higher source of norms, an unwritten realm of the arcana of law that exceeds positive law and is apprehended only by faith, by a method that goes beyond reason and depends therefore upon authority. Second, and related, the properly legal interpretation, the legal deed that takes account of the fathers, is designated, for this reason, *actus legitimi* because it embodies and enacts the mysterious and obscure authority, the 'dark precursor' I am tempted to say, following Deleuze, that structures and marks law as a system (Deleuze 1994: 119).

---

\* Any discussion of *lex amicitia*, Deleuzian or other, must begin with an asterisk footnote (how could it not?) revealing the identifications, networks, revealed amities and hidden enmities, potential citations and evident lacunae of the text. Thanks to the editors, thanks to Nathan Moore, regards to Stanley Fish, beatitude for Linda Mills. *C'est tout.*

Here is where it gets interesting. The third point – the Holy Ghost – lies precisely in the dimension of legality. Why is it necessary to go amongst the fathers to interpret law? Key point, indeed the signal direction of the *New Science*, is that law precedes philosophy, that what the father gives as law is the foundation of all interpretation. We, the contemporary, the moderns, come after the parents, the classics, the ancients. We are dwarves on the shoulders of giants, we are children attending to, and working through, what the juristic tradition has thrown our way. Thus, borrowing another incisive etymology from Vico: *philo-sophia*, the philosopher, the interpreter who comes after the law is at root not merely a lover (*phileō*) of wisdom, not simply a friend (*philia*) of knowledge, but at base a son, at least a child, the root of the word being *phylê* meaning kin group and tribe, and from which the Latins derived *filius* (Vico 1984: 196). *Philien* is cognate with *filius*, and comparably, returning to the fathers amongst whom we wander so as to understand the law, we are inevitably children, as also descendants, the begotten to whom law and thence meaning are given.

First poetry and then mystery found authority and the intuitions of those who seek the norm. The lure of darkness is the adjunct and precursor of meaning, it is the absent source, the invisible hand, the burning bush that dictates the law that we come before in Kafka's alternately demoralising and humorous metaphor.[1] For now, however, the question that I will pose in this essay, the issue to which I will return, is that of the tribe, the kin group and specifically the role of philosopher as *filius*, as child and hence the link between law and friendship, obscurity and meaning, legality and governance as we might mediate them through Deleuze and Guattari's play upon the figure of the friend. The theme is a remarkably persistent one and yet it has been explored to a certain degree in ignorance of law and of lawyers as the originators and most constant promulgators of the *lex amicitia* at the heart of the juristic tradition.[2] How then, and this is my question throughout or at least until I mislay it, how then is friendship tied to the mystery, to the beyond that constitutes law as the precursor of meaning, and as destiny, governance and practice in Agamben's recent lucubrations?

## *Iura imaginaria*

Giambattista, and please excuse the reverse causality, all will unfold in due course, starts his treatise with an image of thought, an emblem to be precise, of the work. (See Figure 1.) This was not uncommon in his day although it was rare to offer such a direct pictorial devising of the

*syntagma* as the treatise used to be termed. Vico appreciated the importance of the symbol, the synecdoche of the work, the impress of the idea which Deleuze would likely term the force that engenders thought, the event of thinking as such. But pause, no need to hurry apparently, according to the latest resurgence of 'slow learning' at least, stay with the image. It is deeply indexical, as images of the period, the baroque so fond to Gilles and Giambattista alike, are prone to be. It is replete with hieroglyphs, with Gods, and mystic rays, fire, a globe, a statue of Homer no less, as well as tablets, ploughs, *fasces*, urns, wings, clouds, *litui* and more. You could write a book. And of course Vico did, but my initial point is a rather different one. The image, emblem or devise, take your pick, is an encoding of a trajectory, a symbolisation of a mode of thought and a representation of providence and law. Take this on two levels. The primary axis is the ray of light that emanates from the divine eye to the breast of the winged 'metaphysic' astride the globe, then to the figure of Homer and thence, less obviously, to the tablet with letters. Light penetrates the darkness, the menacing clouds that would otherwise envelope globe, metaphysic and humanity as such. In Vico's explanation the trajectory here is from law to poetry to art. Interestingly, however, the form of this image of thought is not thought but an image. A series of figures, letters, symbols, hieroglyphs. There is an appropriateness, an ethics even, to this honesty of form that shows everything that will subsequently be told. It can help us. It offers an affect, a face to the world and to thought whereas, at the risk of being critical, Deleuze's image of thought, of dogmatic thought, relies upon eight propositions, eight postulates that 'together form the dogmatic image of thought' (Deleuze 1994: 167).

Deleuze's image of dogmatic thought starts with Descartes – the French like to stick together after all – and the Latin maxim *cogitatio natura universalis* – contemplate/think/cogitate the nature of the universe. Well, first off the Latin, the argot of pontiffs, jurisconsults, Emperors and Romans though not necessarily in that order. There is here a useful depiction of the 'entry amongst the fathers', the trajectory towards the *iura imaginaria*, the legitimacy of empty masks, as Vico so poetically puts it, and which Deleuze here treats as an enigma of origin, Descartes as the fictive source of dogmatic thought, as one of the fathers. A scriptural parent of philosophy to which textual fount Deleuze adopts the ancient formula of the laws, *et ego recipio*, I am bound (to cite the Latin, to promulgate the name, recognise the history, engage the game) (Vico 1984: 388). In juristic valence, this fiction of derivation and authorisation, indirect though it be, places Deleuze and Guattari in the

## Gilles Deleuze and Félix Guattari

Photograph of the authors: © Jerry Bauer

tradition of *filii archivorum*, children of archives. What is more, we can offer an image of this particular filiation, ironic and humorous as it may be. The back cover of the 1977 US edition of *Anti-Oedipus: Capitalism and Schizophrenia* by Gilles Deleuze and Félix Guattari, and forgive this momentary visual digression, has a most unusual 'photograph of the authors' copyrighted by Jerry Bauer. (See Figure 2.)[3] It shows the two authors seated close together, faces turned towards the camera, each in their way smiling, enticing, on a small velvet covered couch. Or so it seems in the black and white image that publishers tend to use for reasons of cost consciousness. It is not a love seat but it is small and the pair are close enough to be almost touching arms. The rest is less normal, or what passes for normal in the post-1960s amongst leftist nomads.

Above the photograph, first hint of irony, *antonomasia*, a playful nomination, are the names of the authors, Gilles Deleuze in bold font, first, Félix Guattari second. You can see it for yourself, courtesy of Jerry Bauer. The names, however, are above the heads of their opposites: Deleuze is above the image of Guattari, and the name of Guattari above the head Deleuze. A carefully staged comedy, it must be supposed, a little disinformation, an inside joke even, especially in so far as in virtually every other photograph of the two, at press conferences, symposia, interviews, it is invariably Gilles on the right and Félix on the left, seated alphabetically, authors all in a row. The three photo portraits used by Dosse in his twin biography, and we must assume that they are emblematic, are each in alphabetical order. The cover picture, the flaunting on the face of the book, shows Deleuze on the right and slightly to the foreground, Guattari leaning back, wearing two pairs of spectacles, making up for Deleuze perhaps, to the right and further back. The other two joint images are not simply in the same order but also play visually upon the identity of the two. They are an identical pair, brothers or in law 'semblables'. Siblings, other selves the pictures seem to say, and in the last portrait, under heavily stacked shelves of books, Deleuze has his enveloping hands on Félix's right thigh.

As for our photo portrait from the back cover of *Anti-Oedipus*, it is very much of its era and epoch, the post-'60s, and it is appropriately – let's say conventionally – unconventional. The background is a plain wood-panelled wall, perhaps wainscotting, the authors on their couch leaning forward earnestly, half smiling, hands clasped philosophically, Deleuze's almost in the mode of prayer, intent and intense. Both philosophers have shoulder length hair, an intimation of the feminine, of the *declassé*, the sympathetic and relaxed, *sans barbe* and so thinkers in a feminine vein as the genealogists of that era would likely say. Then, most striking of all, the two authors, both of the *filii archivorum*, are wearing near identical sweaters. In the black and white photo, both appear to be dressed in grey jumpers, in sartorial terms identical twins, similar colour, similar collar and similar cuffs for the friends, the similars, the other selves. In my copy of the book, dust jacket a little worn, the photograph has the curvature of a TV screen, the authors now apparently and appropriately inside the machine, kids both, desiring the jouissance of the father, and the *iura imaginaria* or imaginary rights that ancient jurisprudence attributed to the *imperium paternum*, the power to invent fictions and elaborate fables that will poetically resolve extant facts into narratives conforming to *nomos*.

The actual frontispiece, the emblem to *Anti-Oedipus*, hidden inside the covers, is indeed the figure of a bloated child, a less flattering filiation tied up in a desiring machine. This is seemingly the underside and backface of filiation and depicts the stupidity of the body, of childish greed, of material want, against the clear lines and mathematical precision of the modernist machine. The picture is by Richard Lidner, from 1954, peculiarly the year of my terrestrial advent, but it is in most respects more obvious and less interesting than the modern frontispiece, albeit that the latter is the recto cover photo. So let me stay, however, with the portrait of boy and machine by Lidner. The child is a friend of the machine, smiling and caught up, entwined in the mechanism. It is a short step to say that the boy is in and of the machine, fulgurating and affiliated in the thought machine, in the fabricator of concepts, the manufacturer of phantasms, the explorer seeking the becoming of thought and the *terra incognita* of distant friends. Deleuze has Guattari, and he sends missives into the darkness, as precursors – who knows? – to Jean-Paul Sartre, Dionysus Mascolo, Henri Bergson, Michel Foucault and more. Time then to address Deleuze's peculiar image of friendship, the anti-Oedipal *lex amicitia*, that we have glimpsed already in the ironically staged cover photograph and the law of desire that pervades the vagabond territories of Deleuzian thought.

## *Carmina*

It is perhaps too easy to say that for Deleuze and Guattari jurisprudence is the study of singularities, of events – pathologies, conflicts, antinomies – that force lawyers to think.[4] There is that, of course, in its varied dimensions, but for Deleuze in particular there is a more trenchant and less expected law of amity which requires, following Vico, that we think first of filiation, of father and son in the classical juristic lexicon, and then latterly of friends. The law of course, a Christian tradition, had long posed amity, *ius amicitiae*, as a dimension of *ius sanguinis*, of blood ties, and Vico simply reminds us not simply of a broadly Lacanian – and again with the reverse causalities, I apologise, enigma following enigma – paternal law, but also of a law that precedes philosophy and the discourse of friends and that indeed gives to such cerebrations their proper meaning. Law, as Vico reiterates, precedes philosophy, and in my turn I am emphasising this because it throws a novel light – a proper darkness – upon the law of amity.

Of the *lex amicitia* itself, which I have treated at length in an unpublished book,[5] I will say only a little. My topic is Deleuze and not I. Let me note a highlight or two. The *lex amicitia* is the law of friendship that according to Aristotle precedes and is more important than legislation. It is the community of friends who make justice possible and law functional. Cicero and later Montaigne, both trained as lawyers, and so too Francis Bacon, the other great advocate of amity, take up the tradition and spell out the law of friends that is identical with the social contract, the being together by mutual affection as expressed most obviously in the Christian *osculum pacis*, the kiss of peace, which gentle or not so gentle insufflation marks membership of the brotherhood of the faith. Derrida, after his turn to law, after his long article on the mystical foundations of justice, picked up this theme, the 'immense rumour' as he calls it, and offers his own view of the brotherhood of friends whose history must remain in ethical and political terms silent and undisclosed. The most indicative lines then, just briefly, towards the end of the *Politics of Friendship*: 'Maligning and cursing, as we have seen often enough, still appertain to the inside of the history of brothers (friends or enemies, be they false or true). This history will not be thought, it will not be recalled, by taking up *this* side' (Derrida 1997: 305). Loyalty to the friend, to the brother of either sex, was Derrida's motto and motif. In his own homoerotic fashion he in the end favoured a species of solidarity, a love in and of the common as Negri wishes it, that transcends the unamicable brother, the brother against whom nothing can be said, and binds him to 'a conjuration and so many unuttered oaths' (Derrida 1997: 305).[6]

Deleuze, by contrast, is in appearance at least not as amicable as Derrida. He believes in the friend, of course, it is hard not to, but at the same time he resists friendship, suspects it and is willing to speak its history of rivalries, competitiveness and frequent banality. When Dionys Mascolo, and the correspondence is quite formal, writes of amity as the sharing of thought, the sharing of the distress of thought, then Gilles Deleuze signs off: 'asking more questions would only hold you back' (Deleuze 2006: 327). Even more poignantly, speaking in another letter to a different correspondent of his intellectual friendship with Félix G., he speaks in essence, as he often does, of his love of concepts, the essential inseparability of affect and concept, and so too of image and amity. Thus, last lines, the best moments of their relationship were when 'under Félix's spell, I felt I could perceive unknown territories where strange concepts dwelt' (Deleuze 2006: 240). Leaving aside the becoming of concepts, the hard and troublesome conception of the conceptual, I wish to attend to the *philia* that Deleuze felt and repeatedly expressed in relation to nominate conceptual *personae* and the theatre of actual thought.

It is the link between affect, image and amity that is most original and singular in Deleuze. Against the scholastic *lex amicitia* and its notion of *philia* as striving for identity and agreement, for the banality of the same, for the lawful and in a sense risk-free *procedere ad similia*, Deleuze offered a much less juridical and much more unwritten sense of the laws of friendship. Thought and friendship, nominate, face to face amity, signature and touch, were much closer to his method. If Vico, and especially his emblem of the divine rapture of metaphysic, represents a bizarre and unorthodox transmission of the classical form of *philia* as *filius*, as family, as parent and child, father and son, he equally poses the question of the distress, the dark and nocturnal substrate and precedent of the *lex amicitia*, the possibility that it can always go horribly wrong.[7] Vico's image of thought is graphically and directly angelological. Metaphysic has her winged helmet and the divinity communicates optically, through a beam of light, a line of sight. By the same metaphor and in the same picture are also the obverse of that which thought divines: darkness, clouds, the 'deep shadows' and obscurity whose principles are hieroglyphic and yet unknown except by their effects (Vico 1984: 7).

Deleuze is fairly constant on this theme. His version of *lex amicitia* takes up Proust's critique of the philosopher as the friend, as agreement, as the same in the other. For Deleuze we must enter a more complex space of reverie and Egyptology, of irony and the unconscious. Thought shatters the complacency of similarity and the tiresome predictability of precedent. The image of the friend, in Deleuze, is bound up with the shadows and the ignorance that Vico had illustrated. In question are 'the dark regions in which are elaborated the effective forces that act on thought, the determinations that force us to think', in short, our desire and our pathology. The truth, in this version of the argument, the proper verdict, the just sentence, 'is not communicated, it is interpreted; it is not willed, it is involuntary' (Deleuze 2000: 95). The friend is a matter of perception, a mystery, a glance, a gesture, an affect image in which a truth is betrayed, and a type of charm revealed. Thus, according to the relaxed, perhaps entranced and certainly benign Deleuze of the *Abécédaire*, the perception of friendship, the image of a friend, begins by denying the father in a momentary reference and then going on to question the virtue of fidelity, similarity and wisdom as such.[8]

As for Deleuze's resistance to the juridified version of amity, it is evident and known, it requires no further elaboration. Not from me at least. The path taken, in thought and in friendship, is that of *terra incognita*, of non-recognition, secrets, betrayals, glimpses in the dark because 'thought is primarily trespass and violence, the enemy . . . everything begins with misosophy' (Deleuze 1994: 139). Watching *L'Abécédaire* it could also be argued that thought begins with foolosophy, with the laugh, as Stivale notes, with comedy as much as hatred. Foolosophy, technically, is associated with the image, it being an expression of *mens emblematica* and specifically of the satirical, of a visual and verbal humour combined in emblems that were variously deemed otiose, nugatory, unserious, playful or obscene because graphically physical, intimately exposing and frequently irreverent in content.[9] Beneath the scorn or superiority that the moderns flung at the emblematic transmission of the norms of justice was a fear of the image and a cognate concern with emblems that showed too much of law, that provided too direct and vivid a picture of a governance that preferred to remain hidden. It is precisely the hidden, the dark precursor, *tenebras antiquitatis*, here meaning the encounter with the fathers that Vico and now Deleuze, the late Deleuze, now properly a child of the archive, addressed by way of the centrality of interpretation.

The conjunction of amity, image and law throws desire and legality into a forced relation. Justice cannot but encounter the machine. There is the entrance and event of what is effectively a non-law, a dark precursor, an interval, a norm both inside and outside of law that gains fleeting recognition in the invention of judgment and in the figures that remain in the text. Foolosophy, mad theories, are one version of this amity that is neither faithful nor predictable, that precedes and subsists within a semantic space, a mode of governance that is neither internal nor external to legality, but rather, as Heidegger would have it, an alien will within. What then does the face of thought, the affect image of a friend, this desire within the contract and law provide? Our foolosopher Guillaume de Perrière, but he is just one instance, offers the remarkably Deleuzian view that the mad speech of emblems expresses a passion, a reverie and fever 'that often symbolizes a mode of vatication'.[10] The humour of the image, the contentment of sight, the visial line all probe towards the expression of an unknown territory, a poetic truth, a light in our darkness that acts as the reverse of the emblematic ray of divine providence that Vico offers. That is not to say that Vico fails to vaticinate, quite the contrary, it is rather to suggest a double reading of the emblem in which the foolosopher looks back and pursues their vision into darkness and non-knowledge as is required in the move from an unknowable providence to the dictates of fate. To be a foolosopher, to look back, to vaticinate, from the Latin *vates*, seer or prophet, means to be inspired, to glimpse things unseen, express thoughts not yet due, provide something new.

Vico's figure of metaphysic could equally stand for the earlier foolosopher. Metaphysic, with her mask and the wings on her head, with her breastplate and theatrical robe, could certainly be taken for the image of a fool. Perrière indeed begins his *Foolosophy* with some suitably drôle images. He has as his opening woodcut a picture of a lawyer weighing cheese and a wand of office in the scales of justice with the moral, 'there is no wisdom so great as not to also be balanced by madness'. His second prefatory woodcut is of a satyr, a cloven hooved divinity, replete with wings, laurels, and three faces looking, Janus like, to past, present and future.[11] The images are linked with extraordinary precision and directness to the foolosopher's quatrains, verses that explain or associate to the image and to the unseen, the darkness and the shadows that lie beyond the immediacy of knowledge, and the limits of reason. It is precisely when the common becomes a singularity, when the *sensibilia* of thought are encountered in the externality of force, that friendship – for wood, for a book, for a concept, for an interlocutor, for an affect image – becomes both possible and laughable (Deleuze and Guattari 1994: 5). Why laughable? Because unexpected, surprising, externally imposed, momentary, epiphanic, part of a process of becoming, unregulated, new.[12]

What do we find? A passionate friendship, faith or love depending upon the vagaries of affiliation, brotherhood or sorority, to a transient image, to *nomos* in its primary sense of rhythm and melody, as well as *nostos* meaning here the poetry of homecoming, of recognising the wildly unfamiliar.[13] It is this sensuous apprehension of amity that provides the first glimpses of thought, the first forces and events that have their proper capture and expression in the poetry of the seers, in the melodies of the bards, in the first laws which gain their expression in vatication. Sydney's *Apologie for Poetrie* is probably the best of the Anglican sources, imbued though it may be with the continental philosophy of its day, as a defence of the inspiration of verse and the origin of thought in metre and rhyme. Without poetry, there would be no law.[14] Vico makes precisely the same point but with a degree of further precision. It is out of the darkness that law emerges in the form of black letters.

## *Religio verborum*

It is the image of the pretext, the visible word in Christian terminology, that gets expressed in the juristic concept of black letters. For the humanists the black letters of law were the testaments of departed friends, the epistles of the fathers amongst whom one has to enter if one is to interpret in the proper sense of *inter-patrari*, of moving amongst the classics, the greats, the patristic poets. The words of the poet legislators emerge from the rhythms of being, from nature and *corpus* as glimpsed in the fleeting measure of verse. Not that lawyers, even practitioners of *lex amicitia*, formulate the notion of law's poetic passport in such a manner. Turning then, and again, to Vico, and his theory of judgment, his concept in particular of the law that precedes philosophy, we can see a series of visual clues in the image of the book of the *New Science*. Take them according to size. The figure of the poet Homer, and the lyre beside him. Then the tablet with letters of ancient Latin and then the modern Latin alphabet. The sword and *fasces*. The several additional hieroglyphs, the *caduceus*, the *litui*, and I could go on. The idea, however, is of several and various signs that mark the uncertainty of origin, and so also the opacity of legal sources, and hence the need for interpretation, divination, as the means of travel towards the image of the source. Law, in that it holds the common together, is religion, it is the most direct expression of the bond, commandment and *vinculum* that defines first legislation and latterly agreement as the modes of social speech. The black letters of *lex amicitia* are the earliest and mythical modes of judgment derived from the beyond, from the divinity, and translated – by angels, by hermeneuts, by the winged metaphysic, by the foolosopher – into images and words. Vico offers the concept of 'extreme verbal scrupulousness' and the name 'religio verborum', religion of the word, to describe the sacred formulae, providential words, the word as received from the fathers. He cites to the old writ: *qui cadit virgula, caussa cadit* ('he who drops a comma loses his case'), and again and frequently to that law of the Twelve Tables which stipulates: *Si quis nexum faciet mancipiumque, uti lingua nuncupassit, ita ius esto* ('if anyone shall make bond or conveyance, as he has declared with his tongue, so shall it be binding') (Vico 1984: 356, 388). Expression of an absolute.

Cattle are bound by their horns and men are bound by their words according to the later aphorism of Loysel. Why so? Vico's answer is that jurisprudence is poetic. Law is first philosophy, an imagined enterprise, the invention of personae and their masks – *iura imaginaria* – which will do justice. Being myth, fable, fiction in origin, it is the form of a law as it emerges from the shadows that gives it both its status as *actus legitimi* and its gravity and reputation.[15] It is, remember, truth that emanates from the sites of justice, fate that is pronounced by lawgivers and hence its black letters, its friendship for the beyond: 'Thus all the fictions of ancient jurisprudence were truths under masks, and the formulae in which the laws were expressed, because of their strict measures of such and so many words – admitting neither addition, subtraction, nor alteration – were called *carmina*, or songs' (Vico 1984: 390). It is an interesting conjunction. Black letter law requires attention to each word, to every syllable, which is, as Sir Edward Coke has it, known and significant to law. Hence the black letters are necessary and obligatory. Not a word can be changed, not a comma missed out, nor a syllable lacking. Black letter is metre and verse. It has to be recited, incanted, and so in a sense sung.

Dark precursors, opaque clouds, black letters alike share a dimension of uncertainty, a visible opacity, a status of partial object because of what cannot be seen. Such is variously their origin, their paternity, their melody, their choral status and expression. I could go on but the point is that it is the opacity, the undisclosed, unbidden and hidden, that generates the passion and attachment to the letter, *ipsissima verba*, the Masochistic intransigence of literalism.[16] The punishment of black letters precedes the pleasure of consummation of the force and effect of law. The prior and so also priority of law is an image, a black letter – and remember if you will the Gothic typography, the multiple colours, fonts, curlicues and sizes of the black lettering – that comes as precursor to interpretation, before philosophy and jurisprudence, the potentiality of freedom and will. It is thus that Deleuze recollects the image of thought, the poetry of invention, the affect of amity as the signature of the concept and the face of thought.

Amity then is the being in common of law, the outside inside, the precursor that has arrived and remained, the momentary refraction of desire between the lines and in the instant of the turn to interpretation. In the end, in sum, and he is dead now, defenestrated, Deleuze sought in the affect image of *lex amicitia* a sign of the force, the externality and possibility of the event that precedes thought.[17] True enough, he mentions that he distrusted this friendship and was distressed by the claims and rivalries, the simulations and falsehoods of pretended friends, mere brothers, but he also kept with him his own sense of humour and his recognition of the affect image that harbours the momentary appearance of the friend and the possibility of a common project, a construction of concepts, a surprise, an event, an intervention in an unknowable world.

There is perhaps finally the question of the image again, not only as the peculiar vehicle of *lex amicitia*, but also as a mode of transmission of law. Why succumb to the image? If Deleuze and Guattari are properly described, as I have depicted them, and I make no claims, I am Gnostic on this, as *filii archivorum*, then is the better figure not positive and epistolary? The answer is no. My apologies. The figure of the archive is already an expression of authority and collection, of staging of texts, of an apparatus of legitimacy, of acts of law. The concept of black letter law, which we inherit and still use for our comfort as lawyers, is also, in its very blackness, as equally in its rigidity and its reference to print a distant progeny of *religio verborum* and the song of law. More than that, however, the image, the face of the friend, the identity of a common project, the figure of becoming all signify what Deleuze elsewhere coins as belief in the world. He was, in his way, even if in conversation Foucault reported reassuringly 'Deleuze is an enigma', also an activist. The image was for Deleuze the slippage of law, the epiphany, the moment of momentary appearance. Here again Deleuze should have the last word, from a conversation on politics, in which he is talking about eluding control and generating new space-times, novel multiplicities. To this he adds: 'It's what you call *pietas*' (Deleuze 1995: 176). Not love, but faith in the world. Faith in the advent of friends, the apparition of ideas, the occasion of events that generate novelties outside the machine. And then, last words, *pietas* defines an age in which the image has priority over the text.

## References

Bottomley, A. (2000), 'Theory is a Process Not an End', in J. Richardson and R. Sandland (eds), *Feminist Perspectives on Law and Theory*, London: Cavendish.
Cartari, V. (1610), *Les Images des dieux, contenant leur pourtraicts, coustumes et ceremonies*.
Critchley, S. (2008), *The Book of Dead Philosophers*, New York: Vintage.
De Sutter, L. (2009), *Deleuze: La pratique du droit*, Paris: Michalon.
Deleuze, G. (1989), *Masochism: Coldness and Cruelty*, trans. J. McNeil, New York: Zone.
Deleuze, G. (1994), *Difference and Repetition*, trans. P. Patton, New York: Columbia University Press.
Deleuze, G. (1995), *Negotiations 1972–1990*, trans. M. Joughin, New York: Columbia University Press.
Deleuze, G. (2000), *Proust and Signs*, trans. R. Howard, Minneapolis: University of Minnesota Press.
Deleuze, G. (2006), *Two Regimes of Madness: Texts and Interviews 1975–1995*, trans. A. Hodges and M. Taormina, ed. D. Lapoujade, Los Angeles: Semiotext(e).
Deleuze, G. and F. Guattari (1994), *What is Philosophy?*, trans. H. Tomlinson and G. Burchell, New York: Columbia University Press.
Deleuze, G. and C. Parnet (2004), *L'Abécédaire*, Paris: Montparnasse.
Derrida, J. (1997), *The Politics of Friendship*, trans. G. Collins, New York: Verso.
Dosse, F. (2010), *Gilles Deleuze and Félix Guattari: Intersecting Lives*, trans. D. Glassman, New York: Columbia University Press.
Goodrich, P. (2001), 'Ad Hominem: Duncan Kennedy, the Man, the Work, his Scholarship and the Polity', *Cardozo Law Review*, 22: 971.
Goodrich, P. (2003), 'Laws of Friendship', *Law & Literature*, 15: 23.
Goodrich, P. (2004), 'The Immense Rumor', *Yale Journal of Law and the Humanities*, 16: 101.
Goodrich, P. (2011), 'Theatres of the Book: Covering, Flaunting, Marketing, Author, and Text', *Law Text Culture*, 33.
Heinzelman, S. (2009), *Riding the Black Ram: Law, Literature, and Gender*, Stanford: Stanford University Press.
McGee, K. (2009), 'Creation, Duration, Adjudication: A Review of Alexandre Lefebvre's *The Image of Law: Deleuze, Bergson, Spinoza*', *Law & Literature*, 21: 480.
Negri, A. (2003), *Time for Revolution*, trans. M. Mandarini, New York: Continuum.
Negri, A. and M. Hardt (2010), *Commonwealth*, Cambridge, MA: Harvard University Press.

Perrière, G. (1553), *La Morosophie*, Lyon: Bonhomme.
Riffard, P. (2004), *Les Philosophes: vie intime*, Paris: PUF.
Sidney, P. (1595), *An Apologie for Poetrie*.
Stivale, C. (2008), *Gilles Deleuze's ABCs: The Folds of Friendship*, Baltimore: Johns Hopkins University Press.
Vico, G. (1984 [1744]), *The New Science of Giambattista Vico*, trans. T. G. Bergin and M. H. Fisch, Ithaca: Cornell University Press.
Wacquet, F. (2008), *Les Enfants de Socrate. Filiation intellectuelle et transmission de savoir XVIIe-XXIe siècle*, Paris: Albin Michel.

## Notes

1. De Sutter 2009: 36–46 provides an excellent analysis of humour, law and its various Kafkaesque divagations. I cannot compete and so will simply refer the reader to that work and its tributaries.
2. Stivale 2008 is an exhaustive and often inspired study of the theme of friendship in Deleuze (and Guattari) but he does not address the *lex amicitia* at all, at least not by name. Dosse (2010) plays upon the theme of friendship and philosophy but focuses on collaboration, intersection, and 'ships passing in the night' rather than on, and allow me the paradox, the black letter of *lex amicitia*.
3. The obscurity of the reference encourages me to mention, on the topic of covers and covering, Goodrich 2011.
4. McGee 2009 offers hints, intimations, gestures towards a theory of law upon such lines. He notes in particular the importance (and subversion) of the Lacanian *nom du père*, the patristic Catholic figure, for Deleuze and Guattari's excursions into jurisprudence.
5. Goodrich, *How Duncan Kennedy Destroyed My Life* (somewhere in a drawer with the author). Parts of this work were published as Goodrich 2001, Goodrich 2003, and Goodrich 2004. But the great treatise, the autobiographical and I thought momentously humorous excavation of the intimate public lives of academic lawyers, the loves and hates of scholarly networks, remains lost in a drawer, filed under incomplete and largely unseen. Publishers thought it variously improper, an upsurge of bile, or that I was not significant enough for my memories to be of interest to a US audience. How about that? *Nil illegitimi carborundum . . . et coetera*.
6. For Negri, see Negri and Hardt 2010: 180 *et seq*.: 'Love is a process of the production of the common and the production of subjectivity.' It is an *oeconomic* power and may usefully be further pursued in Negri 2003: 209 *et seq*.
7. For a beautifully conceived history of such filiations, their amours and bust ups, see Wacquet 2008.
8. Deleuze and Parnet 2004. One aspect of the entrancing is the image in the mirror of a young Claire Parnet, very visible, toying with a cigarette on her lips, throughout the laughter-clad discussion of friendship.
9. Perrière 1553 translates more literally (and inaccurately of course) as the folly of wisdom, and better as the madness of insight, in French *folle sagesse* according to our Toulousian author all that time ago.
10. Perrière 1553: dedicatory epistle, n.p. (*symbolize souvent à vatication*).
11. On the satyr, see Cartari 1610: 167–73.
12. As for the epiphanic, I will engage with my own archives here, child of course that I am, and refer to a rare English jurist Deleuzian, Anne Bottomley; see Bottomley 2000.

13. I am duty bound here, having borrowed the coinage directly, to cite to Heinzelman 2009, which work lengthily and humorously pursues the concept of *nostos* as *nomos*.
14. Sidney 1595: 4–5, arguing that the earliest lawgivers depended entirely upon 'the passport of poetry'.
15. Intriguingly, but predictably, Vico's reference to fiction is to the preface of Justinian's Institutes and the reference there to *antiqui iuris fabulas*.
16. 'We all know ways of twisting the law by excess of zeal' (Deleuze 1989: 88).
17. Riffard 2004: 173 simply places Deleuze in a list of thinkers who had tuberculosis. It is left to the necronaut Simon Critchley to do the medical work and describe Deleuze's emphysema and his plunge for air: 'On a sudden impulse, a high speed fall appears to be one way of forcing air into one's lungs' (Critchley 2008: 237). A disparate friend of windows to the last.

# Chapter 3

# Human Rights in Deleuze and Bergson's Later Philosophy

*Alexandre Lefebvre*

## I

The purpose of this chapter is to develop a concept of human rights congenial to Deleuze's thought. On the surface, this is not a hopeful task. Any reader acquainted with his remarks on human rights knows that they are harsh and curt.

But what is it about human rights that bothers Deleuze so much? In the *Abécédaire* interview (Deleuze 2004), the very mention of them drives him to distraction. He exclaims that they belong to 'impotent thought' (*pensée molle*) upheld by 'imbeciles' (*débiles*). Worse, Deleuze feels backed into a corner in that to oppose human rights one is provoked into holding detestable positions ('*on a envie de devenir, de tenir des propos odieux*'). For, really, how can one be 'against' human rights? Does Deleuze think that individuals should be denied legal appeal beyond the state? Does he dismiss attempts to protect human faculties?

No, of course not. But why do we get the impression otherwise? Why does even Deleuze admit that his thought pulls in this direction? Why does even he feel driven towards positions that deny the value and goals of human rights?

## II

A central difficulty with Deleuze's remarks on human rights is they give the impression of a direct repudiation. It appears as if he rejects the very idea of human rights. Well, does he?

This is a tricky question. On the one hand, Deleuze is careful to specify that his criticism of human rights refers to the *traditions* that advance them. That is, he distinguishes between opposition to human rights as such and opposition to their predominant dispensation. This distinction is crucial for it preserves a concept of human rights from the traditions that vitiate it. He calls the latter 'discourses' of human rights, which, in his intellectual milieu, means discourse ethics and the *nouveau philosophes* (Deleuze 2004: 'G pour Gauche'; see also Deleuze and Guattari 1994: 106–8). On the other hand, it appears that for Deleuze these discourses have monopolised the potential of human rights. It is as if there is no room to think about human rights beyond the traditions he names, which has the practical consequence of collapsing the distinction between human rights and the discourses through which we receive it. Thus, if to oppose the tradition is, *eo ipso*, to oppose the thing itself, then it looks as if Deleuze rejects the very idea of human rights.

This ambiguity between tradition and thing may explain why Deleuze feels painted into a corner in the *Abécédaire*. Indeed, this section of the interview has an extraordinary quality that can't be captured in a transcript. He sighs, pauses, starts and stops; it is as if he wishes to make and retract claims at one and the same time. And this is perfectly understandable: If criticism of human rights discourse shades into criticism of human rights as such, Deleuze walks a fine line between principled opposition and monstrous proposition. A psychological explanation may have a place here. Talking about his friendship with Michel Foucault, Deleuze says 'Being on the same side [means] laughing at the same things, or sharing a silence, not needing to "explain." It was so nice not having to explain things' (Deleuze 1995: 86). Now it's my sense that in the *Abécédaire*, Deleuze wants to make certain claims about human rights as if he were in the company of friends, as if there were no need to explain, as if his remarks would be taken for granted in the right spirit. I take it that he wants his remarks to be understood as criticism of the tradition rather than of human rights, even if he has not, and perhaps cannot readily, distinguish the dangers of the first from the potential of the second. But of course this desire cannot be met in the context of the *Abécédaire* where his audience is unknown. This is why Deleuze is exasperated by the mention of human rights. He can't say what he means; or rather, he says exactly what he means but addressed to company that may very well construe his remarks as monstrous, as he himself knows.

## III

What fault does Deleuze identify in human rights discourses? Transcendence. He repeats this criticism time and again: Human rights introduce transcendence into political thought and practice.

1. 'If you're talking about reconstituting transcendence or universals, restoring a reflective subject as the bearer of rights, or setting up a communicative intersubjectivity, then it's not much of a philosophical advance (*invention philosophique*).' (Deleuze 1995: 152, translation modified)

2. 'These days it's human rights (*droits de l'homme*) that provide our eternal values. It's the constitutional state and other notions everyone recognizes as very abstract. And it's in the name of all this that thinking's fettered, that any analysis in terms of movement is blocked. But if we're so oppressed, it's because our movement is being restricted, not because our eternal values are being violated.' (Deleuze 1995: 122, translation modified)

3. 'Human rights say nothing about the immanent modes of existence of people provided with rights.' (Deleuze and Guattari 1994: 107)

4. 'A concern for human rights shouldn't lead us to extol the "joys" of liberal capitalism of which they're an integral part. There's no democratic state that's not compromised to the very core by its part in generating human misery.' (Deleuze 1995: 173)

Deleuze's definition of transcendence is negative and uncompromising. Transcendence is the immanence of one term to another (Deleuze 2006: 385). Or, expanding the formula, when one term is immanent to another, the latter transcends the former. The definition is negative because transcendence is a function of immanence that negates or 'denatures' itself. In other words, transcendence is essentially derivative: 'transcendence is always a product of immanence' (Deleuze 2006: 388). And the definition is uncompromising because it applies to any situation where we say that something is immanent *to* something else. This ranges from major cases of transcendence, such as 'the world is my representation' (idealism) or 'the world is in God' (religion), to turns of phrase that introduce its trace, such as 'it's raining today' (if we mean some 'it' that is the subject of the action), or 'freedom of speech is in the Constitution' (if we mean that an eminent document contains our freedom). Transcendence, for Deleuze, is everywhere.

What about human rights? As the quotations below show, Deleuze attacks different aspects of transcendence. We can take them one-by-one.

1. Deleuze's baseline criticism of human rights is that they '*suppose a universal and abstract subject of rights*, identified with no one in particular and irreducible to singular, existent figures' (Patton 2005: 58, emphasis added). This characterisation informs his three substantive criticisms.

2. *Human rights inhibit movement and becoming.* On Deleuze's

account, human rights represent a closed set of enumerated qualities. He calls them 'eternal values' because they mark the human being as a stable, given essence. To understand this criticism, it is important to remember that Deleuze is not only concerned with capital C catastrophes, i.e., the kind of major outrage associated with human rights, but also with everyday violence, or rather, the violence of the everyday: ads, magazine quizzes, psychiatric tests, heteronormativity, i.e., anything that works with a fixed concept of the subject. It is this second kind of violence that human rights sustain. Because they reinforce a closed concept of the human, Deleuze implicates human rights within a much broader criticism of representational thought as a limitation on possibility and experimentation.[1] In this respect, his assessment coincides with that of Alain Badiou: 'Let us note that a certain twenty-first century, under the sign of human rights as the rights of the natural living being, of finitude, or resignation to what there is, *tries to return to man as a given*' (Badiou 2007: 169).

3. *Human rights disregard the modes of existence of people provided with rights.* For Deleuze, the criterion for effective political philosophy and practice is that concepts must connect to the 'present milieu' (Deleuze and Guattari 1994: 100). In other words, they must respond to the case at hand, such that both concept and situation are recreated from within the context of their encounter. Because human rights operate as axioms and remain unmodified by intervention, Deleuze calls them abstract and ineffective. Hence his polemic: 'You invoke human rights, what does that mean? It means, "Ah, [you] Turks have no right to massacre Armenians"' (Deleuze 2004: '*G pour Gauche*'). In short, by designating human rights as axioms that transcend concrete situations, Deleuze argues they are *unresponsive* to the problem at hand.[2]

4. *Human rights blind us to harm of our own making.* By positing a transcendent universal humanity, human rights threaten to introduce a spurious sympathy or sentimentality into crises that are (inadvertently) of our own design. As Susan Sontag writes, 'So far as we feel sympathy, we feel we are not accomplices to what caused the suffering. Our sympathy proclaims our innocence as well as our impotence. To that extent, it can be (for all our good intentions) an impertinent – if not an inappropriate – response' (Sontag 2002: 102).

# IV

These criticisms represent, as it were, the traps of transcendence that a positive account of human rights from Deleuze must avoid. To date, commentators have not tried to flesh out a concept of human rights from his work. Instead, those seeking a positive account of law have turned to his concept of 'jurisprudence'.[3] But perhaps strict attention to jurisprudence might eclipse strains of Deleuze's thought useful to human rights. And maybe this focus also overlooks potential models on which to base a Deleuzian conception of human rights. Here, I flag such a model. It comes from his final published piece, 'Immanence: A Life'.

> What is immanence? A life . . . No one has described what a life is better than Charles Dickens . . . A scoundrel, a bad apple (*un mauvais sujet*), held in contempt by everyone, is found on the point of death, and suddenly those charged with his care display an urgency, respect, and even love for the dying man's least sign of life. Everyone makes it his business to save him. As a result, the wicked man himself, in the depths of his coma, feels something soft and sweet penetrate his soul. But as he progresses back toward life, his benefactors turn cold, and he himself rediscovers his old vulgarity and meanness. Between his life and his death, there is a moment where *a life* is merely playing with death.

And Deleuze continues with this commentary:

> The life of the individual has given way to an impersonal and yet singular life, which foregrounds a pure event that has been liberated from the accidents of internal and external life, that is, from the subjectivity and the objectivity of what comes to pass: a '*homo tantum*' with whom everyone sympathizes and who attains a kind of beatitude; or an ecceity, which is no longer an individuation, but a singularization, a life of pure immanence, neutral, beyond good and evil, since only the subject that incarnated it in the midst of things made it good or bad. The life of such individuality is eclipsed (*s'efface au profit*) by the singular immanent life of a man who no longer has a name, though he can be mistaken for no other. A singular essence, a life . . . (Deleuze 2006: 386–7)

Admittedly, this passage does not touch human rights proper. It is not even remotely juridical. Nevertheless, it provides an interpretation of universality, care, life and love, which are four central dimensions of human rights. To this extent, it offers what we might call the inspiration of human rights, free from the sins of transcendence.

The scene from Dickens describes a paradigmatic event of human rights: caring and being cared for. Specifically, it describes the transformation of a set of subjects through the event of care. By this, I do not mean that someone learns or grows from the experience. In fact, the opposite: the despised man emerges no better than before and his caregivers retain their prejudices. In particular, their transformation does not reflect what human theorists urge as the cultivation of an ethos or sensibility.[4] Rather, Dickens describes the transformation of the very fact of subjectivity. The characters lose their individual contours, their oppositions and countable difference; they become, as Deleuze likes to put it, 'counter-actualized' (Deleuze 1990: 150). Indeed, individuation itself is attenuated if not dissolved. In its place, we witness the formation of a sort of bubble created from attention and care. Through a dedication to a life hanging in the balance, to healing and caring for this man, discrete individuals are transformed by an event in which urgency, respect and love gather around a frail life that emits signs and sounds. The basic unit is not the subject but a multiplicity or assemblage (*agencement*). In truth, to persist with the language of subjectivity would hide from view a transformation achieved by the de-actualisation of the subject.

The key concept of this passage, 'a life', is promising for human rights. Given their historic mission to protect the lives of individuals, 'a life' may prepare a foundation for human rights distinct from the subject. The remainder of the essay develops this possibility.

'Immanence: A Life' is a remarkable title. It doesn't just announce its two key terms, but, thanks to the indefinite article, also specifies their relationship. Now the grammatical function of an indefinite article is to introduce a noun and imply that the thing referred to is non-specific. 'Pour me a drink', for example. In Deleuze's essay, this function is philosophically significant in two ways.

1. *The indefinite article makes immanence universal.* The non-specific function of the indefinite article indicates that *every* life should be understood on the model of immanence. It is not this or that life which is explained by immanence; it is any and all life.[5]

2. *The indefinite article combines singularity and universality.* A philosophy of immanence does not subsume concrete multiplicities within a higher order term. Its purpose is to appreciate and release the singularity of a life. In light of this purpose, the indefinite article takes on a double role. As above, it refuses to single out anything in particular: 'a life' is non-specific. But on the other hand, viewed through a philosophy of immanence, it refers to a singularity: 'a life' is unique. In Deleuze's hands, the indefinite article conveys the simultaneous universality and singularity of a life.

Let us turn to the Dickens passage. Deleuze's guiding idea is that the (transcendent) subject and an (immanent) life are convertible into one another. They do not designate different entities. But that is not to say they are of the same order. 'The subject' and 'a life' are at once *coextensive and different in kind*. When the scoundrel falls into a coma, and when his antagonists become caregivers, we witness not simply a change of role but one of being. Subjectivity is de-actualised, and, rather than occupy opposed and ascribed positions, the characters inhabit (a plane of) immanence. That is, they combine to create an event of care; or, as Deleuze puts it, they become 'freed from the accidents of internal and external life, that is, from the subjectivity and objectivity of what happens'. In short, the passage shows how a life, i.e., a position of immanence, is always available; it simply requires an encounter or event to disrupt the subject.[6] We will later explore the significance of this for human rights, but we can see that beneath the rights-bearing subject, perhaps even as its condition, is a life marked both by its difference from, and attachment to, all other lives.

This brings us to the second point: the Dickens passage conceives universality as compatible with singularity. Here we arrive at a marked point of contrast with human rights discourse. What is the universal subject of human rights? – It is the human being stripped of all his or her (or rather, its) particular qualities. Take Article 2 of the *Universal Declaration of Human Rights* (1948): 'Everyone is entitled to all the rights and freedoms set forth in this Declaration, without distinction of any kind, such as race, color, sex, language, religion, political or other opinion, national or social origin, property, birth or other status.' This is a subtractive operation. By peeling away a specific set of qualities, we reach a general human core. Conversely, by adding a specific set of qualities to this core, we reach an embodied individual. In this scheme, the subject of human rights is at once *general* (sharing with all others a common core humanity) and *particular* (individuated by a set of attributes).

Although Deleuze contests this scheme, it is important to note that he replicates and locates it in the Dickens passage. It obtains before and after the event. Take the wicked man: he is of such and such an age, status, etc. He is an amalgam of deeds, opinions and habits, i.e., those recognised and despised as belonging to a scoundrel. What is important to notice is that for Deleuze *this picture of subjectivity can lay claim neither to singularity nor universality*. On the one hand, the scoundrel's uniqueness is that of a type, which provokes typeset responses. He is a particular sort of person, not a singular person. And, on the other hand, his universality is better called abstract generality: a common denominator of the human reached by subtraction. As we would say, beneath it all he is, at the end of the day, a human being and should be treated as such. But again, despite these criticisms, Deleuze does not reject this picture of the subject outright. Indeed, he acknowledges that most of our lives are spent in such roles. We occupy subject positions and take on their appropriate attitudes (e.g., as teacher, father, etc.), and we also see our commonality as generic (i.e., the human).

Nevertheless, there are occasions when this scheme is displaced. The scene of the dying man is just such an event. When the subject cedes his place to a life, the arrangement between the particular and general is displaced by an immediate identification of the singular and universal. Deleuze makes his point by stating an equivalence between *homo tantum* (generic everybody) and *ecceity* (thisness, hereness and nowness): 'The life of the individual has given way to an impersonal and yet singular life ... a "*homo tantum*" with whom everybody sympathizes and who attains a kind of beatitude; *or an* ecceity, which is no longer an individuation, but a singularization, a life of pure immanence...' No doubt this is a difficult quotation but we can see that it repeats the same point in four registers. The transition from 'the' to 'an', the transformation of the 'individual' into 'a life', the association of impersonality and singularity, and the identification of *homo tantum* with *ecceity* all assert that when we pass from transcendence to immanence, a new relationship obtains between the singular and universal. It is a relationship where universality is no longer generality and singularity is no longer particularity. A theory of human rights faithful to immanence must, therefore, address the problem of how to see and protect human universality beyond the transcendent generality of the subject.

## V

At this point, I propose to substantiate the connection between human rights and immanence by turning to Henri Bergson's last book, *The Two Sources of Morality and Religion* (Bergson 1977). Now compared to his commentary on *Matter and Memory*, *Creative Evolution* and *Creative Mind*, Deleuze's attention to this text is negligible.[7] Nevertheless, I hope to show that its treatment of human rights, and especially its concept of love, furnishes a model on which to base a Deleuzian – i.e., purely immanent – picture of human rights. As with our discussion of Deleuze, I begin by outlining Bergson's criticism of the human rights tradition before passing to his alternative account of it.

Bergson made a substantial impact on the intellectual and institutional formation of human rights. On the ground, as it were, he served as the French emissary to the United States during the First World War. He also closely collaborated with Woodrow Wilson to establish the League of Nations and later became president of its committee on international cooperation (Soulez and Worms 1989: 153–70). Moreover, his intellectual influence on John Humphrey, the principal drafter of the Universal Declaration of Human Rights (1948), is profound. As Clinton Curle writes, 'John Humphrey kept a journal of his private thoughts during his early tenure at the United Nations. From these journals, it is apparent that he came to view the Universal Declaration in terms of Bergson's book *The Two Sources of Morality and Religion*' (Curle 2007: 6).

Human rights feature as a central topic in Bergson's *Two Sources*, his only work of political philosophy. Unfortunately, this book has received little attention in both continental and analytical philosophy.[8] How Bergson's thought as a whole came to be overlooked in continental thought is a fascinating and complicated story.[9] But perhaps it is more to the point to ask why the *Two Sources* has never caught on within the analytical tradition. There are any number of reasons, of course: Bergson has seldom found a home there.[10] But what I mean is that if analytical political philosophy did turn to *Two Sources*, I expect it would have special reasons to reject it. I have in mind the argument made by John Rawls and Michael Ignatieff, among others, that it is both unnecessary and undesirable to search for the grounds of human rights. In this view, human rights are purely a political instrument designed to protect individuals and attempts to find a foundation for them are divisive, violent and ultimately ineffective (see Rawls 2001: 15, and Ignatieff 2003: 54).

Bergson's *Two Sources* is in direct contradiction to this line of argument. Its purpose is to argue that there is a single ground for human rights: biological life. Human rights are not simply in the business of protecting life; *they are an expression of life*.

To see the sense and motivation of this surprising claim, it is helpful to place Bergson within a wider context. *Two Sources* is written in dark times. Its publication barely precedes the Nazi occupation of France. And Bergson himself caused an embarrassment for the Vichy government when he refused a special exemption from anti-Semitic regulations and registered as a Jew. In terms of intellectual context, *Two Sources* is published between the two major works of the twentieth century critical of human rights: Carl Schmitt's *Concept of the Political* (1932, the thesis of which first appears in Schmitt 1927) and Hannah Arendt's *Origins of Totalitarianism* (1951). All three books take different paths to a shared negative conclusion: it is an illusion to think that national or political rights can be extended to include all humanity. Worse, failure to acknowledge this difference in kind between political and human rights leads to disaster. That is why it is imperative to either account for the unique foundation of human rights (Bergson and Arendt) or else repudiate the project altogether (Schmitt).

To introduce Bergson it is best, once again as with Deleuze, to turn to a title: *The Two Sources of Morality and Religion*. In truth, it is as much his thesis as his title. Bergson's major argument is that there are *two* sources of morality and religion (and, as we will see, politics). Or, more precisely, he claims that biology or life is the single source but that it is divided into two tendencies that differ in kind: closure and openness. Life's tendency towards closure and its tendency towards openness are the two sources of morality, religion and politics. By granting this primacy to life, Bergson is at odds with all accounts of morality, religion and politics rooted in either reason or society (see Lefebvre and White 2010). He thus provides an alternative to two leading perspectives on human rights: deontological (based in Kant) and sociological (based in Durkheim).

*Two Sources* is not Bergson's first mention of the closed and open tendencies. It appears in an earlier lecture, *The Meaning of War* (1914). In this frankly jingoistic piece, Bergson identifies Germany as a closed society and France as an open one.[11] Whatever our objections, the point to notice is that open and closed tendencies are distributed *between* nations. In *Two Sources*, this scheme is reworked. Now *both* tendencies are found *within* each nation, society and person. And although in *Two Sources* Bergson will persist in discussing 'the' open society and 'the' closed society, we are to understand this as a strictly methodological or heuristic device. It is a way to isolate one of the two tendencies. But the truth is that the essence of humanity is not simple but composite. We are constituted by a dynamic tension between open and closed tendencies.

Let us nevertheless follow Bergson's approach and work through the closed and open tendencies one at a time. We begin with a basic question: what do open and closed mean? – Well, on the one hand, we speak of something as open if it is open-ended, unsettled, up in the air. And this is precisely how Bergson introduces the term in *Creative Evolution* (1907). There, open and closed pertain to different conceptions of time that designate the future as either given in advance (closed) or else as creative and incalculable (open).[12] But, on the other hand, we also speak of open and closed in terms of inclusion and exclusion. For example, an immigration policy can be either open or closed. This is Bergson's primary meaning in *Two Sources*.[13] A closed society is one that includes a restricted set of members; an open society is one that admits everyone. As Bergson puts it, the definition of the closed society is 'to include at any moment a certain number of individuals, and exclude others' (Bergson 1977: 30).

It is also comprehensible to speak of a morality as open or closed. In Bergson's sense, a closed morality is one where we restrict our duties, indeed our love, to a select group of people. Bergson uses a metaphor of circles to describe an ever expanding, yet still closed, set of duties: 'we have a family; we follow a trade or a profession; we belong to our parish, to our district, to our country . . . from the center to the circumference are arranged, like so many ever-widening concentric circles, the various groups to which the individual belongs' (Bergson 1977: 18–19).[14] Each circle has the advantage of making our particular duties concrete, and, taken together, they discharge our duty to society as a whole. The individual and society form a closed circuit made up of crisscrossing networks of obligation.

At this point, Bergson says, a natural illusion arises. We look at these expanding circles of duty and think that with one more step they can be extended to include all humanity.

> Our sympathies are supposed to broaden out in an unbroken progression . . . We observe (*constate*) that the three groups [i.e., family, profession, country] to which we attach ourselves comprise an increasing number of people, and we conclude that a progressive expansion of feeling (*une dilatation progressive du sentiment*) keeps pace with the increasing size of the object we love. (Bergson 1977: 32)

But here Bergson pauses. What about war? If the feelings and duty characteristic of a closed society can be naturally extended to humankind, how is war so much as possible? In other words, if the above picture of sympathy and human rights is adequate, how do we explain the omnipresent fact of war? Where do we place it?

It is a commonplace, especially in liberal political thought, to treat war as exceptional. Or, as Bergson paraphrases from another angle, the suspension of human rights in war is assumed to be temporary and abnormal. '[Society says] that the duties it defines are indeed, in principle, duties towards humanity, but that under exceptional circumstances, regrettably unavoidable, they are for the time being suspended' (Bergson 1977: 31, translation modified). But this explanation is unsatisfying as an account of peace. Indeed, it begs the question. – Why war if we acknowledge duties towards all others? For Bergson, it doesn't make sense. He concludes that if we see peace, underwritten by universal sympathy, as the norm and war as the exception, the latter becomes inexplicable. But if, by contrast, we acknowledge war as the norm and peace as the exception, they both make perfect sense. And this is his position. 'Peace has always been a preparation for defense or even attack, at any rate for war' (Bergson 1977: 31). Peace, however long, is a suspension of hostilities. A stable peace will stay war but it can never hope to eradicate it. All societies, inasmuch as they partake of the closed tendency, inherently march to war.

War is a decisive phenomenon for Bergson because it reveals the closed tendency of society. Specifically, he uses it to anchor two fundamental claims.

1. *The closed tendency is in essence biological.* It is without metaphor that Bergson speaks of an 'original political instinct' (Bergson 1977: 280). And he does not mince words as to what this means: 'murder has all too often remained the *ratio ultima*, if not *prima*, of politics' (Bergson 1977: 279). No society is exempt from this instinct, and, given the omnipresence of war, Bergson takes its naturalness for granted (Bergson 1977: 283–4). But if war is original and natural, it follows that the existence of closed groups to protect and secure existence is contemporaneous with it. Call them tribes, nations, or empires: these too are original and natural. That is why for Bergson, social cohesion is comprehensible as a 'necessity for a community to protect itself against others' (Bergson 1977: 33). The closed society, together with its circles of duties, is life's solution to the problem of war. It is the direction evolution has taken to protect humankind from its own belligerence. Once human beings are given, so too is war, closed societies, and a closed network of rights and duties.[15]

2. *The closed tendency is ineradicable.* Contrary to two of his major interlocutors – Lucien Lévy-Bruhl, the great French anthropologist, and Herbert Spencer, the leading social Darwinist – Bergson does not use the theory of evolution to claim that we have moved past a primitive mentality. To the contrary, if we scrape away all of civilisation's accretions, we will find the human being unchanged from his forbearers. 'We are of the opinion that what was once primitive has not ceased to be so, even though an effort of self-scrutiny (*d'approfondissement interne*) may be necessary to re-discover it' (Bergson 1977: 135). The same closed tendency underlies *all* societies. We never move beyond it. The fact of war dramatises this point: no matter how 'advanced' the civilisation, no matter how refined and committed to cosmopolitan ideals, war will recur. The closed tendency cannot be overcome and it is never remote.

To sum-up, the closed tendency is at the origin of the plurality and fractiousness of human societies. It is a force that encloses human beings in their own nature, and it is innate and ever-present. But for Bergson this is not the end of the story. The closed tendency may be omnipresent but, nevertheless, it marks a limit that human beings are able to overcome. Indeed, that we can even conceive of human rights confirms that we can exceed ourselves. They are proof of our ability to design open political institutions.

But, if this is case, if human rights are a genuinely open phenomenon, why are they so often ineffective? Why does the closed appear to trump the open time and again?

But perhaps this is not the proper way to frame the issue. Or worse, maybe this approach is responsible for the confusion surrounding human rights. For Bergson, it is not that the open tendency is too weak to check the closed. There is no little open angel on our shoulders unable to stop the closed devil. In terms of human rights, it is not that duties to the group carry more force than the love of humanity. In a word, *the failure of human rights is not a result of a conflict between closed and open tendencies*. Rather, Bergson's point is that *human rights fail when they model themselves on the rights and duties of the closed society*. They fail when they attempt to implement an open phenomenon within the framework of the closed.

To repeat, the illusion Bergson attacks is that human rights are extensions of political rights. As we recall, Bergson shares this conclusion with Arendt and Schmitt. But his way of getting there is unique and grounded in biologism. For Bergson, the purpose of political rights and duties is to establish a circuit between individual and community. The circles of duty Bergson describes create social cohesion, which is itself a natural solution to the problem of war. For this reason, it is hopeless to see human rights as a species of political rights. To do so is to try to open what is by nature closed. Thus, it is not merely that 'duties to humanity' are ineffective because they lack the concreteness of those to family or nation. This is true enough but doesn't get to the heart of the matter. Rather, human rights fail by being insufficiently attuned to their origin in a tendency that, while equally rooted in biological life, conceives of our attachment in terms of love.

## VI

Love is a risky ground for human rights. As Richard Rorty observes, what human rights outrage is more common than one caused by love of kith and kin (Rorty 1998: 177)? Bergson too puts his finger on this phenomenon and describes a kind of love fully compatible with hate: '*Homo homini deus* and *Homo homini lupus*, are easily reconcilable. When we formulate the first, we are thinking of some fellow-countryman. The other applies to foreigners' (Bergson 1977: 286). That is how love works in the closed society. There are, therefore, two species of love that respectively correspond to the open and closed tendencies. It is the job of philosophy, and especially political philosophy, to keep these distinct.[16] To ignore this distinction is to indiscriminately treat different phenomena and propose that the same sort of love underlies *both* political and human rights.

One way to locate the tension between political and human rights is as a battle between two kinds of love. In this respect, Bergson profoundly renews a Spinozist theory of parallelism. Briefly put, in the *Ethics* parallelism is the theory that an attribute can be affected only by a like attribute. For example, an idea (thought) cannot affect a body (extension) but only another idea; likewise, a body cannot affect an idea but only another body.[17] In *Two Sources*, Bergson adapts this theory to claim that only an emotion can check another emotion. At the basis of the closed tendency are feelings of pressure and obligation (towards fellow citizens) and hatred and alienation (towards foreigners). Time and again, Bergson repeats that reason cannot work directly on emotion. A mere idea cannot move the will in the way philosophers hope. As he says, 'never, in our hours of temptation, should we sacrifice to the mere need for logical consistency our interest, our passion, our vanity' (Bergson 1977: 23). Here, then, is a theory of parallelism: an idea cannot affect emotion; only another emotion can do that. Hence, the importance of love for Bergson: it is the right kind of phenomenon to check the dangerous (hateful, murderous) impulses of the closed tendency. In what we might call Bergson's theory of political affect, reason does not work to reign in passions, nor does emotion take over once we have run out of reasons; instead, politics is conducted on a plane of countervailing affective forces.[18]

Love thus opposes love: the first is unalloyed, whereas the second has hate as its corollary. But perhaps there is a more fundamental opposition between the two loves. I have in mind the question of object attachment. In the closed society, love is object specific. It always 'alight[s] directly on an object which attracts [it]' (Bergson 1977: 39). As we saw with political rights, duty and affection are always directed towards a determinate thing: a family, a parish, a country, etc. The open, by contrast, has no object. Its love is universal, inclusive. Indeed, in Bergson's formulation, it is almost incomprehensibly objectless:

> The other attitude is that of the open soul (*l'âme ouverte*). What, in that case, is allowed in? Suppose we say that it embraces all humanity: we should not be going too far, we should hardly be going far enough, since

> its love may extend (*s'étendra*) to animals, to plants, to all nature. And yet no one of these things which would thus fill it would suffice to define the attitude taken by the soul, for *it could*, strictly speaking, *do without all of them. Its form is not dependent on its content*. We have just filled it; we could easily empty it again. 'Charity' would persist in him who possesses 'charity', though there be no other living creature on earth. (Bergson 1977: 38, emphasis added)

If love can be described as stark, this is it. The open soul overflows with love but it is never love for anything in particular. Not for one's family or nation, certainly; but also not for humanity or nature or gods or the universe. It is difficult to know what to make of it. If we love our neighbour, it is only incidental: love is not roused by any of its recognizable modes, such as affection, preference, or command. And if love grounds human rights, it is a foundation that is essentially unattached to, perhaps even unconcerned with, human beings. Indeed, I would say that this concept of love is not just unprecedented but unrecognizable. For what is love – with its etymological origin in desire (*libet* for it is pleasing, *libido* for lust or desire) – but affection for something, even, at its limit, for the universe?

This objectlessness of open love is perplexing. But, from a Deleuzian standpoint, it is also promising. Open love avoids the most intractable feature of transcendence: the subject-object relation. By overshooting all objects, by rigorously conceiving of this affect outside attachment, love operates beyond or before the notion of an object. Even Christian love does not do that, directed as it is to the universal neighbour. Perhaps this is the sort of affect Deleuze believes Dickens to have described: not a desire to save this or that person but rather a disposition able to respond to, and be worthy of, the event of a dying man.

Before we attempt further explanation, let us carry Bergson's concept of love to its conclusion. It also dissolves the idea of the subject. This is not, as we might expect, an effect of undercutting the object. Rather, love overcomes the subject by transfiguring the human species itself:

> [Love is] more metaphysical than moral in its essence. What [the lover][19] wants to do, with God's help, is to complete the creation of the human species and make of humanity what it would have straightaway become, had it been able to assume its final shape (*se constituer définitivement*) without the assistance of man himself ... [Love's] direction is exactly that of life's *élan*; it *is* this *élan* itself, communicated in its entirety (*intégralement*) to exceptional men who in their turn would want to impart it to all humanity and, by a living contradiction (*une contradiction realisée*),

convert into creative effort that created thing which is a species, and turn into movement what was, by definition, a stop. (Bergson 1977: 234–5, translation modified)

Love brings us to the heart of Bergson's philosophy of life. To put it as schematically as possible, the essence of life is process, movement and becoming. Or, in a word that means exactly the same thing, its essence is *evolution*: it is life in *time*, in the emphatic sense Bergson gives that word. Evolutionary creativity is paradoxical, however. On the one hand, each species is a genuine invention: it actualises evolutionary creativity. But on the other hand, each species is an immobilisation: it halts evolutionary creativity. As Bergson puts it, a species blocks evolutionary movement. So too with human beings. Notwithstanding the apparent dynamism we call history, our natural constitution destines the species to run 'indefinitely in the same circle' (Bergson 1977: 209). This was Bergson's point with war: it will always come back.

And yet, human beings have a special privilege: they alone love. What does that mean? – Love, for Bergson, is not primarily what we might call a feeling or emotion. Yes, it is that, but, at root, it is something deeper: a drive to create and to include. But isn't this also just the ordinary grammar of the word? – Love begets and love includes. The power of Bergson's concept of love is that it renews these core attributes at the level of the principle of life itself (what he calls the *élan vital*). Love is Bergson's name for a desire and capacity to escape fixed form, both individual and social, and renew the intrinsic creativity of life. Love makes of life what it should have been had it not been burdened by the species that simultaneously actualises and immobilises it. And what should that have been? – Difference, singularity, and the unceasing production of the new.[20] Love makes human beings into outlets for vital creativity.

But, more than that, love overcomes the preferential love at the heart of the closed society. It prevails not by broadening object attachment, which would still participate in the logic of closure, but by affirming movement. That is why love has and does not have an object. The 'thing' we love is not a particular being, nor a quality shared by beings of a certain kind (e.g., reason or morality or the capacity to suffer), nor something beyond all beings, nor even something within all beings. Rather, it is best to say that we are *in love*, which is to say, that we *accept to inhabit an open and interconnected world*.

If this seems complicated and controversial, or just too much metaphysics for a theory of human rights to have to swallow, it is helpful to work back to Deleuze. He opposes human rights on the ground that they introduce transcendence. This makes them not only theoretically inadequate but also practically ineffective. Recall that a theory of human rights based on a universal subject is inadequate for three reasons. 1. It blocks movement by fixing the subject. 2. It fails to respond to concrete situations. 3. It introduces sympathy that covers up harms of our own doing. And further recall Deleuze's equivocal frustration with human rights. Sometimes he has hope for the idea outside its present dispensation in human rights discourses, while at other times he identifies the two and rejects both out of hand.

The purpose of the discussion of love in Bergson was to suggest an alternative ground for a concept of human rights. Love is a relationship free of transcendence. On the one hand, it is without object: it affirms openness. And on the other hand, it is without subject: it counter-actualises the human being as a fixed bundle of attributes. To translate into Deleuze's terms, it is by way of love that we regain 'a life', for love is nothing other than a pure perspective of immanence. The point I wish to make is that love is both a concept and way of being that is fully adequate to immanence. If human rights were love alone, Deleuze could have no objection.

But a theory of love is not a theory of human rights. The latter is obviously not a purely open or immanent phenomenon. Human rights do posit a universal subject, they are limited to the human species, and, not least of all, they are subject to the priorities of the states that codify and enforce them. What, then, is their status? Open or closed, transcendent or immanent? – Both: they are composite. Love is institutionalised and disseminated through human rights. As Bergson says, they '[translate] the dynamic into the static' (Bergson 1977: 274). Although their purpose is to actualise the open tendency of life – and here Bergson is unequivocal: human rights evoke an 'absolute' justice 'incommensurable' with the closed society (Bergson 1977: 74) – they reintroduce elements of transcendence and closure that obscure their source. For Bergson, this compromise with transcendence and closure is acceptable. As with mystics who agree for love to be cooled off by religion so that everyone may 'get a little of what [they] possessed in full', so too do great legislators transform an impulse for justice into a scheme workable within terms understandable to the closed society.

Of course, Bergson acknowledges the risk that the terms that translate the open may, in the end, eclipse their source. The assertion of a universal subject and endless debates as to its attributes may take centre-stage at the expense of the love that inspires human rights in the first place. It is here that we can locate Deleuze's impatience, for he too loses sight of the impulse. Call it the fetishism of human rights: we become blind to the force that produces them. And yet Bergson insists that human rights are unimaginable and impracticable without their foundation in love.

> Humanity had to wait until Christianity for the idea of universal brotherhood, with its implication of equality of rights and the inviolability of the person, to become active (*agissante*). Some may say that it has been rather a slow process; indeed eighteen centuries elapsed before the rights of man (*Droits de l'homme*) were proclaimed by the Puritans of America, soon followed by the men of the French Revolution . . .
> The method [to spread love and justice] consisted in supposing possible what is actually impossible in a given society (*société donnée*), in imagining what would be its effect on the soul of society, and then inducing some such psychic condition by propaganda and example: the effect, once obtained, would retrospectively complete its cause; *new feelings*, evanescent indeed, *would call forth the new legislation seemingly indispensable to their appearance*, and which would then serve to consolidate them. (Bergson 1977: 78, translation modified, emphasis added)

Not just any society can proclaim human rights. It requires a society steeped – one would want to say trained, were it not so awkward – in love. On the one hand, it takes an event – Christian mysticism, on Bergson's account – to so much as reveal a gap to be leaped between open and closed love. And on the other hand, it takes centuries more for love to spread to and sustain a political imagination able to promulgate human rights. In other words, for human rights to be so much as conceivable, not only the legislator but also the public must have broadly acquired a form of love incompatible with exclusion, preference and hatred. In other words, human rights cannot command us to love. Instead, they do two things. Negatively, they protect against the ravages of closed love. They codify and enforce love. Positively, they can initiate us into the form of life Bergson calls love. The intimation of love by human rights may serve as an introduction to it.

In a famous line from *A Thousand Plateaus*, Deleuze and Guattari claim 'a society is defined by its lines of flight (*lignes de fuite*)' (Deleuze and Guattari 1987: 216). It seems to me that Bergson is near this intuition, only he historicises it. For him society is defined by love. Love may start with Christianity, take centuries to spread, and even still be only one half of society, but, nevertheless, it alone appreciates and realises the movement at the heart of life and society. This essay has argued that love is what Deleuze calls immanence (or indeed, philosophy); or rather, love is immanence as a way of life. It overcomes the object, dissolves the subject, and affirms movement. In this sense, when Deleuze claims that society is defined by its lines of flight, he speaks from love; he speaks from a position able to see and accept flight. It takes the same perspective, the same commitment to immanence, to conceive of movement (or flight, or deterritorialisation) as it does of human rights. It takes, therefore, a philosopher (in Deleuze's sense) to properly see the origin, function and value of human rights.

# References

Badiou, A. (2007), *The Century*, trans. A. Toscano, London: Polity Press.
Bergson, H. (1972), *Mélanges*, Paris: PUF.
Bergson, H. (1974), *The Creative Mind: An Introduction to Metaphysics*, trans. M. L. Andison, New York: Citadel Press.
Bergson, H. (1977), *The Two Sources of Morality and Religion*, trans. R. A. Audra and C. Brereton, Notre Dame: University of Notre Dame.
Bergson, H. (1998), *Creative Evolution*, trans. A. Mitchell, New York: Dover.
Braidotti, R., C. Colebrook and P. Hanafin (2009), *Deleuze and Law: Forensic Futures*, London: Palgrave Macmillan.
Curle, C. (2007), *Humanité: John Humphrey's Alternative Account of Human Rights*, Toronto: University of Toronto Press.
de Sutter, L. (2009), *Deleuze, la pratique du droit*, Paris: Machalon.
Deleuze, G. (1990), *The Logic of Sense*, trans. M. Lester and C. Stivale, New York: Columbia University Press.
Deleuze, G. (1994), *Difference and Repetition*, trans. P. Patton, New York: Columbia University Press.
Deleuze, G. (1995), *Negotiations, 1972–1990*, trans. M. Joughin, New York: Columbia University Press.
Deleuze, G. (2004), *L'Abécédaire de Gilles Deleuze, avec Claire Parnet*, Paris: DVD Editions Montparnasse.
Deleuze, G. (2006), 'Immanence: A Life', in *Two Regimes of Madness: Texts and Interviews 1975–1995*, ed. David Lapoujade, New York: Semiotext(e).
Deleuze, G. and F. Guattari (1987), *A Thousand Plateaus, Capitalism and Schizophrenia*, trans. B. Massumi, Minneapolis: University of Minnesota Press.
Deleuze, G. and F. Guattari (1994), *What Is Philosophy?*, trans. H. Tomlinson and G. Burchell, New York: Columbia University Press.
Guerlac, S. (2006), *Thinking in Time: An Introduction to Henri Bergson*, Ithaca: Cornell University Press.
Hunt, L. (2007), *Inventing Human Rights: A History*, New York: W. W. Norton and Company.
Ignatieff, M. (2003), *Human Rights as Politics and Idolatry*, Princeton: Princeton University Press.
Lefebvre, A. (2008), *The Image of Law: Deleuze, Bergson, Spinoza*, Stanford: Stanford University Press.
Lefebvre, A. and M. White (2011a), *Bergson, Politics and Religion*, Durham: Duke University Press.
Lefebvre, A. and M. White (2011b), 'The Politics of Intuition', in Alexandre Lefebvre and Melanie White (eds), *Bergson, Politics and Religion*, Durham: Duke University Press.
Lefebvre, A. and M. White (2010), 'Bergson on Durkheim: Society *Sui Generis*', *Journal of Classical Sociology*, 10 (4): 457–77.

Marrati, P. (2006), 'Mysticism and the Foundation of the Open Society: Bergsonian Politics', in Hent de Vries and Lawrence E. Sullivan (eds), *Political Theologies: Public Religion in a Post-Secular World*, New York: Fordham University Press.
Patton, P. (2000), *Deleuze and the Political*, London: Routledge.
Patton, P. (2005), 'Deleuze and Democratic Politics', in Lasse Thomassen and Lars Tønder (eds), *Radical Democracy: Politics Between Abundance and Lack*, Manchester: Manchester University Press.
Patton, P. (2010), *Deleuzian Concepts: Philosophy, Colonization, Politics*, Stanford: Stanford University Press.
Protevi, John (2009), *Political Affect: Connecting the Social and the Somatic*, Minneapolis: University of Minnesota Press.
Rawls, J. (2001), *The Law of Peoples*, Cambridge: Harvard University Press.
Rorty, R. (1998), 'Human Rights, Rationality, Sentimentality', in *Truth and Progress: Philosophical Papers*, Volume 3, Cambridge: Cambridge University Press.
Schmitt, C. (1927), 'Der Begriff des Politischen', *Archiv für Sozialwissenschaft und Sozialpolitik*, 58 (1).
Sontag, S. (2002), *Regarding the Pain of Others*, New York: Farrar, Straus and Giroux.
Soulez, P. (1989), *Bergson politique*, Paris: PUF.
Soulez, P. and F. Worms (1989), *Bergson*, Paris: PUF.
Spinoza, B. (2002), *Complete Works*, trans. Samuel Shirley, Indianapolis: Hackett.
Waterlot, G. (2008), *Bergson et la religion*, Paris: PUF.
Worms, F. (2004), *Bergson ou les deux sens de la vie*, Paris: PUF.

# Notes

1. See, for example, his critique of recognition as a brake on experimentation in *Difference and Repetition*: 'The form of recognition has never sanctioned anything but the recognizable and the recognized; form will never inspire anything but conformities' (Deleuze 1994: 134).
2. See Lefebvre 2008: 82–7.
3. See, for example, Lefebvre 2008; Patton 2000; Patton 2010; de Sutter 2009; Protevi 2009; Braidotti, Colebrook and Hanafin (2009).
4. See Rorty 1998 and Hunt 2007.
5. The colon in the title reinforces this point. It establishes an equivalence of sense between immanence and a life.
6. Another way to put the matter is that immanence is not chronologically prior to transcendence. It is not as if immanence comes 'first' and is 'then' transformed into transcendence with no hope of going back. Rather, the priority is ontological: behind transcendence, beneath all subjective relations, is immanence waiting to show itself.
7. It is, however, a suspicion of mine that *Two Sources* is the methodological inspiration for *A Thousand Plateaus*. Specifically, I have in mind that the twin concepts of territorialisation and deterritorialisation correspond to Bergson's account of the closed and open tendencies of life. But this is not an insight I can develop here.
8. This is changing, however. See Waterlot 2008 and Lefebvre and White 2011a.
9. See Guerlac 2006: 1–13, 173–96 and Lefebvre and White 2011b.
10. At minimum, these reasons include the influence of Bertrand Russell's polemic, Bergson's failed debate with Einstein, the focus on American rather than French

pragmatism, the rejection of vitalism by analytical philosophy and biology, and, not unimportantly, differences of philosophical style.
11. Philippe Soulez calls the wartime writings polemical and not a genuine treatment of the political. See Soulez 1989: 266.
12. In conceptualising time as open-ended duration, Bergson writes, 'Wherever anything lives, there is, open somewhere, a register in which time is being inscribed' (Bergson 1998: 16).
13. Frédéric Worms observes this change in Bergson's criterion of the 'open' in Worms 2004: 271. Following Worms, we will see that the power of *Two Sources* derives from the link Bergson draws between the two senses of open. It is creative *and* inclusive.
14. *A Thousand Plateaus* uses this metaphor of circles to great effect in Deleuze and Guattari 1987: 209–11.
15. This is not a biologically reductive argument. Bergson does not say that biology dictates a *specific form* of society. Only social cohesion as such, which is designed to counteract the threat of war, is biologically necessary.
16. For a related discussion of a falsely composite emotion, see Bergson's discussion of 'pleasure' and 'happiness' in Bergson 1974: 51.
17. See *Ethics*, Part III, Proposition 2: 'The body cannot determine the mind to thinking, and the mind cannot determine the body to motion, to rest, or to anything else (if there is anything else)' (Spinoza 2002: 279).
18. As Paola Marrati claims, 'Bergson is not calling for a morality and a politics of irrational emotions or sublime sensibility. His claim is rather that no morality and no politics – be it Open or Closed – can ever take place within the limits of reason alone' (Marrati 2006: 600).
19. Bergson's word for pure love is 'mysticism' and its persona is the 'mystic'. I use the generic term 'lover' because we do not need to address the connection between love and mysticism.
20. As Bergson writes elsewhere, evolution is 'succession without repetition, where each moment is unique' (Bergson 1972: 1149).

# Chapter 4
# On 'Cruelty': Law, Literature, and Difference

*Penelope Pether\**

> Thinking *with* AND instead of thinking IS, instead of thinking *for* IS: empiricism has never had another secret. (Deleuze and Parnet 1987: 57)
>
> The whole idea of education is to change and improve things, so that other cultural and political possibilities can emerge, even at moments when so-called pragmatists say it is impossible. (Edward Said, cited in Higgins 2001)
>
> The task of a political literature is to contribute to the invention of this unborn people who do not yet have a language. (Smith, in Deleuze 1997: xlii)

This chapter is grounded in a problem of interdisciplinary theory and practice: how does a scholar working in the critical theoretical traditions account for and then address persistent uses of the interdisciplinary engagement between law and literature that seem first promising and then, rapidly, deeply problematic? These deployments of the 'Law and Literature' interdisciplinary project seem, on the one hand, to approach that 'field' – or intersection of disciplinary fields – seeking to find, in Deleuze's terms, 'productive use[s] of the literary machine' (Deleuze and Guattari 1983: 106). As with Deleuze's interest in 'the processes through which existing forms of government of self and others are transformed' (Patton 2000: 3), they seek change. However, on the other hand, once promise gives way to praxis, they lapse first into tracing old patterns, using the literary text and the pedagogical practices formed around English studies in an impoverished project reminiscent of the discipline's

---

\* This essay is dedicated to my student Cam Cornish, Villanova University School of Law Class of 2012, with profound thanks for bringing me up short; and to my husband, David S. Caudill, whose commitment to the critical informed the teaching that engaged Cam's imagination and provided a forum within the law school for his remarkable voice.

earlier use in inculcating (sexist, racist) sexual morality in the service of engendering governors of Empire.[1] In the equally troubling alternative, they offer an impoverished disciplinary therapeutics, this time using literature to save law from that which besets it.

In Peter Goodrich's terms, law's maladies, or pathologies, consist of its crazed Imperial insistence that it is 'sovereign and unitary', and its concomitant 'jealous[y] of other jurisdictions . . . [and] fear . . . of alternative disciplines'; its reliance for its authority on its claims of scientism, on policing the 'genre and categories of the established institution of doctrine and its artificial and paper rules' (Goodrich 1996a: 2); and the violently disciplining ritualised bodily practice required of its students. This latter has traditionally entailed 'the wasting of youth' (Goodrich 1996a: 80), a prevailing asceticism, a sustained yielding up of the 'becoming' legal professional subject to darkness and to melancholy, and a denial of the body (Goodrich 1996a: 85). It also depended upon adherence to homosocial rituals of the table that systematically excluded 'others'[2] – an uncommon, or all too common, and withal distinctively legal, commons.

The texts I will use here to diagnose the symptoms of the disease besetting the interdiscipline, as much as or more than law itself, suggest the pressing imperative of my project in this essay, the critical and specifically Deleuzian retheorising of 'law and literature' as a means to make change in law's institutions, discourses and practices of professional subject formation. The first group of such texts iterates a persisting methodological argument made by more or less critical scholars of law: that in narrative unjust law meets its match. The others are drawn from a distinctively and curiously literary corpus of texts accounting for the paradigmatic jurisdiction of (post)Modern law: the site of exclusion, zone of apparent excision from the fabric or aegis of law (whether national or international), that is, the prison at Guantánamo Bay, Cuba.

But first, what are the stakes here? Rosi Braidotti's reading of Deleuze in a specifically poststructuralist feminist project, while insisting on women's 'multiplicity', seeking 'to restore intersubjectivity so as to allow differences to create a bond – a political contract among women – so as to affect lasting political changes' (Braidotti 2001: 1417), provides a useful orientation towards the more general 'law and literature' project of refiguring the material practices of the law in pursuit of justice. What, in bell hooks' terms, a '[r]adical postmodernist practice' entails (hooks 1990: 24), Braidotti writes, is 'rethink[ing] alterity and otherness', 'a collectivity resting on the recognition of differences, in an inclusive, i.e. non-exclusionary manner' (Braidotti 2001: 1417).

And what is the particular promise of Deleuzian thought for a diagnosis and critical reassessment of the law and literature interdisciplinary project? I will return to this question in the body of this essay, but two points are in order at this stage. First, Deleuze's work has not just an interest in literary texts – such as 'Bartleby, the Scrivener', and the works of Kafka, that are part of the law and literature canon, but also a particular affinity with interdisciplinarity, arguing, as Paul Patton puts it, 'for the priority of the conjunction "and" over the verb "to be" . . . [as a means of] free[ing] the connective power of relationality':

> as the indeterminate conjunction which subtends all relations, 'and' comes to stand for that which is in-between any two things brought into relation with each other. It becomes an axiom of Deleuze and Guattari's political philosophy that new 'becomings', events or beings always emerge from this 'in-between'. In their view, 'and' is always a border between two elements and as such a potential line of flight along which things happen and changes take place. (Patton 2000: 10)

Next, Deleuzian thought is profoundly oriented to transformation, and what Deleuze has in common with Foucault is a generative conception of power: as Patton reads it, 'Deleuze and Guattari's . . . conception of power is closer to the idea of capacity to act than to the normative notion of action which adversely affects the capacity of others to act' (Patton 2000: 2). A similar commitment to the critical shift from envisioning law and literature pedagogical and scholarly praxis from disciplining and punitive norms to capacity-building, which additionally pays attention to how such capacity-building finds its orientation, undergirds my project in this essay.

If there is any site in legal institutions and disciplinary discourses where transformative 'lines of flight' might seem – given Deleuze's manifest 'lack of sympathy' with law (Vismann 2008: 41) – less than improbable, it might be the law school. In 'Legal Education and the Democratic Imagination', the Law and Literature scholar Ian Ward crisply articulates questions for the legal educator at once besetting and abiding: '"What is a Law School for?" and "What should a Law School be teaching?"' (Ward 2009: 87). On the one hand, as I have just signalled, these are old questions. They lie, for example, below Langdell's push to convince a sceptical university that law could be constructed as a science whose inculcation belonged within the university's institutional domain, and his drive to educate an elite paradoxically – or perhaps inevitably – conceived of as unfit for the business that always was the practice of law (for all that repression in the law school of this other Janus-face of law is as signal as its exclusion of *minorities*, in Goodrich's and Deleuze's terms). Indeed, Langdell's American contemporaries in the project of moving legal education into the university – making it formally a modern discipline rather than the embodied practice of apprenticeship that it had previously been in the colonies and the emergent nation – despised the inevitably commercial practice of law just as much as they did the working-class aspirants to legal practice, 'foreigners' and Jews, whom they sought to exclude from their new disciplinary institutions, the law schools (from which they more or less inevitably excluded women and those whom, registering its anachronism, and flagging its effacing of local and particular historical specificity, I will call 'people of color').[3]

To an academic who became a law teacher in the middle of the 'quiet revolution'[4] in Australian legal education in the early 1990s, these questions – which have been reiterated in the now familiar, if generally unheeded, institutional discourse of the US legal academy from the *MacCrate Report* of the early 1990s to the *Carnegie Report* of 2007 (Sullivan 2007) and the plethora of institutional and disciplinary reform activity and/or publicity that is the latter's rough contemporary – have the character of the enunciations of a Greek chorus: they speak a truth which is inaudible to the drama's protagonists. Likewise, Ward's evident distaste for the 'anti-intellectualism' he sees inculcated by forced obeisance to increasingly insistent 'professional accrediting bodies' (Ward 2009: 88), one imagines, is likely to deepen as the results of the post-Blairite education and budgetary reforms bite harder: one probably does not have to have begun one's postgraduate formation and university teaching career *in medias res* Australia's 'Dawkins reforms' of higher education to discern this, but one's line of sight is inevitably made more acute by such an embodied professional history. A more profound question raised by Ward's passing judgment in this way is whether such professional accrediting bodies might have something imaginative and not 'anti-intellectual' to offer to his project of legal educational reform in the interests of doing justice, a possibility he seems to foreclose.

That said, there is a counter-narrative underpinning and destabilising Ward's jeremiad. Shadowing his condemnation of a curriculum reproducing 'power . . . of the sclerotic Kafkaesque kind' (Ward 2009: 88–9) is an account of legal education familiar from its Australian iteration, at least in the 1990s, but still utterly foreign in the US. There, the *Carnegie Report*, which passes, contextually, for reformist, takes doctrine seriously, albeit recommending its relegation to but one of three sustaining pillars of a distinctively professional education which is instrumentalist and technocratic, affirmatively not *critical*, for all its addition of 'ethics' to a triumvirate of imperatives otherwise consisting of skills and doctrine. 'Scepticism', Ward concludes, in the British legal academy, 'has tended to nurture a culture of subversion', characterised by 'contextual and inter-disciplinary studies', and productive of what Twining (1994: 123, 145) called professorial 'euphoria' (Ward 2009: 89).

However, while he concedes that 'there is nothing politically or even morally neutral about . . . liberal legalism' (Ward 2009: 90), and cites *en passant* Wesley Pue's bleak – and to the Foucaultian, compelling – judgment that education, and a fortiori, legal education, at least as it is practised at this point in history, is 'applied state theory' (Pue 2008: 278–9), Ward's position on what legal education ought both to do and teach is a modestly critical neo-liberal one. His political commitments are democratic and humanist, apparently in sympathy with what he takes to be Dewey's case for a liberal education of the kind Ward desires: its deployment 'to protect and promote a progressive idea of liberal democracy' (Ward 2009: 94).

While his essay opens with the promise of what a 'contextually critical' 'progressive liberal legal education' (Ward 2009: 90, 98) might be imagined as entailing, it then lapses, via accounts of the work of Dewey and Rorty and – inevitably – Nussbaum, into a tragically familiar refrain. The 'peculiar value of the humanities, of the considered narrative, [is] to elevate the imagination' (Ward 2009: 96), he writes, and the uses of literature in general and narrative in particular for reshaping legal education and the legal professional subject's imaginary are identified as the inculcation of empathy; the engendering of the ability to recognise and hear those 'others' the law renders mute; the drawing of the cloistered legal subject into engagement with the world; providing an heuristic for discerning moral touchstones serviceable in that world; and enabling a kind of narcissistic therapeutics of identity, for which Allan Hutchinson's claim that 'legal stories . . . provide the possibilities and parameters of our own self-definition and understanding' is a placeholder (Ward 2009: 104).

Closer to home, and with chastening salience at the end of a gruelling semester trying with decreasing conviction to convey to a class of 85 students in a required upper level course my own passion for close critical reading of the law's texts, for exploring what we might make of and indeed with the traces of the nation's frequently blind faith in liberty and schizophrenic relation to equality, and after a conversation with an especially bright, acute, and constitutionally profoundly humorous student who told me, with utter and evidently heartfelt candour, that the pedagogy of all but one course (it wasn't mine) he had taken at law school made him *angry*, I turned to a recent article more or less in the Law and Literature genre. Co-authored by the writer and (US) law professor Kate Nace Day with her husband, Russell G. Murphy, likewise a law professor, it promised insights into the use of literary texts in the service of generating engagement that might make a difference in the practice of professional subject formation, humanising the core required curriculum, a site of disciplinary power which also engages Ward (2009: 89).

Drawing on Paula Gaber's signal 1990s contribution to critical accounts of the experience of women students in US law schools for what preceded the generic colon (Gaber 1998), the article was titled '"Just Trying To Be Human in This Place": Storytelling and Film in the First-Year Law School Classroom'. Offering a close reading of recent US texts on the failure of the nation's characteristic legal pedagogy, including both the *Carnegie Report* and Elizabeth Mertz's interdisciplinary law and linguistic anthropology study, *The Language of Law School: Learning to 'Think Like a Lawyer'*, the article makes a case for pedagogical techniques that offer a way out of the inculcation of a 'closed epistemology' (Day and Murphy 2009: 253) in legal professional subject formation, and the systematic silencing of students from backgrounds marking them as different from the predominantly white and relatively privileged majority of law students. '"Just Trying to Be Human"' offered some encouraging prescriptions for inculcating awareness of the 'human suffering and vulnerability that lie behind formal legal doctrine' and taking the (considerable and unacknowledged by Day and Murphy) professional risk of putting one's 'humanity on display, requiring ... the expression of a teacher's values, beliefs, and conclusions about course material' (Day and Murphy 2009: 263).

However, its assumptions – that providing a narrative context for the law's texts will humanise both fledgling lawyers and legal education, or in the *Carnegie Report*'s terms 'engage the moral imagination of students as they move toward professional practice' (Sullivan 2007: 188) – took no account of the embeddedness within ingrained cultural stories with which law students enter law school, the alternative sources of narrative they meet there other than the (implicitly) 'progressive', humanising professor. As such, they were all too familiar from most of the scholarship on how the literary might change law.

In none of these hopeful, yet more or less completely untheorised accounts of interdisciplinary law school pedagogy, do I find, when I turn to them, yet again, for strategies that might make a difference at the often (for me) more or less profoundly challenging coalface that is the required or in Ward's terms 'core' class with somewhere between 85 and 130-odd students, for example, any recognition of the incomprehension and resistance with which encounters with challenges to identity formed in significant part by constructions of merit are likely to be met. That same incomprehension and/or resistance meets teacherly challenges to insistently reproduced and thus invisible paradigms of what teaching and learning the law legitimately is or ought to be (which paradigms Tyack and Cuban call 'real school' marked by 'the grammar of schooling' [Tyack and Cuban 1995: 7, 9]); and to what often, unacknowledged, underpins the critique of liberal legalism. This latter entails confronting the brute fact that recognising inequality and exclusion is a necessary, to be sure, but insufficient condition for the redistribution of social and material goods in the skewed allocation of which American law participated, perhaps most strikingly during the eras of slave law and Jim Crow, but also increasingly in the present and more recent past.

Nor yet in the therapeutic legal pedagogy of narrative do I find a glimmer of comprehension of the difficult praxis and ethics of educating law students for an imagined professional community that gives the appearance of being widely desired but has not yet come into being. Characteristic of scholars in this interdisciplinary law and humanities genre, Day and Murphy, reading Elizabeth Mertz's linguistic anthropological analysis of law school pedagogy, engage in a familiar ethical critique of the inculcation of legal disciplinary literacy, which shifts students' pre-law school ways of reading the stories told in appellate opinions 'to a more dispassionate way of reading and storytelling' (Day and Murphy 2009: 271).

Let me leave aside for now interrogating the equally familiar assumption that all entering law students 'naturally' read for the humanity of these narratives, or the phenomenological conception of 'humanity' that assumption entails. To imagine, as Day and Murphy, like so many other scholars of law school pedagogy working in the 'Law and the Humanities' traditions, do, either that disciplinary literacy can be acquired without pedagogical violence or to fail to countenance that law practice might call for the capacity to be both dispassionate and humane, or perhaps even to be violent, seems quite fundamentally naive to a scholar with Foucauldian commitments, or at the very least to any modestly sceptical observer at this point in the history of the material practices of law work.

Don't get me wrong: I profess law and literature, after all, and I have, I think, after 17 years on the teaching side of the legal academic dyad witnessed apparently profound and even transformative legal educational experiences, most of which involved a painful recognition of my own implication as the vector of disciplinary violence. But every time I witness law's grasping for the literary, or (handy for 'progressives', this) literature's ideologically sanitised synecdoche, narrative, as nurse, priest, or therapist, I hear Gerry Wilkes – then Challis Professor of English Literature at the University of Sydney (and a senior colleague during my doctoral studies there), and as such a veteran of a departmental political implosion that putatively turned on pitched ideological battles over the moralising, therapeutic claims of Leavisite literary criticism – intoning with a degree of mordant relish that many of the most venal people he knew were literary critics.

Unlike many who do interdisciplinary work on law school pedagogy, Ward is clearly alert to the sceptical glance a scholar with critical theoretical commitments might cast on his democratising, humanising project, as his wry acknowledgement of Pue and his citation of Lasswell and McDougal on the statist instrumentalism of education both evidence (Ward 2009: 93, citing Lasswell and McDougal 1943: 212). Is there anything, then, to be gleaned or salvaged from his unusually sophisticated scholarly endeavour to locate what interdisciplinary law and literature work might offer a legal academy evidently beset, on both sides of the Atlantic, with variations of a malaise, that might help me work towards an articulation both of my critical and clinical project in this essay and how it might enable praxiological and institutional change? Like Ward, even if not sharing his conviction that a distinctively liberal legal education has as its task the inculcating of the values of a democratic polity (Ward 2009: 93), or his faith in the virtues of either such enterprise, a scholar working in the critical theoretical traditions might conclude with Brighouse and Swift that any conception of education which does not both consciously deploy education's critical role in shaping what Pierre Bourdieu called the *habitus*, and register the ethical implications of so doing, is '"vapid, even pointless"' (Ward 2009: 93, citing Brighouse and Swift 2003: 367), that '[t]he stakes are far too high to permit a pessimism that can debilitate' (Ward 2009: 93).

Ward's most arresting assertion in 'Legal Education and the Democratic Imagination' is that literature, and in his view 'very often fictive literature', 'is the best medium for impressing upon law students the reality of the law'. In particular, he makes the case that when the law's own media, its jurisprudential canonical texts, are 'peculiarly perverse, or perhaps oddly absent', literary texts may be the only ones in which its students can 'read the law'. Ward finds the paradigm case of such perversion or lacuna in the law's contemporary accounting for post-9/11 terrorism, 'supposed to be one of the defining experiences of our generation' (Ward 2009: 104), and in his view rendering law 'essentially silent, effectively impotent', not only at Guantánamo (Ward 2009: 105). Paradigmatic post-9/11 discourse, the fantastical rhetoric of terrorism and counter-terrorism, Ward suggests, at once reveals the narrativity of law, the extent to which its authority is no more – nor in Goodrich's terms less – than rhetorical, and also underscores the 'persuasive[ness]' of 'an alternative literary engagement' (Ward 2009: 105) over a legal accounting for what I have called this 'new exceptionalism' (see Pether 2007).

Against the odds, Ward concludes, with Nussbaum, that 9/11 serves as a therapeutic reminder of liberal democracy's 'deep . . . commitment to the principles of justice' (Ward 2009: 107). He contends that exposure to literature which passes judgment on the inhumanity that always accompanies failures of intersubjective ethics, on what I will call the moral logic of 'us and others', will shake us awake from our '"terror dream[s]"' (Ward 2009: 105, citing Faludi 2007: 2). In particular he holds that familiarity with such literature will inoculate student lawyers against the wages of professional subject formation indicted by Harold Koh's biting (albeit now, given Koh's current job with the US State Department and the persistence of Guantánamo, contextually ironic) assessment that lawyers, who should, decades after the Holocaust, know better, became convinced that 'somehow the destruction of four planes and three buildings has taken us back to a state of nature in which there are no laws or rules' (Ward 2009: 105, citing Koh 2002: 23).

How? 'Terrorist literature . . . provide[s] a testamentary supplement to political, cultural or . . . legal histories of terrorism and counter-terrorism . . . [and] help[s] us – and our students – to engage a more subtle, ethical comprehension' (Ward 2009: 108), through both recognising and profoundly registering our besetting weakness for treating others inhumanely. Interdisciplinary legal education in the law and humanities tradition, he asserts 'make[s] for a better lawyer' (Ward 2009: 109).

Why? Because the expenditure of time and effort plus the 'intrinsic merit in reading Greek plays or modern novels' will lead the law student somehow really to comprehend man's inhumanity to man, possess a context drawn from encounters with 'Euripides and Shakespeare' that enables her to see totalitarianism lurking in populist or legislative texts (Ward 2009: 109–10). Because 'more than any other discipline, literature can make lawyers kinder and more helpful', more empathetic and concerned, by slipping us a spoonful of sugar to make the (ethical) medicine go down. And because kinder, more helpful lawyers are for Ward, as for Day and Murphy, 'better lawyers' (Ward 2009: 111).

Where does the law teacher and scholar of law and the humanities who works in the critical theoretical traditions, who does not profess Ward's more or less unquestioning faith in both liberal democracy and education as practices of freedom, who is all too aware of the disciplinary histories of English studies, begin when confronted with such egregious optimism? And in particular when she, like Ward, hungers as she struggles to challenge her students more, make them think more (Ward 2009: 111), has been profoundly confronted by something near kin to Peter Goodrich's despair in the face of law school's theft of 'intellectual optimism and excitement':

> Law school stole my hopes of change and robbed me of any surviving sense of the relevance of my inner world, of poetry, of desire or dream, to the life of the institution. My experience of law school was of the denial of the relevance of my experience of law school. (Ward 2009, citing Goodrich 1996b: 59)

Where, indeed, to begin? With the invocation of Gerry Wilkes? With my former colleague, the cultural studies scholar Terry Threadgold, when I sought her advice in the face of law student anger because, in teaching the required curriculum rather than in the safe haven of the optional course in law and literature (where one often engages the choir rather than confronts the *vox populi*), I had strayed from the canon, sought to teach differently, critically, to restore law's texts and its disciplinary literacy to contexts which told tales out of school about their partiality? Her words ring in my mind's ear still: 'of course [critical pedagogy] makes [law students] angry', she said.

One place I might begin is with the recognition that Peter Goodrich's sense of betrayal by legal education was subtly, significantly different from that which had made my student angry; that what my student had thought legal education promised was a pedagogy of doing work in the world, of praxis, not poetry; that what he wanted and the poetics – rather than poetry – I thought would be most praxiologically useful to him, were different things; that what was required depended upon recognising that we were *different*. Here Ward offered, finally, something to deploy in retheorising law and literature as a practice of seeking to make law do justice. Close to the end of his essay, which concludes with a celebration of 'a commitment to the democratic [legal] imagination', Ward concedes, without exploring the implications of the concession, that the argument that 'literature makes better lawyers' via fostering the capacity for empathy, should not be taken too far, and we must remain wary of fetish and disciplinary imperialism alike. A reading of Euripides or Shakespeare or Conrad will not alone make for a good lawyer, any more than a reading of *Donohue v Stevenson* or *Rylands v Fletcher* might. But a reading of one without the other will probably sell a law student short. It will challenge them less, make them think less.

It will rob them too, of that sense of intellectual optimism and excitement the loss of which Peter Goodrich famously decried . . . It will rob them, in short, of their humanity. (Ward 2009: 59)

What precedes that unexplored concession is a quotation from David Hume's *A Treatise of Human Nature*, which is apparently perceived by Ward to evidence, *res ipsa*-like, the claim that acquaintance with the (canonically) literary engenders empathy, but which appears rather to speak to empathy's debt to difference, conflict, or critique, and to the commitment to reading what the other has to tell us, perhaps especially, albeit paradoxically, when it is unfamiliar to us, estranging:

No quality of human nature is more remarkable, both in itself and in its consequences, than that propensity we have to sympathize with others, and to receive by communication their inclinations and sentiments, however different from, or even contrary to our own. (Hume 1978 [1740]: 316)

Deleuze was famously a student of Hume, claiming that 'in Hume I found a very creative conception of the institution and right' (Deleuze 1995: 169). Hume's account of human nature was the subject of Deleuze's first book (Deleuze 1991 [1953]), and Deleuze's account of his own work placed it in 'the tradition that runs through Lucretius, Hume, Spinoza and Nietzsche, [entailing] . . . a rejection of negativity, a belief in the externality of forces and relations, a hatred of interiority, and a commitment to the cultivation of joy by means of the invention of concepts', as Patton notes (Patton 2000: 132). Deleuze argues that Hume presents an idea of society that is opposed to that of the social contract theorists.

The main idea [in Hume's philosophy] is this: the essence of society is not the law but the institution. The law, in fact, is a limitation of enterprise and action, and it focuses only on a negative aspect of society . . . The institution, unlike the law, is not a limitation but rather a model of actions, a veritable enterprise, an invented system of positive means or a positive invention of indirect means . . . The social is profoundly creative, inventive, and positive . . . Society is a set of conventions founded on utility, not a set of obligations founded on contract. (Deleuze 1991: 45–6)

Deleuze's critique of the dominant modes of philosophical thought focused on the limiting effects of its characteristic disciplinary discourse. Thus,

> by contrast, he finds in the work of philosophers such as ... Hume ... the outlines of a critical and untimely form of thought that breaks with these prevailing images. It is from the perspective of the approach shared by [Lucretius, Spinoza, Bergson and Nietzsche] that he undertakes the analysis and critique of conservative and conformist images of the nature of thinking, along with the characterization of an alternative form of thinking which would be 'opposed to the traditional image which philosophy has projected or erected in thought'. (Patton 2000: 18, citing Deleuze and Parnet 1987: 16)

As to discourses of law, in Deleuze's exchange with Negri on the influence of Hume's 'representation ... of ... the forms of collective life' on his political thought, he emphasised that 'a constant theme of his work [had] been the conditions under which new institutions can arise. In this regard, it is not the *law* which is interesting but *jurisprudence* in so far as it is "truly creative of rights" ... For this reason, he suggests that this should not be left to judges but should also involve those most directly affected in the elaboration of new principles of right' (Patton 2000: 3, citing Deleuze 1995: 169).

Returning to Ward and his paradigm case for the supplementation of law with literature in the project of legal educational institutional reform, or what we might, following both Deleuze and Marianne Constable, who, writing of law's unjust silences, in Ward's terms its absences and perversions, names as the 'traditional concerns of jurisprudence – law and its relation to justice' (Constable 2005: 178), those most aptly engaged in the productive renewing of different institutions might include both the detainees at Guantánamo Bay, and their lawyers. Among the many literary figurings of the postmodern concentration camp that is Guantánamo, the most striking for me are the remarkable anthology *Poems from Guantánamo: The Detainees Speak*, and human rights lawyer Clive Stafford Smith's account of his representation of Guantánamo detainees, *Eight O'Clock Ferry to the Windward Side: Seeking Justice in Guantánamo Bay*.

*Poems from Guantánamo* is a primary text which shares something of the therapeutic account of the literary for law evident in the work of Day, Murphy and Ward. A revealing triumphalism about the role of the Center for Constitutional Rights in detainee representation suggests that in some way Guantánamo representation saved both lawyers (and those who would become lawyers and who taught them), and democratic values:

This collection would not exist if not for the efforts of the hundreds of volunteer lawyers, professors, paralegals, law students and human rights advocates who have worked tirelessly to restore the rule of law to Guantánamo Bay. Before the lawyers began to open it up, Guantánamo was truly a 'black hole' from which no information – and certainly not the voices of the detainees – could escape.

In this regard, the leadership of the Center for Constitutional Rights has been particularly important. Long before major law firms joined the fold, CCR lawyers were spearheading efforts to mount *habeas corpus* challenges on behalf of the detainees. For more than five years, past and present CCR lawyers . . . have been instrumental in organizing the legal community's response to Guantánamo. (Falkoff 2007: ix)

In addition to celebrating the agency of lawyers who represented their profession's struggle against Guantánamo, framed as a synecdoche of the law's absence, the text's editor here presents the poems anthologised in *Poems from Guantánamo* as the authentic, unmediated voices of those detained, although his narrative goes on to reveal that the material practices of (re)production of the texts involved government classification (Falkoff 2007: 1) and the intermediary work of (amateur) translators (Falkoff 2007: 5) 'who were frequently working under extraordinary conditions both at Guantánamo and in a "secure facility" in Virginia, where our clients' letters and other classified materials are stored . . . [translating] clients' writings, often under tight deadlines and other tools of the trade' (Falkoff 2007: x).

The obstacles [the detainees] have faced in composing their poems are profound. In the first year of their detention, many of the detainees were not allowed regular use of pen and paper. Undeterred, some would draft short poems on Styrofoam cups they had retrieved from their lunch and dinner trays. Lacking writing instruments, they would inscribe their words with pebbles or trace out letters with small dabs of toothpaste, then pass the 'cup poems' from cell to cell. The cups would inevitably be collected with the day's trash, the poetic inscriptions consigned to the bottom of a rubbish bin. Two of these poems – by Shaikh Abdurraheem Muslin Dost, a Pakistani poet who was released from Guantánamo in April 2005 – were reconstructed from memory [the text is silent as to who undertook such 'reconstruction'] and are included in this collection.

After about a year, the military granted the detainees access to regular writing materials, and for the first time they could preserve their poems beyond the end of a meal. The first poem I saw was sent to me by Abdulsalam Ali Abdulrahman Al-Hela, who had written his verses in Arabic after spending extended periods in an isolation cell. The poem is a moving cry about the injustice of arbitrary detention and a hymn to the comforts of religious faith. Soon after I read it, I learned that Adnan Farhan Abdul Latif – another of our clients who has been mercilessly abused while in Guantánamo – had composed a poem of his own called 'The Shout of Death.' (I cannot comment more on these poems, because the Pentagon has refused to clear them for public inspection.) After querying other lawyers, I learned that Guantánamo was filled with amateur poets. (Falkoff 2007: 3)

Flagg Miller's scholarly essay, 'Forms of Suffering in Muslim Prison Poetry', which follows the Editor's introductory 'Notes on Guantánamo', reading like nothing so much as a curatorial catalog raisonné for a visual arts exhibit which needs supplementation by expertise so that it might be 'read' correctly, explained for the purposes of consumption by mystified amateurs who do not know what they see, provides a rather more sophisticated account of the generic tradition of protest literature in which the Guantánamo detainee poems partake. It registers, too, that in Islamic political history, 'poets were important allies to political leaders . . . [and] could be formidable adversaries' (Falkoff 2007: 7).

So too Ariel Dorfman, in his afterword to the poems, 'Where the Buried Flame Burns', locates them in a tradition represented by a survivor of a victim of torture at the hands of the Pinochet regime, who used the escape to poetry (remembered and, in silence, recited, rather than composed) as a practice of resistance to her torturers, a way to access and insist on her humanity, keep something of herself and her history precious, paradoxically safe through reading a message from beyond the grave:

> It was poetry . . . which had allowed her to survive. In the fierce darkness of her ordeal, she repeated to herself those verses sent from some dead poet, she said, as a way of differentiating herself from the men who were treating her body like an object, like a piece of meat. That was how she protected her besieged identity, the one thing those jailers could not touch, could not deny her, could not erase: just some words, just some precarious, almost evanescent, words from the past as a defense against what seemed an eternity of pain and humiliation. (Falkoff 2007: 69)

Taking the matter of genre seriously, more striking than many of the poems themselves (Dorfman aptly concludes that 'some of the words they composed are haunted with beauty . . . Others are less accomplished; [some of the poets] are almost fanatically militant [while others] crave the serenity of home, the absent mother, father, son' [Falkoff: 70]), however, are the bluntly unadorned, militantly unpoetic biographies of the 'Guantánamo poets' that precede the contributions of each:

**Abdullah Thani Faris Al Anazi**
Abdullah Thani Faris al Anazi was teaching in Pakistan when he was arrested by mercenaries and sold to allied forces. A religious scholar who dislikes hostility and was once a candidate for a judgeship, he has a daughter, born just three months before he was captured, who is now five years old. During a military administrative hearing, he was told, 'If you are considered to be a continued threat, you will be detained. If you are not considered a threat, we will recommend release. Why should we consider releasing you?' Al Anazi's response was, 'In the world of international courts, the person is innocent until proven guilty. Why, here, is the person guilty until proven innocent?' (Falkoff 2007: 64)

Equally striking is the text's lawyer-editor's insights into the way the US state regarded these poetic texts. Not only did the Pentagon destroy and confiscate many detainee poems, including in the latter group 'nearly all twenty-five thousand lines of poetry composed by Shaikh Abdurraheem Muslim Dost, returning to him only a handful upon his release from Guantánamo', to his evident pain (Falkoff 2007: 4). Additionally,

> the Pentagon refuses to allow most of the detainees' poems to be made public, arguing that poetry 'presents a special risk' to national security because of its 'content and format.' The fear appears to be that the detainees will try to smuggle coded messages out of the prison camp ... In addition, most of the poems that *have* been cleared are in English translation only, because the Pentagon believes that their original Arabic or Pashto versions represent an enhanced security risk. (Falkoff 2007: 4–5)

The Pentagon thus seems to nurse a degree of the understanding of the subversiveness of poetry equal to that of law and literature scholar Kenji Yoshino (see Yoshino 2005). My own experiences with those doing the government's (putatively legal) work at Guantánamo certainly suggests its consciousness of the uses of narrative: twice in the past few years I have had conversations with those laying down the law on behalf of the military at the prison, one in a professional context and the other social. Both of these men, one a military lawyer and the other a member of a combatant status review board, made a point of telling me scurrilous stories about the anti-death penalty advocate and Guantánamo lawyer Clive Stafford Smith which struck me, positioned as I am, as at once spectacularly (if in one case crudely) defamatory and manifestly fanciful, but which were clearly conveyed as an attempt to persuade me of the danger of interested civilian law in the 'national security' context.

While Stafford Smith's memoir, *Eight O'Clock Ferry to the Windward*

*Side*, fits neatly in the genre of heroic lawyer war story, and while he is apparently a 'criminal justice paradigm Romantic' in his approach to what legal institutions and professional subjects ought properly to do about the considerable challenges contemporary 'Islamic' terrorism confronts them with (Stafford Smith 2007: 276–8), Stafford Smith is too good a lawyer not to be aware of the baggage his representation of his clients in the memoir bears with it. Conceding that 'many people find themselves unable to work up much sympathy for someone like Sheikh bin al-Libi, even if he has been repatriated [from a 'secret location' where he had been interrogated by the US] to Libya to face persecution', Stafford Smith goes on to categorise al-Libi as a refugee or asylum-seeker, arguing that 'the rules regarding refugees were not written just for him – they apply to people who used to be our heroes, those willing to languish in prison cells for their beliefs. A refugee might have challenged totalitarianism in the Soviet Union, an authoritarian regime in South Africa, or a tyrant in Libya' (Stafford Smith 2007: 252).

A long-time death penalty defence and abolition cause lawyer, with an acute eye for manifestations of what he names 'the politics of hatred' (Stafford Smith 2007: 252), the logic of us and others, Stafford Smith epitomises the *interested* advocate. As such, he reads the legal culture in which he deploys his capability to make change, in Deleuzian terms, 'with love' (Deleuze 1995: 9). That is, Stafford Smith knows that lawyers, like writers, both practitioners of the art of telling tales, and thus what Deleuze, following Nietzsche, called 'clinicians of civilization' (Deleuze 1990: 237), read according to their orientation. Narrative will not necessarily humanise; encounters of the legal with the literary will not inevitably engender 'lines of flight' that are productive, rather than destructive, of radical change, 'affirmative', rather than 'negative' (Deleuze 1983: 89, 102). For as the law and literature scholar Brook Thomas registers of the constitutional stories that engage him, like Stafford Smith, and me, all students in our own way of America, whose literature (and politics) was in significant part Deleuze's subject (Deleuze and Parnet 1987: 36–51), 'literature can serve the dominant ideology, as well as challenge it' (Thomas 1987: 6).

Readers, too, matter. For Deleuze,

> this intensive way of reading, in contact with what's outside the book, as a flow meeting other flows, one machine among others, as a series of experiments for each reader in the midst of events that have nothing to do with books, as tearing the book into pieces, getting it to interact with other things, absolutely anything . . . is reading with love. (Deleuze 1995: 9)

This account of interdisciplinary engagements with literature at once clinical, in its orientation to cultural diagnostics, is also critical, in that its practitioner, like Deleuze, 'do[es] not present [herself] as a commentator on texts. For [her], a text is merely a small cog in an extra-textual practice. It is not a question of commentating on the text by a method of deconstruction, or by a method of textual practice, or by other methods; it is a question of seeing what use it has in the extra-textual practice that prolongs the text' (Smith in Deleuze 1997: xvi). Miller, too, reminds us that we always already are and must be interested readers:

> Linking broader trends in Muslim prison poetry to the contributions in *Poems from Guantánamo* begs the question of the nature of the Guantánamo poets' dissent. Do the detainees call upon the vocabulary of radical Islamic militancy to defend themselves? Do they evoke other discussion of social justice? To what extent do their verses confirm their designations as global Islamic jihadists and 'unlawful enemy combatants', as the U.S. administration and military tribunals have maintained?
> 
> Part of the challenge of answering such questions lies in the role of poetry as a figurative enterprise. If our aim is to study verbal artistry in a way that is maximally useful, we need to be prepared to consider answers not about the poets' intentions but about our own intentions as analysts responsible for distinguishing fact from fiction. We need to assess not only the detainees' own tendencies toward radicalism but also our own assumptions about detainees' identities, goals, and motivations. (Falkoff 2007: 11)

Deleuze's own interdisciplinary praxis, his 'thinking alongside literary works, [his] engagement of philosophical issues generated from and developed through encounters with literary text' (Bogue 2003: 2) is shaped by his philosophical method, as by his politics, with its 'anti-capitalist thematic', its 'philosophy of desire' informed by its participation in the 'political and theoretical orientations common to the post-1968 libertarian left' (Patton 2000: 6). His readings of literary texts make productive, methodologically self-conscious use of the way these texts articulate critical shifts in what might conventionally be called the history of ideas, viewing literature at once 'as a machine, producing certain effects, amenable to certain use' (Deleuze and Guattari 1983: 109), and as the material for the mosaic the political philosopher, shadowing the literary artist, fabricates as he reads into it 'all the meanings [he] wants it to have according to its functioning' (Deleuze 1972: 138).

*Eight O'Clock Ferry*, Stafford Smith's hybrid of memoir and advocacy, closing as it does with a primer for readers on what they can do 'to take action against Guantánamo and the secret prisons' (providing, as he tacitly acknowledges, that he has converted them to this lawyering cause) (Stafford Smith 2007: 296), is one kind of exemplar of how what we learn from Deleuze about interested reading might be applied in productively changing the legal educational institutions which shape the work that lawyers do. The great uncertainty with the practice of cause lawyering, as with scholarly and pedagogical practices of law and literature, however, is about whether in exploring what our bodies can do (lifting an expression from Spinoza) we may engage with other bodies to reproduce the molar 'overcoding' (Deleuze and Guattari 1987: 208) of the seductively familiar logic of 'us and them', practice interdisciplinary scholarship and pedagogy such that in our 'micropolitics of perception, affection, conversation, and so forth', we knit together the 'supple fabric [of the disciplines, instantiations of the molecular] without which . . . [the] rigid segments [of the molar binary of "us and them"] would not hold' (Deleuze and Guattari 1987: 213). On the most basic level, theory-work such as Deleuze's, in its very textual strangeness, its contestation of the fiction that we all read the same common sense, might rupture the insistent reproduction of the molar; so too might introjecting literary discourse into the legal discursive domain.

Contesting Ward's implication that the 'real' is accessible to all of us, regardless of race, class, sex and the world view we take from our embodied experience of the cultures in which we are constituted, I would assert, rather, that some literature can be made to tell tales about law that strip it bare of its claims to viewpointless authority, if we learn and then teach how to read it that way. A scholarly and pedagogical practice of law and literature that is highly conscious of the ethics it seeks to engender, which understands that the work minority literatures as Deleuze conceives of them must be made rather than expected to do when they tell stories fashioned from symptoms about law and society, and confronts its own ethical challenge as a practice of disciplinary violence, is another such exemplar. For if law's judgments, on the one hand, and justice, on the other, are, as Deleuze asserts, different things (Deleuze 1997: 127), their apparent binary is unsettled by cruelty (Deleuze 1997: 126–35), at once 'everywhere opposed to the doctrine of judgment' (Deleuze 1997: 128), and 'not without a certain cruelty toward itself' (Deleuze 1997: 135). Perhaps most productive of all is what is suggested when we bring insights generated by Deleuze's critical and clinical engagements with literature to bear on how the texts on legal educational institutions, discourses and practices I have assembled in this essay might be read with a companion-text to the apparently stripped-bare yet evocative biographies which punctuate the anthology of *Poems from Guantánamo*. Rather than resorting to an interdisciplinarity of intertextuality, *Death in Camp Delta*, the incisively forensic narrative produced by faculty and students at Seton Hall University School of Law, draws on an interdisciplinary heuristics, using the law's characteristic forensic rhetoric to read its own texts as fabrications. The non-fictional murder-mystery *Death in Camp Delta* is a mosaicisation of the law, a ripping apart at the seams of governmental accounts of what *Poems from Guantánamo* inadequately indicts as suicides prompted by despair, albeit reinscribed in 'Orwellian' fashion by the Pentagon as 'incidents of "manipulative self-injurious behavior" ... [and] acts of "asymmetric warfare"' (Falkoff 2007: 2). It can be made to tell a story of how law schools might make change if law teachers, drawing on Deleuze's *Essays Critical and Clinical*, make legal discourse *stutter*:

> [w]e have to see creation as tracing a path between impossibilities ... A creator who isn't grabbed by the throat by a set of impossibilities is no creator. A creator's someone who creates their own impossibilities, and thereby creates possibilities ... Without a set of impossibilities, you won't have a line of flight, the exit that is creation, the power of falsity that is truth. (Deleuze 1995: 133)

Let me close, first, with Said. 'Critical reading', he wrote, 'provides students with an awakened understanding' and 'furnishes the engaged mind with an alertness to the lazy rhetoric and automatic language-use that has so often covered up abuses of power' (Said, in Higgins 2001). But let me equally, opening as I close, hazard a line of flight that that might get 'out of the black holes ... connecting with other lines and each time augmenting its valence' or might turn, rather '*to destruction*' (Deleuze and Guattari 1987: 229). For if, as Albrecht-Crane and Daryl Slack suggest, creative cruelty is kissing kin to reading with love, the transformative pedagogy they seek to imagine is dangerous:

> It is the immanence of [the line of flight] that spurs Ashton-Warner to write repeatedly about 'an energy that is almost frightening when released', that 'so severely opposes a teacher when imposing knowledge'. This 'energy' constitutes a line of flight that escapes the molar function of the classroom. It is a line she both values and fears. (Albrecht-Crane and Daryl Slack 2007: 104)

# References

Albrecht-Crane, C. and J. Daryl Slack (2007), 'Toward a Pedagogy of Affect', in A. Hickey-Moody and P. Mullins (eds), *Deleuzian Encounters: Studies in Contemporary Social Issues*, Basingstoke: Palgrave Macmillan.

Baldick, C. (1983), *The Social Mission of English Criticism 1848–1932*, Oxford: Clarendon.

Bogue, R. (2003), *Deleuze on Literature*, New York and London: Routledge.
Braidotti, R. (2001), 'Toward a New Nomadism: Feminist Deleuzian Tracks; or Metaphysics and Metabolism', in G. Genosko (ed.), *Deleuze and Guattari: Critical Assessments of Leading Philosophers*, Vol. 3, London and New York: Routledge.
Brighouse, H. and Swift, A. (2003), 'Defending Liberalism in Education Theory', *Journal of Education Theory*, 18: 367.
Constable, M. (2005), *Just Silences: The Limits and Possibilities of Modern Law*, Princeton: Princeton University Press.
Day, K. N. and R. G. Murphy (2009), '"Just Trying to Be Human in This Place": Storytelling and Film in the First-Year Law School Classroom', *Stetson Law Review*, 39: 247.
Deleuze, G. (1972), *Proust and Signs*, trans. R. Howard, New York: George Brazillier.
Deleuze, G. (1983), *Nietzsche and Philosophy*, trans. H. Tomlinson, London: Athlone Press.
Deleuze, G. (1990), *The Logic of Sense*, trans. M. Lester and C. Stivale, ed. C. Boundas, New York: Columbia University Press.
Deleuze, G. (1991), *Empiricism and Subjectivity: An Essay on Hume's Theory of Human Nature*, trans. C. Boundas, New York: Columbia University Press.
Deleuze, G. (1995), *Negotiations, 1972–1990*, trans. M. Joughlin, New York: Columbia University Press.
Deleuze, G. (1997), *Essays Critical and Clinical*, trans. D. Smith, Minneapolis: University of Minnesota Press.
Deleuze, G. and F. Guattari (1983), *Anti-Oedipus: Capitalism and Schizophrenia*, trans. R. Hurley, M. Seem and H. Lane, Minneapolis: University of Minnesota Press.
Deleuze, G. and F. Guattari (1987), *A Thousand Plateaus: Capitalism and Schizophrenia*, trans. B. Massumi, London: Athlone Press.
Deleuze, G. and C. Parnet (1987), *Dialogues*, trans. H. Tomlinson and B. Habberjam, London: Athlone Press.
Denbeaux, M., et al. (2009), *Death in Camp Delta*, Newark: Seton Hall University School of Law Center for Policy & Research.
Falkoff, M. (ed.) (2007), *Poems from Guantánamo: The Detainees Speak*, Iowa City: University of Iowa Press.
Faludi, S. (2007), *The Terror Dream: Fear and Fantasy in Post-9/11 America*, New York: Metropolitan Books.
Gaber, P. (1998), '"Just Trying to Be Human in This Place": The Legal Education of Twenty Women', *Yale Journal of Law and Feminism*, 10: 166.
Goodrich, P. (1996a), *Law in the Courts of Love: Literature and Other Minor Jurisprudences*, London: Routledge.
Goodrich, P. (1996b), 'Of Blackstone's Tower: Metaphors of Distance and Histories of English Law Schools', in P. Birks (ed.), *What Are Law Schools For?*, Oxford: Oxford University Press.
Higgins, J. (2001), 'Critical Thinking on the Path to Peace', *Times Higher Education Supplement*, 9 March, <http://www.timeshighereducation.co.uk/story.asp?storycode=158007> (accessed 6 Feb 2012).
hooks, b. (1990), *Yearning: Race, Gender, and Cultural Politics*, Toronto: Between the Lines.
Hume, D. (1978 [1740]), *A Treatise of Human Nature*, Oxford: Oxford University Press.
Koh, H. (2002), 'The Spirit of the Laws', *Harvard International Law Journal*, 43: 23.

Lasswell, H. and M. McDougal (1943), 'Legal Education and Public Policy: Professional Training in the Public Interest', *Yale Law Journal*, 52: 212.
LeBrun, M. and R. Johnstone (1994), *The Quiet Revolution: Improving Student Learning in Law*, Sydney: Law Book Co. Ltd.
Mertz, E. (2007), *The Language of Law School: Learning to 'Think Like a Lawyer'*, Oxford: Oxford University Press.
Patton, P. (2000), *Deleuze and the Political*, London and New York: Routledge.
Pether, P. (2002), 'Measured Judgments: Histories, Pedagogies, and the Possibility of Equity', *Law and Literature*, 14 (3): 489.
Pether, P. (2007), 'Editor's Introduction: The New Exceptionalism: Law and Literature Since 9/11 Symposium', *Law & Literature*, 19 (2): 155.
Pue, W. (2008), 'Legal Education's Mission', *Law Teacher*, 42: 270.
Stafford Smith, C. (2007), *Eight O'Clock Ferry to the Windward Side: Seeking Justice in Guantánamo Bay*, New York: Nation Books.
Sullivan, W. et al. (2007), *Educating Lawyers: Preparation for the Profession of Law*, San Francisco: Jossey-Bass.
Thomas, B. (1987), *Cross-Examinations of Law and Literature: Cooper, Hawthorne, Stowe and Melville*, Cambridge: Cambridge University Press.
Twining, W. (1994), *Blackstone's Tower: The English Law School*, London: Sweet and Maxwell.
Tyack, D. and L. Cuban (1995), *Thinking Toward Utopia: A Century of Public School Reform*, Cambridge, MA: Harvard University Press.
Vismann, C. (2008), 'The Archive and the Beginning of Law', in P. Goodrich et al., *Derrida and Legal Philosophy*, Basingstoke and New York: Palgrave Macmillan.
Ward, I. (2009), 'Legal Education and the Democratic Imagination', *Law and the Humanities*, 3 (1): 87.
Yoshino, K. (2005), 'The City and the Poet', *Yale Law Journal*, 114: 1835.

# Notes

1. See Baldick 1983.
2. See Goodrich 1996a, especially Chapter 3.
3. See Pether 2002 for a general account of this institutional history.
4. To student-centered legal education of the kind anatomised in LeBrun and Johnstone 1994.

Chapter 5

# Law, Space, Bodies: The Emergence of Spatial Justice

*Andreas Philippopoulos-Mihalopoulos*

### In the Ocean

Law's recent spatial turn should not be confined to a disciplinary connection between law and geography. While the emergence of the connection is relevant, it tends to parochialise the issue by placing the emphasis only on law's interaction with local or global geographies. The importance of the spatial turn, however, is much larger and somehow much more threatening than that. It requires a spatialisation of law and its processes, namely a serious engagement with contemporary definitions and operations of space, and a close observation of the changes the law undergoes through this new conceptualisation. The changes are both radical and immanent, brought from within the law yet wholly unsettling for current legal practices. Law's spatiality is a line of flight the law has a responsibility to follow. Indeed, there is very little choice for a body of law that aims at remaining open to future developments.[1]

In what follows, I construct a concept of spatial law as well as an emerging concept of spatial justice. Deleuzian and Deleuze/Guattarian thought is invaluable for this kind of conceptualisation. On a processual level, it is the task of the thinker to construct concepts that forge new ways of thinking by assembling various elements together (Deleuze and Guattari 1994). This forging can only take place on a *plane of immanence* (or what Deleuze has called an 'image of thought' [Deleuze 2004c]), that is, the parameters of thinking that determine the problem in answer to which the concept comes forth (Deleuze and Guattari 1994). This is neither a clean-cut epistemological exercise, nor a representation of the way things work. On the contrary, the plane of immanence is a continuous exploration that becomes unsettled with the changing conditions of movement within it; as Moira Gatens writes,

## Law, Space, Bodies: The Emergence of Spatial Justice 91

it is 'a plane of experimentation, a mapping of extensive relations and intensive capacities that are mobile and dynamic' (Gatens 1996: 165). It is also something that lies outside the control of either the thinker or the concepts rehearsed on it. It is affected, but not solely determined by (specific shoots of philosophical) thinking without succumbing to historicisation. Its loyalty is limited to whatever emerges at any point, a truly intensive cartography and thus an unstable playground. Lab sociological conditions are left behind in order to embrace the often unpredictable and sometimes violent movement that takes place on the plane. Thus, Deleuze and Guattari write:

> Precisely because the plane of immanence is prephilosophical and does not immediately take effect with concepts, it implies a sort of groping experimentation and its layout resorts to measures that are not very respectable, rational or reasonable. These measures belong to the order of dreams, of pathological processes, esoteric experiences, drunkenness, and excess. (Deleuze and Guattari 1994: 141)

Following this, let me clarify that the plane of immanence on which this text moves does not easily square with existing understandings of the field in which law operates, nor with conceptualisations of bodies merely as human beings moving against a geographical background. It is a drunken, excessive plane of immanence that demands the collapse of existing boundaries and the erection of new ways of delimitation based on movement and rest, speed and slowness, flows and flow conjunctures. The order of dreams that conjures the present plane of immanence is properly speaking liminal and insular. The text closes in on a desert island, albeit a literary one, that contains an embattled configuration of a manifold space striated and destratified by laws, and trammelled by bodies that move along sharp lines of flight.[2] As I show below, the island erected out of this order of dreams and within the immanence of the plane is the body of spatial justice.

In what follows, I define more fully the plane of immanence from which an understanding of law's spatiality emerges. This I do by mapping Michel Tournier's novel *Vendredi*, which, at least according to my reading, is characterised by an obsessive normative spatiality. To this effect, I partly follow Deleuze's reading of the novel, and partly employ my own Deleuzian reading that explicitly reveals the strata of legality. At that point in the text, I reach a flow conjuncture, a clot that alters the flow and pushes it into another line of flight. This clot, right in the middle, is a Deleuzian-inspired understanding of law as immanent, spatial and posthuman. End of clot, and the flow has now been overcoded, a paroxysm of erected singularity that unfolds with the emergence of the body of spatial justice as radically immanent to this very clot.

## On the Island

Gilles Deleuze's essay on Michel Tournier's *Vendredi ou les Limbes du Pacifique* (in English, the title has been simplified to *Friday*)[3] maps a self-enclosed, immanent island.[4] Deleuze uses Tournier's *Vendredi* as a diagrammatic text, as something that 'does not function to represent, even something real, but rather constructs a real that is yet to come, a new type of reality' (Deleuze and Guattari 1988: 142). This new type of reality is immanent to the space of its emergence, to its own plane of immanence, the latter both on the basis of and beyond the control of such reality. Whatever emerges out of the diagrammatic never quite abandons it but stays within its future-promising immanence. Here, the plane of immanence is a desert island. Its coastline, brimful with movement, pushes out its desert, living the island overflowing with bodies. 'What is deserted is the ocean around it' (Deleuze 2004a: 11). Ready to be populated, the island offers itself to the shipwreck.

Tournier's *Vendredi* is the story of Robinson-meets-Friday. It differs radically, however, from the Defoe original, of which incidentally Deleuze has written that 'one can hardly imagine a more boring novel, and it is sad to see children still reading it today' (Deleuze 2004a: 12). Deleuze's dismissal of Defoe's Robinson is on account of the novel's preachy, capitalist, property-obsessed tone that makes 'any healthy reader' dream 'of seeing [Friday] eat Robinson' (Deleuze 2004a: 12). In some ways, Tournier's treatment of the topic is Deleuze's dream come true. Although no cannibalism is practised between the two men, there is a certain reciprocal ingestion that characterises the whole novel. Indeed, Tournier's version begins with an initial Defoe-like storyline of Robinson's attempt to master his surroundings, only quickly to move to a meditation on a becoming-elemental – a becoming-tree, becoming-Friday, and eventually becoming-island. Tournier's Robinson ends up in an assemblage consisting of the insular earth and Friday's body. Rather eccentrically, however, Robinson's sexual becoming couples with the former rather than the latter. Sexual or not,[5] the connection between bodies and space is one of double-capture, a wasp-orchid ingestion. Desire flows and rests, throws itself wildly around, and forms clots of thick craving. Its movement is in accordance with a law that trammels the whole assemblage. This law, however, does not determine the assemblage any more than it is determined by it. The law in *Vendredi* cannot be dissociated from either the body or the space of its appearance.

Deleuze's reading of *Vendredi* offers a thesis on the connection between space and body.[6] Both elements are explicitly present in the novel. Let me start with space first. In another difference to the Defoe original, *Vendredi* is flooded by a sense of spatiality and in many respects entirely measured by it. The space of the island is never a mere backdrop but an active force. The two men follow languidly the movement of the island, to the final point at which the space of the island becomes no different from the bodies that walk over it. The island as destination, imagination and geography hosts these 'heavenly nuptials, multiplicities of multiplicities' (Deleuze and Guattari 1988: 35), of bodies and space flowing together in an elemental dance. Thought, memory, movement, future projections, philosophical enquiries, desire, fear, nostalgia: they are all mediated by the space of the island. Above all, *hope* is the island's main function, which is why Robinson quickly names it *Speranza* ('hope' in Italian). Envisaged initially as Robinson's hope to be saved from the elements, the cannibals, the solitude, it quickly embodies the hope of saving Robinson from himself and his human nature.

What is more, space does not only appear in its abstract quality as the field on which the story unfolds, nor in its concreteness as just an as yet unmapped territory in the ocean. On the contrary, the space of the island is material, tangible, a body in itself that floats on the ocean. Its extension includes the ocean of the voyage as well as that last vestige of transcendence, the shipwreck itself, now well ingested in the spatial immanence of the island. As Deleuze writes, 'humans would have to reduce themselves to the movement that brings them to the island' (Deleuze 2004a: 11). The movement *to* the island becomes one with the movement *of* the island, thus fusing imagination with the materiality of geography and the voyage with the desert island. It is in this sense that the endeavour is not a utopia, at least in its usual sense of successful failure that the voyage towards an *ou*-topos entails. On the contrary, the voyage is immanent to the (eventual) joy of becoming one with the *topos*: it is folded in the coastline of the island. The voyage is no longer anything more than the shipwreck from which one can still draw useful tools and useless rituals.[7] The voyage has become a space of the island, simultaneously a potential means of striation, organisation, categorisation, *and* a space from which the origin prepares the island for its teleology, its emergence as pure spatiality. One must not forget the voyage; nor, however, must one lose oneself in it. The island remains desert and the perfect case of what DeLanda (2005) has called *manifold* (which is a spatially pronounced description of multiplicity), namely a field of rapidities and slownesses defined internally, by and through itself and its inclusive immanence. The island as manifold includes the space of all possible states the island can have, as well as the invariant structure of that space (Buchanan and Lambert 2005), the part of the organism needed for the organism to reinvent itself.

Through its gravitational pull, its fully spatialised *here*, the island demands one's emplaced body. For Deleuze, 'a body can be anything: it can be an animal, a body of sounds, a mind or idea; it can be a linguistic corpus, a social body, a collectivity' (Deleuze 1988: 127). What connects these bodies is matter. But matter is not inert. On the contrary, 'matter is molecular material, not dead, brute, homogeneous matter, but a matter-movement' (Deleuze and Guattari 1988: 512). In its movement, matter is generative of both order and chaos. It is supple, molecular, folding, heterogeneous. It is unrepresentable, uncontainable, infinite, bearing in its folds singularities and their encounters with other singularities, bodies that in their movement affect and are affected by other bodies. Robinson, Friday, the goats Robinson has tamed, the island are bodies. But so are the log that Robinson keeps and the body of the law that he builds as soon as he lands on the island. Bodies emerge all the time from the folds of matter, defined less by their extensive qualities, namely the space that they occupy, and more by the way they affect and are affected by other bodies. Bodies form other bodies, arranged not in hierarchy but in a system of movement and rest in which positions change and power balances are being constantly restructured. The island is moving in that direction, eventually to become, as I show below, this most exquisite of bodies, a body without organs.

While space and bodies are explicitly dealt with in Deleuze's text on *Vendredi*, the law is less so. Deleuze anchors law on the concept of perversion. He writes: 'Perversion is a bastard concept, half-juridical, half-medical. But neither law nor medicine are entirely suited to it' (Deleuze 2004b: 343). Law (along with medicine) constitute the system in which the pervert introduces his desire and tries to make it work as an internal limit. In so doing, the law does not see the pervert as someone who desires but as a threat to a well-established system of desire. Deleuze's understanding of law as a capturing machine runs throughout his work. It is little surprise, therefore, that direct references to law are limited and generally dismissive. Still, in his essay on *Vendredi*, the law is constantly and implicitly there. In the text, the law determines the space between the self and the Other with regards to desire. Thus, the Other gives depth to the world because she is assumed to be able to see what I cannot see:

# Law, Space, Bodies: The Emergence of Spatial Justice 95

'I desire nothing that cannot be seen, thought, or possessed by a possible Other' (Deleuze 2004b: 345). Her presence determines what is *possible* by delimiting and thus defining my perceptual field. The Other appears here as the normative frame that determines what I see, where I move, what I can touch. The Other is the authority that subsumes my perception into a specific perspective. Just as the Other operates spatially by rendering things available to me, in the same way the law, itself always spatially emplaced, offers to me the possible, thereby excluding the things that are to remain out of reach for me. The law, just as the Other, is 'neither an object in the field of my perception nor a subject who perceives me: the Other is initially a structure of the perceptual field, without which the entire field could not function as it does' (Deleuze 2004b: 346). This is the '*a priori Other*', 'the absolute structure' that places things into categories and distributes space according to the organisation of its own structure. The presence of the Other manifests itself through a spatial law, what we can call the *law of the Other*. This law striates the very space on which it operates; it determines distances and propinquities between bodies; it restricts, enables or forces movement; it renders visible bodies with which a connection is possible while obscuring others, thus rendering the connection impossible. The Law of the Other is the law that society needs in order to carry on functioning according to its pre-given structure. Tournier writes: 'He knew now that man resembles a person injured in a street riot, who can only stay upright while the crowd packed densely around him continues to prop him up' (Tournier 1969 [1967]: 40 [38]). Just as the Other, the law 'is the structure which conditions the entire field and its functioning, by rendering possible the constitution and application of the preceding categories' (Deleuze 2004b: 348). The law of the Other is the great categoriser, finding its breath in the body of the Other. The law emplaces my body on an island of controlled flows, where only the bodies revealed to me by the law can be part of my field of perception.

And so it is in *Vendredi*. Robinson begins with an obsessive normativity that striates the island. He divides it in excruciatingly delimited spaces that contain resources, or are designated for the ritual of log-keeping, or for church-like spiritual concentration. He also divides the island in present and future visibility, thereby keeping the seed stock well hidden while using a small portion for his present needs, thus deferring most of it to a future promise. Smelted in the rocks of the island and the sinews of Robinson, the law determines the assemblage between the body of Robinson and that of the island. This is an angular, rectilinear assemblage that reterritorialises the desert island and produces capital accumulation on the cutting edge of further deterritorialisation. As Tournier's Robinson reflects in his log, 'Robinson is infinitely rich only when he coincides with the whole island' (Tournier 1969 [1967]: 67 [70]). The assemblage is productive because it is determined by the law of the Other. Robinson constructs the Other, indeed represents the Other in the form of rituals, dressed-up ceremonies, self-imposed limits or even a ban on the consumption of crops, calendar division of time, and a desperate self-imposed obligation for vocal articulation of all thinking. The reader witnesses the collective enunciations of 'acts and statements, of incorporeal transformations of bodies' (Deleuze and Guattari 1983: 88). Robinson obsessively controls the way his senses thematise space. Right from the start he codifies everything in a *Charte de l'Ile* (Tournier 1969 [1967]: 69 [71]. The English translation is *Charter*), namely a code of several articles and paragraphs *and* a map of the island, a cartography of movement and a striation, not only of the body of the island but also of his own body, his effluxes and ingestions, his position on the island at any time during the day, his breathing and his vocality. Robinson needs the law because he is still dependent on the Other as structure. Tournier writes: 'Once again he found that to build, to organize, and to make and abide by laws were sovereign remedies against the dissolving effect of the absence of the Other' (Tournier 1969 [1967]: 76 [79], translation modified). Through normative fortification, he constructs his desire for the society that he is missing (which is, according to Deleuze and Guattari, the function of the law: 'so, *that's* what I wanted!' [Deleuze and Guattari 1988: 125]). The Other is present in her absence.

Yet, as Deleuze remarks, Tournier's novel 'develops the very thesis of Robinson: the man without Others on his island' (Deleuze 2004b: 344). Robinson's thesis, his position on the island, is one of shifting juxtaposition. Indeed, initially the absence of the Other manifests itself with an asphyxiating presence that leads to frenetic juridification. But then, the Other is finally ingested in her absence and nothing is left: the Other's presence is finally absent. In a beautiful, almost Kierkegaardian passage, Robinson indulges the Nietzschean ecstasy of what he subsequently calls 'a moment of innocence' (Tournier 1969 [1967]: 90 [94]). Robinson returns to a pre-edenic state of atemporality and aspatiality, when he is caught unawares by a pause in his daily routine caused inadvertently by the stopping of his salvaged hourglass. This pause operates like a legal lacuna, an abrupt estoppel of the legal flow. The legislative gap cracks open the subject/object distinction that Robinson has constructed for himself in relation to the island, and dramatically minimises the distance between them. The body of the law is wounded and leaking. A moment of innocence that supercodes any judgment of guilty or not-guilty, pushes Robinson on a new line of flight, radically immanent to his existing assemblage: it exposes him to an awareness of his *affect*, '*these nonhuman becomings of man*', and edges him to let it flow together with the island as a *percept*, or what Deleuze and Guattari have called the '*nonhuman landscapes of nature*' (Deleuze and Guattari 1994: 169, original emphasis). The 'barrier of the skin which separates the inner from the outer world' (Tournier 1969 [1967]: 69 [70]) collapses, and Robinson becomes aware of progressively shedding his human nature when 'he perceived, when he awoke one morning, he realises that his beard, growing in the night, had begun to take root in the earth' (Tournier 1969 [1967]: 130 [138]).

Robinson slowly abandons the law of the Other and slides into a new assemblage with the body of the island. The emerging assemblage is an insular one, the island being more potent than Robinson. He becomes one with the elements and loses completely the presence of the absence of the Other as structure. Robinson passes from the representation of the Other as juridical structure in the form of law's compulsive spatial striation to a different juridical structure: that of the demise of the Other. Law is no longer mediated through the Other but emanates directly from within Robinson's assemblage with the body of the island. The law is no longer simply spatial but becomes posthuman. A newfound freedom that is a direct product of Robinson's *encounter* with the island smoothens the territory by whispering a different law altogether – the law of *becoming other*. This is no longer a law of striation but of continuous, uncontrollable, nomadic perambulation. Robinson is finally free to fall, literally into the depths of the island, deep into her womb, losing time and rendering visible another cavernous insular space. He spends an unspecified amount of time in a deep dark hole in the ground, an intense claustrophobic space in the novel that leaves a Robinson blanched out, weak, savage, smooth. He emerges in a milky consistency, new-born and healed, one with the body of the island.

It is remarkable that Friday appears when Robinson's becoming-other is well under way. Friday arrives too late to be able to resuscitate the order of the Other, yet a little too early to slide along the Robinson-island assemblage. So the assemblage changes again. Friday's legality is a different one to that of Robinson, a legality of surface rather than depth, and in this more *profound*.[8] Thus, while Robinson enjoys withdrawing underground in an arborescent move, Friday spreads his body on the island, grass-like, exposed and seemingly without need for shelter, and even reversing the available surfaces by replanting trees upside-down, or using the element of wind to make music on an Aeolian harp. Not without a certain envy, Robinson draws a parallel between him and Aphrodite, perennially emerging and free-floating on the sea spray. While Robinson's transition from the law of the depth to that of the surface is progressive and hesitant, Friday is firmly based on the *here* of the island. Friday's minor spatiality, unhierarchical and elemental, deterritorialises Robinson's relics of structure that manically hold onto the vertical and the royal. The deterritorialisation occurs not in an opposition but from within the structure, *in equal measure invited and invaded by the structure*. The movement is always immanent, always from within: the minor from within the royal. The law of surface moves across the law of depth and captures it while luring it.

## Clot: In the Middle

To begin in the middle is every time a new beginning. Beginning in the middle repeats the previous beginning while maintaining its singularity, it does 'not add a second or third time to the first, but carr[ies] the first to the "nth" power' (Deleuze 2004c: 2). The middle can never call itself the centre or the origin. The middle is the topology of the rhizome which 'has neither beginning nor end, but always a middle [*milieu*] from which it grows and which it overspills' (Deleuze and Guattari 1988: 21). So, to begin in the middle is not beginning but carrying on, taking a line of flight and establishing a deterritorialising cutting edge right in the middle of the plane of immanence.[9] A series of beginnings that demolishes the original beginning, drags it from its tail and throws it again in the middle. This new beginning, the *repeated* beginning that maintains difference rather than identity (Deleuze 2004c), is the beginning of the law. The law begins in the middle. And since every middle is immanent to the plane of immanence in which it finds itself undercut and interfolded, the law finds itself in the middle of the law of depth and the law of surface, furtively spreading itself in the movement between these two laws. But are these two laws ever distinct or do they always appear inextricably assembled?

To begin with, for Deleuze and Guattari there is *logos* and *nomos*. In spatial terms, *logos* is the abstract machine that guides striation from within, namely the organisation of space into a 'space of *pillars*' and of homogeneity (Deleuze and Guattari 1988: 408), 'striated by walls, enclosures, and roads between enclosures' (Deleuze and Guattari 1988: 420). *Nomos*, on the other hand, is the law as distribution (νομή – 'nomé' in Greek), 'the law ... without division into shares, in a space without borders or enclosure'. This is the law of smooth space, the variable open boundless space characterised by a 'polyvocality of directions' (Deleuze and Guattari 1988: 421), a space 'wedded to a very particular type of multiplicity: nonmetric, acentered, rhizomatic multiplicities' (Deleuze and Guattari 1988: 409). In the parlance of this text, logos is the law of the Other that made Robinson excavate the island, erect edifices dedicated to specific functions, and place fences and limits everywhere. Robinson's law of depth striated the island with cavities of past crops and observatories of future salvation perched on the highest peak. When, however, Robinson began to become-island, and especially after the advent of Friday, the law of depth (logos) gave way to the law of surface (nomos). Space is now manifold, emergent and spread out, a playground of nomadic existence where one never gets lost because there is no centre, no measure, and no one direction. The surface has surfaced (especially after a spectacular explosion caused by Friday that destroys the cave with the provisions) and the island becomes a smooth, elastic membrane.

One has to be careful though with the seeming binarism of logos/nomos. The two are never found independently, whether this is the law of the land or the law of the island. The insular plane of immanence contains the two in overlapping events. Robinson's law contained spaces of smoothness, Sundays, periods of rest and sleep, and allowances for cave retreats and moments of innocence. Likewise, Friday's law striated the space around which he could lie about and enjoy the sun. An example: Friday made full use of every single part of the grand goat that he had killed after a battle. The goat in its various manifestations as food, clothing, tools, toys, musical instruments could only be made thus by following an intensive and exhausting series of actions in strict order and with a view to (elemental) possession. Even in its progressive formation, the assemblage Robinson-Friday-Speranza moves between the two laws and on the two spaces, overlapping, in *glissando* or in convulsions, resting or rushing. There is no value judgment here. What is important is that it moves: *eppur si muove!* as Galileo whispered, gravitationally forced to remain within the confines of the centre. But here, the centre is in orbit, folded with its bodies, celestial or otherwise.

I begin again in this space of the middle in the following section, where the body of justice emerges precisely in the middle of these two laws and in a paroxysm of repetition. In the remainder of this intermezzo, however, I want to make a case for a Deleuzian conceptualisation of a broadly understood (but not metaphorically) spatial law that floats on the melange nomos/logos. In what can be understood as a *conjuncture* in the flow of the text, and in an attempt to ground what is coming next but without necessarily following the same line, the law squats here in the middle of the text and with an eye to overcoding the end, offering a teleology that resists transcendence. The usual disclaimer that Deleuze did not often engage with the law aside, a Deleuzian understanding of the law that moves along the lines of his philosophical project and employs the conceptual tools he offers has three fundamental characteristics.

First, law can only operate on a plane of immanence that nurtures the possibility of encounters between law and other bodies. Bodies here are understood in their Spinozan/Deleuzian sense as bodies of discourse or material bodies, natural or artificial, undefined or future bodies. Law proceeds in encounters that constantly alter its potential, every time remoulding its virtuality as a new actual singularity. This is not only a question for Deleuzian jurisprudence, namely law's engagement with the particular case and its outcome in its concreteness and singularity.[10] It affects the law as the whole, its production, its consumption and its movement across the plane of immanence. This is what I would call the joyful moment of encounter between law and other bodies – law on its own cannot deliver itself. It needs to drive itself to its edge and there to produce its becoming. However, joy should be understood as positive, vitalistic force (Braidotti 2006) that pushes law from within and into forceful encounters with other bodies. The encounter encompasses the possibility of violence, of mutual destruction, of cannibalistic ingestion but also of new becomings and different power configurations:

> Heretofore it was only a question of how a particular thing can decompose other things by giving them a relation that is consistent with one of its own, or, on the contrary, how it risks being decomposed by other things. But now it is a question of knowing whether relations (and which ones?) can compound directly to form a new, more 'extensive' relation, or whether capacities can compound directly to constitute a more 'intense' capacity or power. (Deleuze 1988: 126)

It is obvious that this goes significantly further than interdisciplinarity. It strikes in the middle of the law's ability to remain the law and yet to compound with economy, politics, science, revolution, gossip, fear, natural catastrophes and whatever else might enter into an encounter with law, thus generating intensive or extensive relations that redefine the plane of immanence on which the law finds itself.

Second, law is becoming aware of its spatiality. This does not refer merely to specific legal branches, such as the obvious property or environmental law, but the law as a whole and in all its particular manifestations. By spatiality I mean an emplaced materiality that affects the form of the law. Just as with any Spinozan/Deleuzian body, the body of law is defined by its *longitude* and *latitude*, by the material elements that comprise its body in its movement and rest, and its capacity to enter into affective connections with other bodies (Deleuze and Guattari 1988: 287). Law's materiality is not just courts and wigs but the way the law emplaces itself, its measures, commands and prohibitions, between other bodies, or between objects and thoughts, in the distance and propinquity between them. Law determines these spaces through its longitude but also defines which bodies are to be brought into affective contact with the law, and through the law with each other. At the same time, law is affected by these bodies and connections. Its intensive qualities (latitude) change to such an extent that the law has to move, thereby affecting its extensive qualities, its spatial emplacement (longitude). Law moves from one assemblage to another, changing masters as it were, without tying itself to any one in particular and without any predictability. In the process, it deterritorialises as well as becoming deterritorialised. Law is not just logos that striates but also nomos that destratifies. Law's movement pushes other bodies to their extreme, to the cutting edge of their intensity, and then releases them into finding different assemblages. This movement of destratification goes hand in hand with legal stratification, namely the reterritorialising and overcoding of space both in terms of matter and in terms of semantics. Law provides readily available avenues of thought and action, it binds expectations of how to move, and in that way binds thought and behaviour in narrow, blind corridors of striation. But at the same time, law makes its own walls collapse, betrays expectations, reveals smoothness where once there were only pillars. Even in being disobeyed, the law opens up smooth spaces of new distances and proximities. This is an intensely spatial process – nothing metaphorical here – grounded on material, shifting space.

Third, law is becoming posthuman. Law is thrown in the middle of what I have elsewhere called *open ecology*,[11] to a large extent following Guattari's concept of three ecologies, namely a 'mental, a natural and a cultural ecology' (Guattari 2000: 20). Guattari's triad of body (and its connection to mind as a thinking multiplicity), nature (in its sense of *earth*) and the movement of the social (in the sense of assemblages operating on the plane of immanence in ways that, despite delusions to the contrary, cannot be controlled by subjectivities/haecceities) demands an ethicopolitical articulation of the law that will address the connections between these three ecologies. This is a process rather than value-based ecological turn that discredits the tired legal debate between anthropocentricity and ecocentricity. To quote Deleuze and Guattari, 'we make no distinction between man and nature: the human essence of nature and the natural essence of man become one within nature in the form of production of industry' (Deleuze and Guattari 1983: 4). In this absence of any boundary between the two, human law becomes posthuman by moving into new assemblages with bodies previously excluded from its remit.[12] An example of new ecological spaces opening up for the law is the challenge of material inscription of the law within the body of genetically modified crops.[13] The law acts in ripples, by moving in and keeping out, in the violent paradox of the *nomic* and the *logic*. Donna Haraway has famously declared that 'the boundary between human and animal is thoroughly breached', and cyborgs, oncomice and coyotes are posthumanist dimensions of more traditional feminist bodies that transcend the natural/cultural, organic/mechanical, physical/non-physical divides (Haraway 2004: 32). Katherine Hayles's digital subjectivity is built on a discontinued and inherently unpredictable conception of the human (Hayles 2005). Rosi Braidotti's vitalist philosophy grounds the law on precisely such a space of joyful encounters (Braidotti 2009). The question of whether trees should have court standing has been long and validly rehearsed in legal thinking (Stone 1974). A posthuman law is one that couples with abandon with the natural, the artificial, the uncategorisable, and constructs new jurisprudential assemblages with all of them.

Any conceptualisation of spatial justice must be determined by the above fundamental qualities of Deleuzian law. Justice is not detached from the law but radically, rhizomatically immanent to it. Justice is the abstract machine of the law, directing the law from within. An immanent, spatial and posthuman law vibrates with the kind of clashes needed for the emergence of spatial justice.

## The Second Island, or Justice Erected

Back on the island, everything is precipitating towards its final apotheosis. According to Deleuze, Tournier puts the story 'in terms of end, and not in terms of origin' (Deleuze 2004b: 342). Indeed, right from the start the novel moves headlong to its edge and with a teleology that is foreshadowed as both irresistible and inevitable. By treating the voyage and the shipwreck (the origin) as a space within the island, Tournier is trapped in an immanence that 'makes it impossible for him to allow Robinson to leave the island' (Deleuze 2004b: 342). The challenge with any manifold surface however is to carry on unfolding it, 'not how to finish the fold, but how to continue it, to have it go through the ceiling, how to bring it to infinity' (Deleuze 2006: 39). Tournier's solution is to bring infinity down, ground it on the elements and thus liberate it from the desire to transcend. The end of the novel follows Robinson's ends: both are defined in terms of their insular immanence. Although 'these ends represent a fantastic deviation from our world' (Deleuze 2004b: 343), they remain inalienable to the world that has been progressively constructed by the various movements on the island. The end has been present well before the law of the Other is fused with the law of Friday. In fact, even before the shipwreck takes place, the end is revealed to Robinson onboard the ship by a tarot reader:

> A snake biting its tail is the symbol of that self-enclosed sexuality, in which there is no leak or flaw. It is the zenith of human perfectibility, infinitely difficult to achieve, more difficult still to sustain. It seems you are destined to rise even to these heights, or so the Egyptian tarot cards say. My compliments, young sir. (Tournier 1969 [1967]: 12 [12])

The tarot image brings to mind the Jungian uroborous snake with its paradoxical flow constitutive of its immanence (Jung 1963). Indeed, every closure is characterised by *enantiodromia*,[14] Jung's alchemic loan of a vitalistic paradoxical force that flows simultaneously in two opposing directions.

Compare the above to what Deleuze writes: 'the power of the paradox therefore is not at all in following the other direction, but rather in showing that sense always takes on both senses at once, or follows two directions at the same time' (Deleuze 2004b: 88). 'Sense' is understood as both 'meaning' and 'direction'. Every direction endows the body that moves with a different meaning. In their opposition, the two directions form a perfect immanence, or to paraphrase Edgar Morin, a closure that rests on its openness.[15] The plane of immanence simultaneously accommodates smooth and striated spaces, logos and nomos, state and nomads, Robinson and Friday. The enantiodromic movement of these opposites *is* the abstract machine of the plane of immanence. The paradox behind Deleuze and Guattari's thinking is, convincingly argued (Deleuze and Guattari 1988: 8ff), not a binarism but a conflict that is resolved nowhere outside the two opposites. There is nothing outside except for the infinity of elongation. Even in Friday's law, the law without the Other, striation persists. Likewise, in Robinson's law, smoothness is always round the corner. In the law of the Other, there is identification with society, with the missing Other, with desire as determined by the structure. In the law without the Other, there is diversity, a multiplicity that 'gives itself a singularity' (Deleuze 2004b: 87).

Let me return briefly to Deleuze's paradox. In one of his treatments of *Alice in Wonderland*, Deleuze plays with the various levels of common sense/good sense. Impressionistically and rather schematically, common sense is about identification with the Other, whereas good sense is singular thinking. Common sense is shared sense but also (self-)imposed sense, a frame through which the path is revealed, the decision is sanctioned. Society, in its presence or absence, is embodied in common sense and imposes the law of the Other through the unity of the 'I'. Good sense on the other hand is the direction from the singular to the regular with a teleology and in some ways a responsibility to stretch the former over the latter. Even though I have crudely simplified the intricacies of the two senses, I must stress that the two are not contradictory. As Deleuze writes, 'the force of paradoxes is that they are not contradictory; they rather allow us to be present at the genesis of the contradiction' (Deleuze 2004b: 86). The genesis is multiple and explosive, its effects trickling in the way one sense flows into each other.

> Good sense could not fix any beginning, end, or direction, it could not distribute any diversity, if it did not transcend itself toward an instance capable of relating the diverse to the form of a subject's identity . . . Conversely, this form of identity within common sense would remain empty if it did not transcend itself toward an instance capable of determining it by means of a particular diversity, which would begin here, end there, and which one would suppose to last as long as it is necessary to assure the equalization of its parts. (Deleuze 2004b: 90)

The two senses cross each other, annul each other while feeding into each other from within. Their connection is more complex than simple dialectical dependence. There is no final resolution and no transcendence but simply a repetition of such emergence. The Deleuzian paradox is the space where the superlative body emerges, the body without organs. No organism, just flow and flow that stops the flow, organs that throw themselves in space, on the surface, and then move against each other, molecular explosions, violence of clots and nerves, clashes of Otherness and elements. Nothing is thrown away; all is recycled in the infinite closure of the plane of immanence.

The laws of Robinson and Friday in their reciprocal assemblages are both needed, paradoxically crossing over and within each other in order to materialise the grand teleology of the novel: the other, *second* island. Thus Robinson:

> Now I have been transported to that other Speranza, I live perpetually in a 'moment of innocence'. Speranza is no longer an uncultivated land that

must bear fruit, nor Friday a savage towards whom I bear the duty of civilising. Both demand my undivided attention, a careful contemplation, an ecstatic surveillance, for I think – nay, I am certain – that every moment I am seeing them for the first time. (Tournier 1969 [1967]: 205 [220], translation modified)

The other island is not merely a smooth space of nomadic movement. It is that too, but it is also a space that demands surveillance, contemplation, vigilance – in short, striation: 'you don't reach the Body without Organs, and its place of consistency, by wildly destratifying it' (Deleuze and Guattari 1988: 161).

But let me move to what emerges from the paradox of the two laws. For the second island, according to Deleuze, is not simply another island but a *double* that 'is not a replica of things. It is, on the contrary, the new upright image in which the elements are released and take possession of themselves again, having become celestial and forming a thousand capricious elemental figures' (Deleuze 2004b: 351, translation modified). The second island is the product of the flow between the two legalities, yet it reaches beyond them. For the second island is neither Robinson's, nor Friday's: '[Friday] indicates *another*, supposedly true world, an irreducible double which alone is genuine, and in this other world, a double of the Other who no longer is and cannot be' (Deleuze 2004b: 355). Friday 'indicates' it but is not it, nor can he provide for it. The second island emerges out of the various bodies and their relations of mutual striation and destratification. The emergence, however, is not simply a product of dialectic interpenetration. No doubt the law of Robinson cross-fertilises the law of Friday and the two orient themselves towards the teleology of law. No doubt either that the second island emerges in the middle of these two laws. But this is not a calculation of unities. The emergence is violent, tremor-like and uncontrollable. Its immanence in the law is tempered by an opposite movement, an opening of space of infinity. The opening is filled with a sense of arriving, of delivering the teleology of the law, of administering *justice*. The second island is overflowing with the elemental luminosity of justice arrived.

Let me sum up before I proceed to the final topos of the argument: Robinson's law, the striating law of the Other, couples with the law of Friday, the nomic law of smooth space, in an assemblage that generates its very own teleology. Orientated towards the emergence of the second island, the two insular laws find themselves unable to calculate the topology of this second island. Itself immanent to the legal paradox yet moving beyond it, the second island is the elemental space of legal teleology, of justice. Justice emerges from within the law in 'capricious elemental figures'. This is the connection between law and justice – the latter emerging from the conflicts of the former but not necessarily and not always. No formula can be followed, and no calculation can take place, either in striation or in smoothness, that can guarantee the emergence. What either law can do is orient themselves to the teleology of justice, to put themselves 'in terms of end, and not in terms of origin' (Deleuze 2004b: 342). But even this orientation is counter-intuitive. For the moment of emergence of spatial justice is that of a movement *away* from the goal: '*withdrawal, freaks*'.[16]

I have contextualised this movement of spatial justice elsewhere, in the context of bodies withdrawing from spaces claimed by other bodies (Philippopoulos-Mihalopoulos 2010). Here I want to pursue the same movement, but this time in terms of the insular legal bodies, namely the body of law of Robinson and that of Friday. In both cases, the movement is the same: a mutual withdrawal from the space in which spatial justice *might* emerge. This is a concession to a risk that stands the chance of ending up being uncontainable, for here withdrawal refers both to the oppressive machine of striating law *and* the smooth distribution of nomadic law. Both laws withdraw from the space in which the second island, the island of justice, might emerge. While this means that the space of justice is a lawless space, in both the striating and the nomic way, it does not mean that there is no law there. The elemental legality of the meteors that Tournier describes is yet another form of legality, but one that is pure materiality, without the image of law. No law is represented on the second island, yet the island moves along its own spatial normativity. What remains is a sedimented law, a law without representation that is infinitely repeated, thus producing singularity.[17] *Spatial justice is the movement of withdrawal of the law with the aim of a possible emergence of a space of a different, second legality: the lawless legality of justice.*

The second island is the body of Deleuzian jurisprudence. If the latter is that which 'acts as the event or abstract machine of the legal assemblage' (Moore 2007: 43), then spatial justice is simply another name for Deleuzian jurisprudence. Deleuze's engagement with the concept of jurisprudence was sporadic and incidental, and in many ways leaves an open space for concept construction. My aim therefore is to add to the existing subsequent literature on jurisprudence by emphasising two things that I believe emanate directly from Deleuzian thought: spatiality and immanence. Spatiality in spatial justice is as much a statement of something painfully obvious (can there ever be a justice that is not spatially emplaced? an abstract, universal justice that transcends the concrete?), as it is a political gesture that aims at moving law away from its traditional historicisation and into the open, fragmented, material space of geography, of earth and geophilosophy, of violent falls and dirty fingernails. My other aim is to emphasise the immanence of justice, namely its self-enclosed generation that is, however, necessarily based on a connection of withdrawal with the law. Spatial justice is immanent to law, flowing along the legal orientation towards justice, yet overcoded by the withdrawal of the law. Spatial justice is jurisprudence that retains the law within, in withdrawal and perennial movement, like the empty square of the chessboard. As Deleuze writes, 'there is no structure without the empty square, which makes everything function' (Deleuze 2004b: 61). The second island orients everything on account of its empty space, a space of withdrawal within. And Deleuze carries on by urging us to keep moving the square: 'today's task is to make the empty square circulate' (Deleuze 2004b: 84). The space of withdrawal is always there but needs to be constantly flowing, for otherwise justice becomes frozen in the regime, a pillar amidst other pillars. Just as justice cannot be disengaged from the law in its paradoxical flow of the logic and the nomic, in the same way there is no telling how much of either needs to be withdrawn for the empty square to follow the lines of escape and keep on moving. Withdrawal is a revolutionary, dangerous move that takes risks by allowing spaces to discover their immanent legality.

The second island is the product of a Deleuzian encounter, pulsating with its infinitely repeated singularity. It is the space of *here* into which the law throws itself, the luminosity of 'erected' spaces, the singularity of 'erected' times: 'each day stands separate and erect, proudly affirming its own intrinsic value . . . They so resemble each other as to be superimposed in my memory, so that I seem to be ceaselessly reliving anew the same day' (Tournier 1969 [1967]: 204 [219]). The space of justice is the space of 'second origin', which is 'more essential than the first, since it gives us the law of repetition, the law of the series' (Deleuze 2004a: 13) that repeats to the 'nth' degree the encounter every time anew. The second island, the space in which spatial justice emerges, is then the *desert island* par excellence. It is uncharted, unreachable except through the conjuncture of a shipwreck, closed, 'a sacred island' (Deleuze, 2004a: 13). But to retain this sacredness, the island must remain desert yet open to shipwrecks and people arriving: 'far from compromising it, humans bring the desertedness to its perfection and highest point' (Deleuze 2004a: 10). Humans pierce the island, make it a 'holey space' that 'communicates with smooth space and striated space' (Deleuze and Guattari 1988: 415), they set the ground on which the 'perfection and highest point of desertedness', namely of the world without law, might eventually emerge.

# References

Braidotti, R. (2006), *Transpositions: on Nomadic Ethics*, Cambridge: Polity Press.
Braidotti, R. (2009), 'Locating Deleuze's Eco-Philosophy: Between *Bio/Zoe*-Power and Necro-Politics', in Rosi Braidotti, Claire Colebrook and Patrick Hanafin (eds), *Deleuze and the Law: Forensic Futures*, Basingstoke: Palgrave Macmillan.
Buchanan, I. and G. Lambert (eds) (2005), *Deleuze and Space*, Edinburgh: Edinburgh University Press.
de Sutter, L. (2008), *Deleuze: La Pratique du Droit*, Paris: Michalon.
DeLanda, M. (2005), 'Space: Extensive and Intensive, Actual and Virtual', in Ian Buchanan and Gregg Lambert (eds), *Deleuze and Space*, Edinburgh: Edinburgh University Press.
Deleuze, G. (1967), 'Une Theorie d'Autrui (Autrui, Robinson et le Pervers)', *Critique* 241: 503–25.
Deleuze, G. (1988), *Spinoza: Practical Philosophy*, trans. R. Hurley, San Francisco: City Lights Books.
Deleuze, G. (1995), *Negotiations*, trans. M. Joughin, New York: Columbia University Press.
Deleuze, G. (2004a), *Desert Islands and Other Texts, 1953–1974*, trans. M. Taormina, Los Angeles: Semiotext(e).
Deleuze, G. (2004b), *The Logic of Sense*, trans. M. Lester with C. Stivale, London: Continuum.
Deleuze, G. (2004c), *Difference and Repetition*, trans. P. Patton, London: Continuum.
Deleuze, G. (2006), *The Fold*, trans. T. Conley, London: Continuum.
Deleuze, G. and F. Guattari (1983), *Anti-Oedipus: Capitalism and Schizophrenia*, trans. R. Hurley, M. Seem and H. R. Lane, Minneapolis: University of Minnesota Press.
Deleuze, G. and F. Guattari (1988), *A Thousand Plateaus: Capitalism and Schizophrenia*, trans. B. Massumi, London: Continuum.
Deleuze, G. and F. Guattari (1994), *What is Philosophy?*, trans. H. Tomlinson and G. Burchell, New York: Columbia University Press.
Foucault, M. (2003), *Abnormal: Lectures at the College De France 1974–1975*, trans. G. Burchell, London: Verso.
Gatens, M. (1996), 'Through a Spinozist Lens: Ethology, Difference, Power', in Paul Patton (ed.), *Deleuze: A Critical Reader*, Oxford: Blackwell.
Guattari, F. (2000), *Three Ecologies*, trans. I. Pindar and P. Sutto, London: Athlone.
Haraway, D. (2004), *The Haraway Reader*, London: Routledge.
Hayles, K. (2005), *My Mother Was a Computer: Digital Subjects and Literary Texts*, Chicago: Chicago University Press.
Herzongerath, B. (ed.) (2008), *An [Un]Likely Alliance: Thinking Environment[s] with Deleuze|Guattari*, Newcastle: Cambridge Scholars Publishing.
Herzogenrath, B. (ed.) (2009), *Deleuze|Guattari & Ecology*, Basingstoke: Palgrave Macmillan.
Jung, C. (1963), 'Mysterium Coniunctionis: An Inquiry into the Separation and Synthesis of Psychic Opposites in Alchemy', *Collected Works* 14, trans. R. F. C. Hull, London: Routledge and Kegan Paul.
Lefebvre, A. (2008), *The Image of Law: Deleuze, Bergson, Spinoza*, Stanford: Stanford University Press.

Moore, N. (2007), 'Icons of Control: Deleuze, Signs, Law', *International Journal for the Semiotics of Law*, 20: 33–54.

Morin, E. (1986), *La Méthode II: La Connaissance de la Connaissance*, Paris: Seuil.

Pottage, A. (2011), 'Biotechnology as Environmental Regulation', in A. Philippopoulos-Mihalopoulos (ed.), *Law and Ecology: New Environmental Foundations*, London: Routledge.

Philippopoulos-Mihalopoulos, A. (2007), 'In the Lawscape', in A. Philippopoulos-Mihalopoulos (ed.), *Law and the City*, London: Routledge.

Philippopoulos-Mihalopoulos, A. (2010), 'Spatial Justice: Law and the Geography of Withdrawal', *International Journal of Law in Context*, 6 (3): 1–16.

Philippopoulos-Mihalopoulos, A. (2011a), 'Law's Spatial Turn: Geography, Justice and a Certain Fear of Space', *Law, Culture and Humanities*, 7 (2): 1–16.

Philippopoulos-Mihalopoulos, A. (2011b), '"...the sound of a breaking string": Critical Environmental Law and Ontological Vulnerability', *Journal of Environmental Law and Human Rights*, 2 (1): 5–22.

Ruddick, S. (2004), 'Domesticating Monsters: Cartographies of Difference and the Emancipatory City', in L. Lees (ed.), *The Emancipatory City*, London: Sage.

Sharpe, A. (2007), 'Structured Like a Monster: Understanding Human Difference Through a Legal Category', *Law and Critique*, 18 (2): 207–28.

Stone, C. (1974), *Should Trees Have Standing? Toward Legal Rights for Natural Objects*, Los Altos: William Kaufmann.

Tournier, M. (1967), *Vendredi ou Les Limbes du Pacifique*, Paris: Gallimard (*Friday*, trans. N. Denny, Baltimore: Johns Hopkins University Press, 1969).

# Notes

1. For a discussion on law's spatial turn, see Philippopoulos-Mihalopoulos 2011a.
2. Space, law and body combine to create what I have elsewhere called a *lawscape* (see Philippopoulos-Mihalopoulos 2007), namely an assemblage of space and law characterised by motion and rest, in which the body (in the broader Deleuzian/Spinozian sense) affects and is being affected continuously and inescapably.
3. Tournier 1967 and English translation 1969. In what follows, I give the translated page reference followed by the page of the original (in its folio edition) in brackets, stating whenever I have modified the translation. The novel operates on multiple levels, such as the animistic, the sexual, the intercorporeal, the philosophical, the reflective, the 'perverse'. In many respects, it is a paradigm of what a Deleuzian programmatic novel might be. The novel appears to be a source of inspiration for Deleuze's philosophy.
4. Deleuze was a friend of Tournier's and has referred to the latter's novels in his work. The essay cited here was first published in 1967, subsequently incorporated as a postface in Tournier's book and as an appendix in Deleuze's *The Logic of Sense* (2004b). I have used the latter edition of the essay.
5. Deleuze's essay focuses on sexual perversion, a reading readily offered by the novel itself. While law can be read through desire (indeed one could argue that the two are inseparable), for reasons of textual consistency, I am obliged to focus on the connection between space and bodies in relation to the law.
6. Although arguably its most explicit focus is the connection between the self and the world. However, unsurprisingly for Deleuze, both are discussed in their material dimension, namely as bodily affects in space.
7. As Deleuze writes, 'we need only extrapolate in imagination the movement they [the shipwrecked] bring with them to the island. Only in appearance does such

a movement put an end to the island's desertedness; in reality, it takes up and prolongs the *élan* that produced the island as deserted' (Deleuze 2004a: 9).
8. 'Is it the case that every event is of this type – forest, battle and wound – all the more profound since *it* occurs at the surface?' (Deleuze 2004b: 12).
9. 'The middle is by no means an average; on the contrary, it is where things pick up speed. *Between things* does not designate a localizable relation going from one thing to the other and back again, but a perpendicular direction, a transversal moment that sweeps one and the other away, a stream without beginning or end that undermines its banks and picks up speed in the middle' (Deleuze and Guattari 1988: 28).
10. 'What interests me isn't the law or laws (the former being an empty notion, the latter uncritical notions), nor even law or rights, but jurisprudence. It's jurisprudence, ultimately, that creates law, and we mustn't go on leaving this to judges' (Deleuze 1995: 169). See Lefebvre 2008 for an analysis of the use of the term and Moore, who defines jurisprudence as 'the mode of practising the law, where the law is engaged with anew in each and every situation' (2007: 34). Deleuze uses the term creatively, as a contextualised, positive and problem-specific thought located in the middle of concrete situations. Jurisprudence is a philosophical thought that amounts to praxis, and that facilitates the production of radical encounters between bodies and, consequently, the 'prolonging of singularities'.
11. See Philippopoulos-Mihalopoulos 2011b.
12. See Foucault 2003, and indicatively, see further Ruddick 2004; Sharpe 2007; Braidotti 2006. See also Herzogenrath 2008 and 2009.
13. See Pottage 2011.
14. From Greek *enanti* which means 'opposite' and 'across', and *dromos* which means 'route', 'path', 'flow'.
15. '*L'ouvert s'appuie sur le fermé*' (Morin 1986: 203).
16. 'But the revolutionary knows that escape is revolutionary – *withdrawal, freaks* – provided one sweeps away the social cover on leaving, or causes a piece of the system to get lost in the shuffle. What matters is to break through the wall' (Deleuze and Guattari 1983: 277).
17. I have chosen here not to focus on Deleuze's return to perversion in his text on Tournier because I feel that it deals with a different kind of legality to the one I am interested in here. Still, it is indicative that the second island for Deleuze, to some extent following Lacan and de Sade, is the embodiment of a perversion that comes out of an aberrant *withdrawal* from structure. Logos sees this as harm to another (see Deleuze 2004b: 358), and this is according to Deleuze a basic legal misinterpretation. However, perversion, this bastard 'half juridical, half medical' concept (Deleuze 2004b: 343), reveals a world without the Other yet with its own immanent and teleological structure – once again, a legality of the middle.

Chapter 6

# Institutions and Interactions: On the Problem of the Molecular and Molar

*Marc Schuilenburg*

In a filmed interview with Claire Parnet, Deleuze gives the example of smoking in taxis to explain what 'jurisprudence' is (Deleuze 1997a: 'G'): a man sues the owner of a cab for the right to smoke in his taxi; the owner loses the case on the grounds that when someone takes a taxi, he is renting it, and the renter has the right to smoke in his rented location. According to the judge's verdict, the taxi is a rolling apartment, and the customer is the renter. Ten years later, Deleuze continues, the taxi is no longer seen in this way, it becomes assimilated instead to being a form of public service, and no one has the right any more to smoke in taxis. In response to Parnet, Deleuze points out that jurisprudence is 'a question of situations that evolve'. A clearer answer on the meaning of the practice of jurisprudence would be hard to find in his work. According to Deleuze, jurisprudence operates in concrete situations and on specific problems. It is 'law in action' (working case-by-case) and has the capacity to invent or create rights and rules. As such, the practice of jurisprudence 'deals with singularities' (Deleuze 1995: 153; 2006: 350) and concerns a process that is already active prior to its normalisation on the level of the law.

It is interesting to notice that in his book on Hume Deleuze draws a similar contrast between 'the law' and 'institutions'. For Deleuze, Hume's distinction between 'the law' and 'institutions', and his argument on the positivity of an institution rooted in the social world, imply a new conception of law, one more open to the psychological and social dimensions of humans (Dosse 2010: 113–14). The law, Deleuze writes in *Empiricism and Subjectivity*, is a 'limitation of enterprise and action, and it focuses only on a negative aspect of society' (Deleuze 1991: 45). Criminal law, for instance, does not tell us how to behave, but only which types of conduct are forbidden and the punitive response to wrongdoers. The assumption in classical punishment theory is that effective punishment of the offender will deter the commission of further acts of harm against society (Beccaria 2009). Institutions, however, comprise 'the essence of society' and are 'a model of actions, a veritable enterprise, an invented system of positive means or a positive invention of indirect means' (Deleuze 1991: 45–6; 2004: 19–21). Given this conception of the social as 'profoundly creative, inventive, and positive', the law, Deleuze concludes, 'is not primary, it presupposes an institution that it limits' (Deleuze 1991: 46). In other words, the issue of law and order is a secondary issue. Initially there is the permanent process of creation and invention. Order and stability always follow later. They emerge from the dynamics within the social, as a temporary congealing point of continually branching series of relations that do not represent 'things', but events that never obtain their final meaning. This raises the question how such a combinatory of two levels proceeds.

Rather than tracing this combinatory between them through a judicial framework, I want to suggest that Deleuze's concepts of 'molar' and 'molecular' provide a way to answer this question in detail. Reading 'molar' for 'the law' and 'molecular' for 'institutions' (and 'jurisprudence'), enables us to see how at the most basic level of coexistence, interactions can cause the disruption of an existing social-cultural field, which subsequently develops in a way not laid down in advance or thought possible.[1] I would further suggest that this approach is best expressed in the work of the French sociologist Gabriel Tarde (1843–1904). The microsociology of Tarde is an important inspiration for Deleuze's concept of molecular processes, which have the potential to bring about significant changes on the molar level of the social order. Against this background, three problems need to be addressed. First, where the concepts of molar and molecular come from and how Deleuze and Guattari transform them into a sociological problem. Second, the way Tarde shows how to move from molar representations to molecular interactions (and the other way around). Third, the way in which the relation between the molar and molecular comes about in complex assemblages (*agencements*).

## The Molar

The term 'molar' is used in physics, especially in the science of thermodynamics (the first science of complexity), which studies the interactions between large collections of particles on a macroscopic level. The term refers to the Avogadro Constant, a constant number of particles the value of which is $6.023 \times 10^{23}$ mol$^{-1}$ (like a dozen is 12 and a score is

20). This number of particles defines the amount of substance called the 'mole'. One mole of any substance is $6.023 \times 10^{23}$ particles of it, which may be atoms, molecules, ions or electrons, depending on the substance. The Avogadro Constant is named after the Italian chemist and physicist Amedeo Avogadro (1776–1856), a specialist in the field of chemical gases, who discovered in 1811 that equal volumes of all gases under the same conditions contain the same number of particles. In other words, a mole of any gas always takes the same volume at a certain pressure and temperature. It is impossible to count such an enormous number of particles, but it can be weighed. A mole of any substance is that substance's atomic or molecular mass expressed in grams, and this mass is called the 'molar mass'. The number of moles of any substance is the amount of it (Beavon and Jarvis 2003: 20–1).

It's only a small step from Avogadro's number, which indicates the absolute number of molecules in one mole substance, to the approach taken in social scientific research to studying what Deleuze and Guattari in *Anti-Oedipus* call large 'molar aggregates' (*ensembles molaires*) (Deleuze and Guattari 1983: 181, 183, 340). These molar aggregates ('the state', 'society', 'the market', 'social classes', 'sexes') represent functional, stable entities or large-scale structures and have a specific use in social theory. According to Deleuze and Guattari, they 'presuppose pre-established connections that are not explained by their functioning, since the latter results from them' (Deleuze and Guattari 1983: 181). Simplifying social reality like this, scientists divide it into part–whole relations, which are presented as more or less homogeneous. This allows them to isolate and control specific matters. As a consequence, researchers study the parts in terms of what they contribute to the whole or 'any sort of original totality' (Deleuze and Guattari 1983: 42). In doing so, they make their object of research distinguishable from the rest of the world. They draw boundaries around that which is to be researched or scrutinised. The causes of what people do are then located in a system which is supposed to determine human behaviour, e.g. economic dynamics, culture, values, mentality, and so on. They are supposed to precede interaction and develop in a knowable and predictable way (Van Calster and Schuilenburg 2011).

In sociology, this is reflected in the work of one of the founders of French sociology, Emile Durkheim. According to Durkheim, a social fact, i.e. the description of what the social precisely entails or defines, is characterised by the power of external coercion it exerts upon individual behaviour, and the influence it has on personal attitudes or needs. An example of such a social fact is the language in which we speak and communicate. After all, the language we learn to speak from birth is inescapably imposed upon us. It has a compelling and invisible force, so to speak, which no one can escape. According to Durkheim, a social fact is not only identifiable because of its external influence on what individuals do and say, it additionally has a reality of its own that cannot be reduced to the qualities of separate individuals. In other words, it is an independent entity that imposes certain views and ways of acting on the individual, which he or she would not have displayed spontaneously. From that perspective, a social fact is not only coercive and supra-individual, it can also be understood as objective (in the meaning of a 'thing') (Laermans 1995).

The characteristics of a social fact feature most clearly in Durkheim's thesis of a *conscience collective*, the largest common denominator of the content of the consciousness of individuals in a society. This collective consciousness manifests itself as a separate variable and forms the foundation for cohesion in a community. It not only generates emotions that are qualitatively different than individual perceptions, it has specific characteristics as well (Durkheim 1973). If we apply those characteristics to society itself, then society will have a reality of its own, a philosophical point of departure called 'realism'. In 'realism' society has its own nature. The independence of society as a whole brings forth convictions, norms, ideas and perceptions that are shared by the members of that society.[2] Although psychological insights about associations of individuals can be of importance for understanding changes in solidarity in a society, it is up to the science of sociology to subsequently study that solidarity as an independent social fact. This can be accomplished through scientific methods and models, as Durkheim demonstrates, which can be used to objectify and verify statistics about birth rates, marriage rates, suicide rates and criminality rates. It is possible to analyse the annual average of marriages, births, voluntary deaths and the degree of criminality, which expresses the collective consciousness or morality of a society as a whole, without discussing the related individual circumstances.

But, according to Deleuze and Guattari, this kind of thinking is trapped in a representational logic that does not acknowledge social reality as such. Behind the part/whole distinction lurks the hypothesis that parts exist because of the whole ('something that already exists'). Not only are they part of the whole, they maintain the whole in existence. Therefore, the problem of the molar is a sociological problem 'so long as the whole is considered as a totality derived from the parts, or as an original totality from which the parts emanate, or as a dialectical totalization' (Deleuze and Guattari 1987: 44). In fact, there is no sort of evolution that will cause parts to form an integrated whole, any more than there is an original totality from which they can be derived. Instead of society being an organism or 'collective self', we must understand that every society is 'constantly escaping in all directions, never stops slipping away' and, Deleuze asserts in an interview with Paul Rabinow and Keith Gandal, is 'flowing everywhere' (Deleuze 2006: 280). From this point of view, the main emphasis is no longer on abstract quantities, but on the fluid character of social reality itself, what Deleuze and Guattari call 'the molecular'. This molecular medium (*milieu*) refers to 'singularities, their interactions and connections at a distance or between different orders' (Deleuze and Guattari 1983: 280). With a reference to the work of F. Scott Fitzgerald, they speak of subtle and supple (but no less disquieting) breaks, '*which occur when things are going well on the other side*' (Deleuze and Guattari 1987: 198).

## The Molecular

The dominant position of molar thought in contemporary scientific research is not surprising. Social scientists, like all researchers, tend to break down reality into wholes that consist of parts in order to focus attention on 'large numbers and statistical laws' (Deleuze and Guattari 1983: 280). It is a molar approach, 'manifesting the statistical aggregate and state of equilibrium existing on the macroscopic level' (Deleuze and Guattari 1987: 57). However, social reality is much more complex than the molar approach can or will research. According to Deleuze and Guattari, the molar cannot be understood without the molecular. What the molecular offers, at a minimum, is 'an entire world of unconscious micropercepts, unconscious affects, fine segmentations that grasp or experience different things' (Deleuze and Guattari 1987: 213). As such, the molecular approaches the fluid character of social reality, which is always incomplete and cannot be made absolute in an all-encompassing whole.

If we again look at the way physics deals with the molecular, it first assumes that elements exist apart from each other and are constantly in motion (Kubinga 2003: 65). Physicists and chemists therefore speak of interactions between molecules (proteins, lipids, metabolites and so on). Although scientists consider the molecular as the most fundamental level of interaction, they recognise that information in this area is still poor and incomplete. Specific knowledge as to why interacting molecules group into spontaneous order is lacking (Sijbesma 2007). Nature offers nice examples of such 'self-assemblage' or 'self-organisation', by which molecules adopt a defined arrangement without guidance or management from an outside source. However, controlling the shape and structure of self-assembling systems still generates many questions.

From a philosophical point of view, it is clear that on the molecular level things are different than on the level of the molar, where concepts of 'control' and 'functionality' are predominant. This is important because the molecular composition is more concerned with flows (including poles, mutations, connections, accelerations, singularities and quanta), while the molar is about segmented lines, i.e. 'the binary, circular, and linear' (Deleuze and Guattari 1987: 209). Alliez (2009) is therefore right in stating that the molecular level revolves around 'small complex relations', rather than 'huge dialectic structures' that direct the whole. In terms of the social, it means that attention is turned to interactions that have no reference to a centre, standard or norm. The focus lies on 'becoming', as Deleuze and Guattari write in *A Thousand Plateaus*, and not on 'being' (Deleuze and Guattari 1987: 275, 277). Unlike with the molar, inhabited by unchanging essences or laws with a permanent identity, small changes can have huge and unpredictable effects on the molecular.

In developing this idea, I would like to distinguish three characteristics of the molecular. It is important to note that these characteristics do not present new abstract principles intended to provide a new representation of reality. Rather, they coincide separately with each 'event' or each 'case'. First, the molecular is about the *immediate*. It deals with 'beliefs and desires' (Deleuze and Guattari 1987: 219) that represent the world 'here and now' and which transcend actions from a rational-calculating portrayal of mankind, as represented in the classical judicial works of Beccaria (2009) and Hobbes (1985). The latter assume that people prefer to choose an action (for example obeying rules or violating them) from which they think they will benefit. The problem with this approach, Deleuze states in his book on Hume's empiricism, is that rationalism 'expects ideas to stand for something which cannot be constituted within experience or be given in an idea without contradiction: the generality of the idea, the existence of the object, and the content of the terms "always," "universal," "necessary," and "true"' (Deleuze 1991: 30). As is well known, another problem with such rationalism is its all too narrow time-frame. After all, the effects of such a choice are spread over a long period of time. The immediate instead deals with interactions (such as pride, frustration, pleasure, anger, shame and so on) which exist in *real time*, that is here and now. From a molar perspective these interactions are seen as exceptional and are largely kept outside 'the order of the discourse', to quote Foucault (1971). In fact, they fall outside the structural frame of uniformity or a knowable goal (Schuilenburg 2008; 2009: 210).

Second, the molecular is characterised by *heterogeneous* series that produce difference. Rather than representation by means of 'identity, opposition, analogy and resemblance' (Deleuze 1994: 137), a system of series is a differen*c*iating of differences by means of the coupling of heterogeneous series (whose elements are already heterogeneous). This actualisation is not a unilateral process, but rather the result of a whole series of mutually reinforcing effects, e.g. non-linear relationships, series of events and affairs, non-intentional acts and open series of interactions that lead in directions not previously agreed or established. As such, molecular relations are made possible by other acts making other acts possible in turn. They are in a constant state of flux and permit an infinite number of connections, creating with every connection something new. This means that – against the laws of classic causality – coincidence must be seen as a cause of social change(s).

Third, the molecular is about *perspectivism*, i.e. accepting that all truth can only be known in the context of one's own perspective. Perspectivism, which takes root in Hume's empiricism and Kant's idealism and was further developed by Schopenhauer and Nietzsche, rejects the idea of a specific interpretation of social reality that would be 'complete' or 'total'. Perspectivism claims that all knowledge is perspectival. Concrete circumstances and behaviour will always been seen from different viewpoints. Or, as Nietzsche points out in *The Will To Power*: 'In so far as the word "knowledge" has any meaning, ... it has no meaning behind it, but countless meanings – "perspectivism"' (Nietzsche 1967: §421). Yet perspectivism has nothing to do with relativism. Perspectivism may develop sensitivity for different points of view or interpretations. It compels people to see the conditions and actual circumstances under which a certain view may appear.

In short, contrary to the molar, the molecular knows neither univocal definition nor individual boundaries. It is fundamentally ambiguous and paradoxical. Perhaps it is this intangibility that raises suspicion and mistrust among social researchers towards the idea of researching the molecular. Researchers in sociology and economics, for instance, tend to categorise interactions in terms of 'usefulness' and 'interest' for the larger whole (profit, sales, and so on). By so doing they focus their attention on the molar. Even criminologists who research group processes actually focus on the characteristics of a group, such as rivalry, structure or leadership, which underline the static and therefore spotlight the molar. Hence instead of limiting sociology to molar structures, at least implicitly always based on a juridical model,[3] Deleuze wants to focus on the question of genesis or the emergence of relations through which existing structures are themselves constituted. For Deleuze, the work of Tarde bears witness to how the molecular, as opposed to molar aggregates, could lead to an understanding of the emergence of new social phenomena or new stratifications (see also van Tuinen 2009). What does this mean in terms of interactions between people of flesh and blood?

## Tarde: Interactions

Whereas Durkheim, simply put, held that social facts should be analysed as separate entities, his contemporary and main opponent, Tarde, argued that sociology should focus precisely on the interpersonal interactions that provide society with some degree of social structure. In *A Thousand Plateaus*, Deleuze and Guattari compare the polemic between Tarde and Durkheim to the never-ending debate between Geoffroy Saint-Hilaire and Cuvier: 'the sweet and subtle Geoffroy and the rigid specialist Cuvier' (Deleuze and Guattari 1987: 45–7, 254–5). Both positions need not necessarily be diametrically opposed to each other. However, they do focus on a different field of research. Contrary to Durkheim's molar view, which concentrates on studying the shared convictions produced by a group or a collective as a whole, Tarde considers the interpersonal interactions themselves as a social fact worthy of scientific research. We should understand this to mean that the 'metaphysical meaning' Durkheim attaches to a social fact has no absolute validity or value to Tarde. One could say that Tarde's interests lie in the dynamics of social life. He thus draws our attention to an essential aspect that remains unanswered in Durkheim's thought, namely: How can so many different individuals together form one whole? Or, put differently: How can the 'similarity of millions of people' (Deleuze 1994: 313–14 n.3; Deleuze and Guattari 1987: 218) be explained?

Instead of disputing Durkheim's concept of social facts or questioning his scientific analysis of suicide, criminality, etc., Tarde uses a different approach. On the one hand he questions the rigidity of Durkheim's assumption of a collective whole that underlies a society's shared solidarity, morality and culture, on the other he asks how a social fact can exist outside the individuals themselves (see Rhoads 1991: 119). After all, Durkheim's postulate of a social fact is based on the never-tested assumption that such a 'shared conviction' exists. Tarde does not deny the possibility of solidarity and morality between individuals, but he shifts the attention to how resemblances between individuals (that entail a degree of solidarity or morality) are brought about. Durkheim had simply assumed that resemblances multiply, and that these resemblances form a reality of their own that more or less transcends the individual level. Acting morally then simply means that someone subjects themselves to the force of a collective, which externally imposes rules, norms and codes on individuals. But that assumption, Tarde argues, is merely an 'ontological illusion', and basically implies a revival of Plato's doctrine of Ideas (Tarde 1969: 115, 117). Similar to Durkheim's social facts, Ideas to Plato represent eternal, stable and archetypical things that can only be known through spiritual experience. The Ideas themselves are not confined to matter, time and place, but lie in a higher world that, according to Plato, is fixed forever, and that leads an autonomous existence independent from thought.

Tarde, however, prefers, as he terms it, a 'pure sociology' or a 'general sociology' (Tarde 1962: ix–x) which interprets the general character of social interactions, and which can be applied to every social fact. He uses the term 'general laws' (Tarde 1912: 326) in that respect, when he discusses series of molecular interactions that are perpetual rather than temporary. Although the terms 'general laws' and 'general sociology' may seem to suggest otherwise, Tarde's method should not be defined as molar or structuralist (see Barry and Thrift 2007). While Durkheim places the emphasis of social science on structures underlying social relations (structures that are therefore not directly visible), Tarde shifts the attention to concrete relations between people. Thus before we can deal with the question whether an underlying structure exists, and, if so, how it affects daily life, we should – according to Tarde – explore how resemblances in the behaviour of all these different individuals, who constitute social life, develop. According to Tarde such resemblances are brought about by repetition. 'All resemblance is due to repetition', he writes in *The Laws of Imitation* (Tarde 1962: 14). This does not mean, however, that a linear process unfolds in which people repeat each other's behaviour continuously, or as a monomaniac would. In *The Laws of Imitation* Tarde also writes that 'repetition exists for the sake of variation' (Tarde 1962: 7), and a little earlier he postulates: 'resemblances and repetitions . . . are the necessary themes of the differences and variations which exist in all phenomena' (Tarde 1962: 6).

In his general sociology Tarde essentially attempts to find a mean between the Scylla of absolute relativism and the Charybdis of absolute absolutism. In his approach, a society corresponds with a 'group of beings who are apt to possession of common traits which are ancient copies of the same model' (Tarde 1962: 68). In *The Laws of Imitation* he analyses such resemblances as series of imitations, which he links with notions such as somnambulism and hypnosis – frequently debated notions at the end of the nineteenth century. Entirely in line with his thinking, society then is 'imitation and imitation is a kind of somnambulism' (Tarde 1962: 87). The emphasis on somnambulism and hypnoses reappears in *Penal Philosophy* (Tarde 1912: 192–201), where Tarde discusses in detail the idea of hypnosis as 'the experimental junction point of psychology and sociology: it shows us the most simplified sort of psychic life which can be conceived of under the form of the most elementary social relation' (Tarde 1912: 193). In his later work, Tarde yields to a more abstract and horizontal approach to molecular interactions, which he terms 'repetition, opposition, and adaption' (Tarde 2000: 8). Proceeding from this conditional formulation of action, Tarde further stretches the notion of society. In *Monadologie et sociologie* he writes that 'all things are society and any phenomenon is a social fact' (Tarde 1999: 58), a view which Latour describes as a 'a flat society argument' (see Latour 2002).[4] In the framework of this chapter, however, it is important that, from Tarde's perspective of interactions, the Durkheimian issue of structure and order is a secondary one. Initially there is change, movement and difference (Tarde 1962: 71; Latour 2007: 13–16; Deleuze and Guattari 1987: 218–19). Order and stability always follow later.

## Imitations and . . .

To find an answer to the question of how molecular interactions take place in general and, more specifically, with what variation, Tarde introduces a systematic distinction between processes of 'imitation' and 'invention': two series of interactions that each form a reality in themselves, but that also influence each other. Tarde defines imitation as the movement by which something is repeated and diffused (Tarde 1962: 17). In the preface to the second edition of *The Laws of Imitation*, he speaks of 'the action at a distance of one mind upon another' and of 'every inter-psychical photography, so to speak, willed or not willed, passive or active' (Tarde 1962: xiv). Concretely, this means that people consciously or unconsciously imitate each other's behaviour. They copy certain methods or preferences which, for instance, may include the way they work (process or technique) or the way they dress (fashion), or the music (style) they prefer. But imitation is found in smaller things as well, in the minute adjustments in behaviour when youngsters copy each other's body movements, for example, or when they adopt certain expressions.

Here it is important to note the branching character of series of imitations. This means that in the dissemination of behaviour, all kinds of *new* series will form that may produce *new* relations, which in turn may generate other series of imitations. Adding new series to existing ones leaves open the possibility of creation, and keeps the social-cultural field in motion and thus alive. This, according to Tarde in *Penal Philosophy*, is how criminality should also be approached, that is, as 'a phenomenon of imitative propagation' (Tarde 1912: 362). Forms of criminality spread 'like every industrial product, like every good or bad idea' (Tarde 1912: 338). Tarde does not claim here that criminality can be studied as a separate entity, independent from other developments in society. The question, he states, is

> whether the many other phenomena of imitative propagation, which taken all together are called civilization ... foster or impede the progress of the propagation of crime. Or rather, the aim is to discover, if that were possible, which among these various spreadings of example which are called instruction, religion, politics, commerce, industry, are the ones that foster, and which ones that impede, the expansion of crime. (Tarde 1912: 362)

To elucidate the process of imitation, Tarde (1962: 140 ff) distinguishes two laws. He speaks of a 'logical law' when imitation starts from the idea that it will contribute to a higher objective, or because it is expected to solve a problem better than other inventions. More often than from rational or well-thought-out considerations, however, imitation takes place according to 'extra-logical laws'. In these laws the emphasis is on cultural elements, but psychological and sociological influences also play a role. Tarde shows that certain forms of crime occur increasingly frequently as the number of interactions between different people also increases (through processes of urbanisation, for example, or following the move from the aristocracy to the bourgeoisie). He exemplifies this with the notorious case of the nursemaid Henriette Cornier, who in 1825 decapitated a nineteen-month old child. Cornier took the girl into her room and sliced her head off with a big knife. When the mother came looking for her daughter, Cornier took an apron, put the head in, and threw it out of the window, because, so she said, 'the idea presented itself'. Not long after that, other nursemaids also yielded to an 'irresistible impulse to cut the throats of their employers' children' (Tarde 1912: 340).[5]

## ... Inventions

With the term 'general laws' Tarde indicates that the process of imitation not only plays a role in social life, but also in other areas, such as geology, astronomy and chemistry. But even though he refers to these laws as 'general', their effect is different in each area. The process of invention is distinctive in this regard. An invention is not social until it is imitated in social life, Tarde writes in *Social Laws* (Tarde 2000: 23, 78). From a societal point of view, inventions that are not imitated are not relevant (Tarde 1912: 396 n.1). This means that an invention does not produce effects until it is included in series of imitations 'which have fallen one after another into the domain of the commonplace, the traditional, and the customary' (Tarde 1912: 118). This involves small and large imitations; imitations that take place short-term and long-term.

Tarde (1969: 153) defines an invention as the combination of dissimilar imitations. For inventions, too, branch into series, according to Tarde, like links in a chain with 'highly variable intervals, sometimes of a few days or months, sometimes of several centuries' (Tarde 1969: 160). They merge into series of imitations, as a result of which they expand like an oil stain, leading a social cultural field to increasingly achieve sameness. How are we to understand this? Inventions spread, to use one of Tarde's favourite analogies, like ripples in water, moving steadily towards the shore until they hit an obstacle. According to Tarde, that obstacle will often be the imitation of a previous invention, and their collision (in dialectic terms: 'opposition') will generate a new product, that is, a new invention which in turn may be imitated, until it too hits new obstacles (Tarde 1969: 21). Extending this analogy, society is one large irrigation system, with constantly moving currents, undercurrents, and counter-currents (Van Ginneken 1992: 200).

Although invention and imitation are not to be considered hierarchical opposites (as they are mutually influencing forces), in his approach to inventions Tarde seems to adhere to the classical notion of 'genius' as found in, inter alia, Kant's *Critique of Judgment* (1790). To Kant, a genius is characterised by an autonomous creativity (autonomy meaning literally 'self-legislating'). He appreciates positively what others consider to be merely coincidental or trivial. In a similar fashion, Tarde attributes inventions more than once to the ability of 'true great men'. In *Penal Philosophy*, for example, he asserts that such people can reform the crowd and gradually make it conform to themselves (Tarde 1912: 164–5). At the same time, for Tarde, this rationalist view only partly explains why we are 'more imitative than innovative' (Tarde 1962: 98). Contrary to the more rationalist approaches of Durkheim and Weber, Tarde, following Théodule Ribots' *Essai sur l'imagination créatice* (1900), also points to other factors that influence the generation of new inventions, such as emotion or desire ('fear or anger, sadness or joy, hate or love') (Tarde 1969: 150). In *The Laws of Imitation*, therefore, he refuses to distinguish between conscious and unconscious inventions:

> I have certainly applied this name [invention] to all individual initiatives, not only without considering the extent to which they are self-conscious – for the individual often innovates unconsciously, and, as a matter of fact, the most imitative man is an innovator on some side or another – but without paying the slightest attention in the world to the degree of difficulty or merit of the innovation in question. (Tarde 1962: xiv)

Nevertheless, Tarde seems to imply that an invention is a strictly individual matter, while imitation requires two separate individuals. In other words, to what extent is Tarde's approach nothing but a plea for practising psychologism or spiritualism? In *Difference and Repetition*, Deleuze refutes the criticism that a psychology lay hidden behind Tarde's sociology. According to Deleuze, Tarde realises a '*microsociology*, which is not necessarily concerned with what happens between individuals but with what happens within a single individual: for example, hesitation understood as "infinitesimal social opposition", or invention as "infinitesimal social adaptation"' (Deleuze 1994: 314 n.3). With this, according to Deleuze, Tarde demonstrates that besides the issue of structure, there is always a second issue. More than on the molar level of order and stability, this involves a 'molecular' level, which has a very different rhythm and speed. This level is not necessarily manifest or noticeable. Conversely, it does have the strength to destabilise, break open and transform a social-cultural field.

## What Difference Does it Make?

Although Deleuze and Guattari write that the division between the molar and the molecular is meant 'to isolate two different processes' (Deleuze and Guattari 1987: 212), it would be a mistake to see the molar and molecular as two separate levels of existence: 'molecular escapes and movements would be nothing if they did not return to the molar organizations to reshuffle their segments, their binary distributions of sexes, classes and parties' (Deleuze and Guattari 1987: 216–17).

As Tarde showed so eloquently in his work on interactions, they coexist and revolve around the interaction between stability ('imitation') and transformation ('innovation'). Change or transformation can therefore emerge out of even the smallest expression or gesture of an arbitrary actor. Such an approach, which already works brilliantly in the beta sciences, is underdeveloped in the field of social sciences. Maybe this is caused by the view that the molecular is confused with a minimal order or – even worse – conceived as chaos and disorder.[6] Perhaps researchers assume that the molecular is capable of neutralising the molar? In that case, the force of the molecular would be more powerful than that of the molar. It may be clear by now that these assumptions are misconceptions. It is not about the molecular as chaos or revolution, nor about the molar as dogmatic and conservative. Let us therefore remove four errors concerning the difference between both levels.

First, the molar and molecular do not refer to 'the collective' on the one side and 'the individual' on the other (Deleuze and Guattari 1983: 280). In reality, both levels are not distinguishable in terms of size or scale. It would be better to speak of a difference in composition, organisation and consistency between the elements on each level. The molar and molecular are not defined by the amount of elements that they bring together, and therefore not by their multiple characters, but by the nature of the relationships between their elements. In the case of the molecular, its features are nomadic, rhizomatic, many-voiced, smooth, intensive and indivisible. The molar is connected with features that are sedentary, arborescent, unanimous, striated, extensive and divisible (Deleuze and Guattari 1987: 33, 505).

Second, the distinction between molar and molecular is not one between form and substance. In fact, both operate through form and substance. 'Substances are nothing other than formed matters' (Deleuze and Guattari 1987: 41, 57). Earlier I suggested that the molar concerns the whole and its isolated and controllable parts. That means the molar is more visible, because its actions are (at first sight) fixed and framed by univocal and compelling laws and regulations. However, it would be a mistake to reduce the molar to an abstract or judicial form (for example Hobbes' and Beccaria's *social contract* or Durkheim's *conscience collective*), which may be unrelated to human actions. In that case, the molar would be reassuring, while the molecular would be a matter of disruption. Each segmentation brings into play both forms and substances. As such, the molar is not an interaction-free structure or lacking in interactions. Characteristic for the functioning of the molar is the 'centering, unification, totalization, integration, hierarchization and finalization'

(Deleuze and Guattari 1987: 41) of the molecular by inserting it into larger wholes. Foucault (1975) would speak here of 'disciplinary techniques' (allocation, classification, consolidation, normalisation, etc.), to make visible the insertion of human activities in the institutions of the disciplinarian society, in its schools, prisons, factories, hospitals, army barracks.

Third, the two forms are not distinguished by the size of their elements, as a large form (molar) and a small form (molecular). That would mean dealing with social institutions and the state at the macro level and with a micro-politics involving a theory of human agency at the micro level.[7] In the words of Deleuze and Guattari: 'Although it is true that the molecular works in detail and operates in small groups, this does not mean that it is any less coextensive with the entire social field than molar organization' (Deleuze and Guattari 1987: 215). Essentially what they are arguing here is that the two levels must be treated as relative to a particular scale. As a simple example of this, one can look at a person as a molar identity if studying the beliefs and desires out of which he or she individuates. But a person can at the same time be considered on a molecular level in relation to the organisation he or she is a part of. In fact, the movement of the molecular combines to produce molar entities which in turn re-act on the molecular, forcing it to change and adapt.

Fourth, the difference between the molar and the molecular is not an absolute or a 'dualist opposition' (Deleuze and Guattari 1987: 34). There is no Chinese wall between them. In fact, neither can exist independently of the other. To put this differently, 'there is not one molecular formation that is not by itself an investment of a molar formation' (Deleuze and Guattari 1983: 340). Both levels are 'constantly interfering, reacting upon each other, introducing into each other either a current of suppleness or a point of rigidity' (Deleuze and Guattari 1987: 196). As a consequence 'their disjunction is a relation of included disjunction, which varies only according to the two directions of subordination, according as the molecular phenomena are subordinated to the large aggregates, or on the contrary subordinate them to themselves' (Deleuze and Guattari 1983: 340–1). So everything always functions at the same time ('and-and') and in parallel. Although both levels are usually studied separately (as if concerning two different kinds of social reality), both are intertwined in a single process. The two levels are constantly running into each other and are connected in what Deleuze calls a 'zone of indiscernibility' (Deleuze 1997b: 78), a play of forces, which he characterises as pure intensity.

## Assemblages

It is important to recognise that the molar is only one way of looking at social reality. At the same time, paying attention solely to the issue of functionality and stability leads to a drastic simplification of that reality. Then, the molar is affirmed as the positive general, without taking into account what occurs at the molecular level: the immediate, unpredictable and heterogeneous. It is striking that the molar approach cannot encompass these matters and leaves them out of its research framework. The consequence of this is that the molar only manages to grip of a small part of the question at hand in social reality. For that reason it needs to put its own position in perspective. Moreover, it should address a more permanent and dynamic system that is difficult or impossible to formalise, i.e. that cannot be interpreted in terms of mandatory categories or abstract forms, structures and properties (Schuilenburg and Van Calster 2010). In fact, the more molar an organisation is, the more it induces a molecularisation of its own elements, relations and elementary apparatuses. This raises the question of how the complex relation between the molecular and the molar can be understood.

As mentioned earlier, a whole or totality consists of a collection of heterogeneous elements that relate to each other. This implies a certain consistency and coherence. Viewed from a molecular perspective, a whole is always an open set or combination because the different elements are related to specific circumstances and are constantly mediated by the relations between them. In a philosophical sense, this means that an element is immanent to specific and local conditions and the relations in which it exists. In fact, essence and unity are replaced by a dynamic 'middle' that connects different elements to each other. This 'middle ground' is 'not an average' (Deleuze and Guattari 1987: 293) or principle that gives reality a new direction and unity, but a process where new relations pop up and connections are made.

In a more general sense, the middle is related to the changing conditions by which something new can appear and with everything that differs. Illustrative for the middle is the verb 'connect'. This principle can be physical, linguistic or conceptual, and ensures that elements are connected together into a larger whole. Especially important here is that at any time a connection can ensure that a separate element changes, and as a consequence so does the whole. Moreover, the connection makes it possible for new elements to be taken up in a whole and old elements to disappear or be plugged into a new whole in which the interactions are different. One element may dislodge and go on to function in another assemblage. It can be taken out of one assemblage and incorporated in another context (DeLanda 2006; Schuilenburg 2009). In turn, this context is formed by new variables, unforeseen interactions and other outcomes. This guarantees that 'the whole' can change constantly. Or, put another way, the dynamic between the elements at a molecular level allows for the possibility that the interactions between different parts may result in new syntheses.

If we translate this 'principle of connecting' in terms of relations between the different elements of the molecular, this means that each interaction ensures that a social field goes adrift, meaning that an existing field of organisation is broken up and moves in directions which are not formally established or legally regulated. Relations are in fact always in the middle and with each connection create something new. In this respect, they mediate the elements in the whole permanently. It is therefore important to understand that relations exist before they connect elements and continue to exist if elements become detached from the whole. In that sense, they are external to the elements and remain in force after certain events have occurred, specific forms or structures are created, or social acts are performed. This means that they cannot be traced to the elements they connect. Relations can change without the elements changing (Deleuze and Parnet 2002: 55). But also the properties of the elements do not explain all the relations that give the whole a certain autonomy. In this light, the elementary social fact is not the individual or the whole, but a molecular series of interactions that produce a difference; movements that differentiate something qualitatively and quantitatively (Barry and Thrift 2007).

It will be obvious by now that we are far removed from the classical way of considering meaning or purpose, in which the human subject is at the centre of attributing meaning and purpose, a logic inspired by Descartes' magical maxim 'I think, therefore I am'. In this way of thinking, the actions of a person are the product of a free, autonomous and immutable actor. This individual is in opposition to his immediate environment without forming part of it. From an external position he can comprehend and grasp social reality in its entirety. However, given the relation between the molar and the molecular we should assume that interactions cannot be reduced to the action of the individual, that is, of the substance or subject it refers or is ascribed to. The interaction is an autonomous process, which makes discerning causes or consequences problematical. Moreover, the relation between cause and effect is ambiguous and difficult to determine. Order and unity are therefore not provided *a priori*. They emerge immanently 'from below', from interactions on a molecular level, rather than being constrained from above by large molar aggregates.[8]

## Conclusion

Deleuze employs the distinction between 'the law' and 'jurisprudence' in different ways. Although, this relation never received the attention in his philosophical work as, for example, did painting, cinema and literature, there is a consistent treatment of the theme throughout his work (see also de Sutter 2008; Lefebvre 2008). Whereas 'the law' corresponds with a Durkheimian strand of thought, in which social reality is identified with great collective or molar representations, 'jurisprudence' can be characterised by the work of Tarde, where emphasis is placed on molecular flows and fluids as the reality. Against this background, a simple opposition between both positions is misleading for they always overlap and become entangled. The point is one of knowing 'how to move from molecular perceptions to molar perceptions' (Deleuze 1993: 87). It is clear that this cannot be understood through a process of totalisation in which the parts form a whole or any sort of original totality. In fact, we are dealing with 'two segmentarities simultaneously: one molar, the other *molecular*' (Deleuze and Guattari 1987: 213). Far more than focusing on the molar level in isolation, therefore, we must also look at the molecular level and its ever-emerging effects. For even when everything appears to function well, the smallest of actions and passions may have unexpected consequences on the molar level. Or, in the words of Deleuze and Guattari: 'Good or bad, politics and its judgements are always molar, but it is the molecular and its assessment that makes it or breaks it' (Deleuze and Guattari 1987: 222).

## References

Alliez, E. (2009), 'Gabriel Tarde', in G. Jones and J. Roffe (eds), *Deleuze's Philosophical Lineage*, Edinburgh: Edinburgh University Press.
Barry, A. and N. Thrift (2007), 'Gabriel Tarde: Imitation, Invention and Economy', *Economy and Society*, 36 (4): 509–25.
Beavon, R. and A. Jarvis (2003), *Nelson Advanced Science: Structure, Bonding and Main Group Chemistry*, Cheltenham: Nelson Thornes.
Beccaria, C. (2009 [1764]), *On Crimes and Punishment*, New Brunswick, NJ: Transaction Publishers (fifth edition).
de Sutter, L. (2008), *Deleuze: La pratique du droit*, Paris: Michalon.
DeLanda, M. (2002), *Intensive Science and Virtual Philosophy*, London: Continuum.
DeLanda, M. (2006), *A New Philosophy of Society: Assemblage Theory and Social Complexity*, London: Continuum.

Deleuze, G. (1988), *Foucault*, trans. S. Hand, Minneapolis: University of Minnesota Press.
Deleuze, G. (1991), *Empiricism and Subjectivity: An Essay on Hume's Theory of Human Nature*, trans. C. Boundas, New York: Columbia University Press.
Deleuze, G. (1993), *The Fold: Leibniz and the Baroque*, trans T. Conley, Minneapolis: University of Minnesota Press.
Deleuze, G. (1994), *Difference and Repetition*, trans. P. Patton, New York: Columbia University Press.
Deleuze, G. (1995), *Negotiations 1972–1990*, trans. M. Joughin, New York: Columbia University Press.
Deleuze, G. (1997a), *L'Abécédaire de Gilles Deleuze* (DVD), Paris: Montparnasse.
Deleuze, G. (1997b), *Essays Critical and Clinical*, trans. D. Smith and M. Greco, Minneapolis: University of Minnesota Press.
Deleuze, G. (2004), *Desert Islands and Other Texts, 1953–1974*, trans. M. Taormina, New York: Semiotext(e).
Deleuze, G. (2006), *Two Regimes of Madness: Texts and Interviews 1975–1995*, trans. M. Taormina, Los Angeles/New York: Semiotext(e).
Deleuze, G. and F. Guattari (1983), *Anti-Oedipus: Capitalism and Schizophrenia*, trans. R. Hurley, M. Seem, and H. R. Lane, Minneapolis: University of Minnesota Press.
Deleuze, G. and F. Guattari (1986), *Kafka: Toward a Minor Literature*, trans. D. Polan, Minneapolis: University of Minnesota Press.
Deleuze, G. and F. Guattari (1987), *A Thousand Plateaus: Capitalism and Schizophrenia*, trans. B. Massumi, Minneapolis: University of Minnesota Press.
Deleuze, G. and C. Parnet (2002), *Dialogues II*, trans. H. Tomlinson and B. Habberjam, New York: Columbia University Press.
Dosse, F. (2010), *Gilles Deleuze and Félix Guattari: Intersecting Lives*, New York: Columbia University Press.
Durkheim, E. (1984 [1893]), *The Division of Labor in Society*, New York: Free Press.
Durkheim, E. (1973), *On Morality and Society: Selected Writings*, Chicago: University of Chicago Press.
Foucault, M. (1971), *L'ordre du discours*, Paris: Gallimard.
Foucault, M. (1975), *Surveiller et punir: Naissance de la prison*, Paris: Gallimard.
Foucault, M. (2003), *Abnormal: Lectures at the Collège de France 1974–1975*, Picador: New York.
Ginneken, J. Van (1992), *Crowds, Psychology, and Politics, 1871–1899*, Cambridge: Cambridge University Press.
Guattari, F. (2009), *Chaosophy: Texts and Interviews 1972–1977*, Los Angeles: Semiotext(e).
Hobbes, T. (1985 [1651]), *Leviathan*, London: Penguin Books.
Kubinga, H. (2003), *De molecularisering van het wereldbeeld*, Deel I., Hilversum: Verloren.
Laermans, R. (1995), 'Sociologie vandaag: enkele stellingen en notities', *Tijdschrift voor Sociologie*, 16 (2): 133–41.
Latour, B. (2002), 'Gabriel Tarde and the End of the Social', in P. Joyce (ed.), *The Social in Question: New Bearings in History and the Social Sciences*, London: Routledge.
Latour, B. (2007), *Reassembling the Social: An Introduction to Actor-Network-Theory*, New York: Oxford University Press.
Lefebvre, A. (2008), *The Image of Law: Deleuze, Bergson, Spinoza*, Stanford: Stanford University Press.
Nietzsche, F. (1967), *The Will To Power*, trans. W. Kaufmann and R. Hollingdale, New York: Random House.

Prigogine, I. and I. Stengers (1984), *Order Out of Chaos: Man's New Dialogue with Nature*, New York: Bantam Books.
Rhoads, J. K. (1991), *Critical Issues in Social Theory*, University Park: Pennsylvania State University Press.
Schuilenburg, M. (2006), 'De kracht van een revolutie. Mensenrechten en de democratie', in R. de Brabander (ed.), *Het Uur van de Waarheid. Alain Badiou – revolutionair denker*, Kampen: Ten Have.
Schuilenburg, M. (2008), 'The Dislocating Perspective of Assemblages: Another Look at the Issue of Security', in *Open. Cahier on art and the public domain*, 15: 18–35.
Schuilenburg, M. (2009), 'Assemblages', in E. Romein, M. Schuilenburg and S. van Tuinen (eds), *Deleuze compendium*, Amsterdam: Boom.
Schuilenburg, M. and P. Van Calster (2010), 'Molair en moleculair onderzoek in veiligheidsstudies', *Panopticon*, 31 (4): 59–66.
Sijbesma, R. (2007), *Pakkende verbindingen. Zelf-organiserende moleculen voor functionele materialen*, Intreerede, uitgesproken op 23 februari 2007 aan de Technische Universiteit Eindhoven.
Tarde, G. (1912 [1890]), *Penal Philosophy*, Boston: Little, Brown, and Company.
Tarde, G. (1924 [1886]), *La criminalité comparée*, Paris: Librairie Félix Alcan.
Tarde, G. (1962 [1890]), *The Laws of Imitation*, Gloucester, MA: Smith.
Tarde, G. (1969), *On Communication and Social Influence*, Selected Papers, edited with an introduction by T. N. Clark, Chicago: University of Chicago Press.
Tarde, G. (1999 [1893]), *Monadologie et sociologie*, Paris: Les empêcheurs de penser en rond.
Tarde, G. (2000 [1898]), *Social Laws: An Outline of Sociology*, Kitchener, Ontario: Batoche Books.
Tuinen, S. van (2009), *Mannerism in Philosophy: A Study of Gilles Deleuze's Development of Monadology into Nomadology, of Leibnizian Approaches to the Problem of Constitution, and of Deleuze's Concept of Mannerism*, Dissertatie Universiteit Gent.
Van Calster, P. and M. Schuilenburg (2011), 'Governing Security: Including the Molecular into the Molar', in M. Hildebrand, J. Blad, M. Schuilenburg and P. Van Calster (eds), *Governing Security Under the Rule of Law?*, Amsterdam: Eleven International Publishing.

# Notes

1. Deleuze changes his terminology in every one of his books. Very few concepts retain their names or identity. As DeLanda notes in *Intensive Science and Virtual Philosophy*: 'The point of this exuberance is not merely to give the impression of difference through the use of synonyms, but rather to develop a set of different theories on the same subject' (DeLanda 2002: 167).
2. We should not infer from this that a society exists eternally and completely on its own, as if functioning totally separate from the individuals who compose it. Durkheim opposes a transcendental view of society as an entity operating independently from its constituent individuals. To Durkheim, society, through the associations of individuals, brings about specific behaviours that together form a collective unity. In *The Division of Labor in Society* (Durkheim 1984), for example, he analysed the development of a moral solidarity in different types of society. While the primitive society enjoyed a mechanical solidarity based on equality, the modern society is characterised by an organic solidarity based on differences and inequality, caused by factors such as the new division of labour

and the strong growth of population that further increased the number of mutual interactions.
3. Here we can invoke Foucault's thesis concerning sovereign forms of power. As Deleuze writes in *Foucault*: 'What is common to both republics and monarchies in the West is that they raised the whole entity of Law to the status of the assumed principle of power, in order to give themselves a homogeneous representation of jurisdiction: the "juridical model" became the blueprint for all strategies' (Deleuze 1988: 30).
4. DeLanda speaks of a 'flat ontology of individuals' (DeLanda 2002).
5. Foucault (2003) treats the case of Henriette Cornier in his lectures of 5 and 12 February 1975, in which he investigates the formation of the concept of abnormality in the history of the modern West by the transition from 'the monster' to 'the abnormal'. One of the most interesting aspects of this case is the fact that there is no 'rational' explanation according to the law. Cornier had no motive, no reason, and no interest. But also, according to the indictment, Cornier shows none of the traditional signs of illness or madness. According to Foucault, the fundamental principles of the judicial apparatus and the penal mechanism are here 'questioned, challenged, disturbed, put back into play, cracked, and undermined by this nonetheless paradoxical thing of the dynamic of an act without interest that pushes aside the most fundamental interests of every individual' (Foucault 2003: 129).
6. The concept of 'molecular chaos' is, for instance, used in thermodynamics for the description of the behaviour of independent molecules before they collide (Prigogine and Stengers 1984).
7. The relativising of the distinction between a micro- and a macro-politics removes the conceptual mistake that there are only two levels of politics operating in social processes. Although in *A Thousand Plateaus*, Deleuze and Guattari still use the term 'microsociology' in honour of the work of Gabriel Tarde, their goal is to move the binary opposition between the macro and micro toward multiplicity and a generalised fragmentation. As Deleuze notes: 'The macro-micro distinction is very important, but it belongs more to Guattari than to me. I'm more about the distinction of two multiplicities. That's what I find essential' (Dosse 2010: 235–6).
8. Note the difference here with the position of Alain Badiou and Slavoj Žižek, who argue that change can only occur with a radically unpredictable, unknown and unknowable event, such as the French Revolution or the Cultural Revolution in China. By this, they undeniably maintain the modern view that in politics anything new can only emerge from an external event that is beyond any form of representation (Schuilenburg 2006).

# Chapter 7

# The Perception of the Middle

Nathan Moore

'The hesitation of the nomad is legendary' (Deleuze and Guattari 1988: 418).

## P. Image: [2008] UKHL 48

In law, it seems as though we have to always start again. That is, we look for the proper ground in the belief that, once it is discovered, all else will follow. In this sense, law does not aim for utopia so much as it sets out from it. It begins with the proper divisions, and the suitable allocations of men and things. To be sure, law acts in this manner most of the time, inasmuch as it provides the solutions to disagreements in advance. When really successful, it does this to the extent that a disagreement cannot even appear as such – it is already resolved before it begins. In which case, the disagreement is nothing new, but simply the banal repetition of a legal problem already discovered at some point in the past. It is, then, those cases that cannot be referred to a previous problem – which would include *every* case that requires a decision, judicial or otherwise – that make it necessary to search anew for how things should be arranged, to assemble once more the relevant ground. In this necessity, the law is not so much applied as repeated. The repetition is not banal, however, but a repetition of the legal assemblage in its entirety, to the extent that a new ground calls for the rearrangement of the legal assemblage from bottom to top.

There is no need to limit oneself to matters of public or international law to see this process at work. It is there in the most seemingly mundane of cases, to the extent that any case is a situation where the ground is lacking. Nevertheless, it tends to be constitutional questions that both highlight the absence of a ground, whilst simultaneously trying to ignore it as a legal matter. For reasons that are contingent to law, we are told that the problem is, instead, political and/or economic, and so must be resolved in those terms (Foucault 2008). Whilst it is of little interest to argue that somehow law has been toppled from its rightful place by geopolitics, the geopolitical turn repeats, in its own way, the fact of law's lacking a ground. For this reason many recent writers have been encouraged, once again, to address the apparently fundamental problem of modern law: on what grounds can effective legal order be established? (see Loughlin and Walker 2007). In truth, it seems that little advance has been made since the problem was formulated in terms of a social contract by writers such as Hobbes and Rousseau, inasmuch as the recurring theme is how to think the relationship between the ruler and the ruled. In other words, how are the grounds of law to be established, either internally (for example, Kelsen), or externally (for example, Schmitt).

The banality of case law has a great advantage over the problem as set out in public and international law: it is not directly concerned with the origin of legal power. This is not to say that origins don't appear, but that they are treated differently, as a function of the case at hand. In the problem as conceptualised by constitutional theory, the cart is put before the horse, and a pure ground is sought from which the legitimacy of all cases then follows. This thinking tends to be limited by the idea of emanation, so that a legal assemblage is constituted by no more than chains of increasing/decreasing legitimacy, depending upon the direction one travels in. In short, the problem is still dominated by the thinking of political theology. This thinking is characterised by an unbreakable circle and, like all such circles, it works very well: either the constituent is too absent, by being represented by the constituted, or it is too present, by being equated with the constituted (Lindhal 2007). Similarly, one cannot hope to leave this circle: the grounds of law are either theological (precisely, an *ens increatum*), or simply secularised theology.[1] Together, these two circles create a double bind from which legal thinking has little chance of escape.

Alternatively, rather than carrying on the search for the solution to these problems, it is more productive to adopt the method of Bergson and ask whether the problem itself is a good one. Is it a problem that has been well formulated? With respect, our response must be no. Our reason for this is straightforward, and is indebted to Bergson's arguments in *Time and Free Will* and *Matter and Memory*: the formulation of the problem of the grounds of law has occurred within the context of the philosophical tension between idealism and materialism. Consequently, the problem is continuously played out in terms of representations or things, and absence or presence. In short, it remains theological. The challenge is then the following: what does it mean to think of law as an assemblage of images, and nothing but images? Here, we must be clear that 'image' is intended not as an image of something – it is not a representation – but rather as a pure image, meaning something that is constituted by other images, and is itself part of further images. As Bergson describes it, the image is between a representation and a thing, meaning that it is neither, whilst at the same time being the mechanism by which both are grafted onto one another. This means that, in their most extreme form as pure memory and pure perception, representation and thing pass into each other as duration (Bergson 1991).

This is significant for the thinking of legal assemblages. If we understand the assemblage to be an assemblage of images, and thus nothing but an image itself, then what becomes apparent is that the issue is not, 'How do images come to be bound together?', but rather, 'How does an image distinguish itself from the universe of images?' In posing the question of the contract or bond, legal thought has obscured the problem by setting it always as a question of origins – how was the bond formed? Bergson's philosophy allows us to bypass this question, replacing it instead with one of how an image is carved out, or perception made sufficiently narrow. The answer is that perception arises in relation to the interests and requirements of a body-image, so that perception is made dependent upon the actions an image can take (that is, the effect it can have on other images, this effect itself conditioned by the images that effect the image in question). It is not a matter of forming a body or state so that it might take action. Rather, the potential for action creates a body by hewing it out from the universe of images, like a sculpture emerging from a block of granite.

It is useful at this point to overlay the Bergsonian image with elements drawn from the Spinozist one. According to Deleuze (1988), Spinoza's image is one that is tied inextricably to affect. Affect is the passion or power an image has as a result of its contact with other images, in the process of either perceiving or of being perceived. This passion or power is not a steady state, but is either an increase or decrease depending upon the nature of the contact in question (that an image either adds to the power of another image, by combining with it, or detracts from its power, by disassembling it in some way). Thus, an image is also movement, in the sense of being transitional from one level of excitation to another. Being transitional, an image is also durational: an image necessarily takes the time of transition, not merely in the abstract sense of one image moving from one place to another, but rather that the image *is* the time in question. Consequently, duration is a complex interfolding of various states of transition, speeds of movement, and intensities of affect.

What we draw from this is that all images, despite being in contact or passing through every other image (Deleuze 1992b), are nevertheless distinct and unique when taken individually. Their distinctness is entirely dependent upon their power, and this power is, in addition, responsible for creating the ability to perceive; meaning that what an image perceives is determined by the power it has to act upon what it perceives. However, we should not think that the action and perception of images is linked to a freedom of action, if we mean by this an intended or voluntary choice. For Bergson, freedom means not perceiving entirely clearly, in the sense that there is a zone of indeterminacy in perception caused by the *potential* for action. This freedom is not well thought of as a matter of choice (in the sense that an image chooses which images, from a number of potentials, to affect), but rather as a sort of hesitation (see Guerlac 2006). Hesitation follows from the complexity of an image, in the sense that, the more complex an image is (for example, the greater the number of images it is itself assembled from), the greater the power of action it enjoys. Freedom as hesitation arises from power, so that we might say, in a more Spinozist register, that an image is more free the greater its power of being affected (and thus its power of affecting) is.

Another important aspect of this, and one that, crucially, frees us from the wearying debate around the origin of law, is that any image is both preceded and followed by other images. Consequently, there is neither an origin, nor an end point, to the universe of images. As Deleuze draws from Nietzsche, if we correctly understand images as forces of becoming, then not only was becoming not set in motion (there was no being before becoming) but also, given becoming's infinite past, there is no end to it either (Deleuze 1983). There is no prime mover or *ens increatum* in Deleuze's philosophy: there is no Being from which all other beings consequently emanate. Rather, there is expressionism, which allows us to think of being as the expressed of all images. As Ansell Pearson points out, Deleuze is a thinker of both the one *and* the plural (Ansell Pearson 2002).

This means that we can speak of 'individual' or specific images only to the extent that we are sufficiently empowered to be able to perceive them as something that we might act upon. In addition, we cannot think of an individual image as either better or worse than any other image except in relation to our own power – that is, in terms of whether or not an image might increase or decrease our power. Perhaps the most important consequence is that there is no possibility of a total or pure image: there is no image of being. There are only ever partial images, shot through with other images, that all express being in a partial and specific way. It is not possible to add up all of the images to make a complete or whole image, because they do not emanate from being as so many bits *of* being, but rather express being as that which – as becoming, movement, affectation, and so on – must necessarily differ from itself: being cannot be made present as a unified thing. There is no aspect of lack in this because the question of presence is made redundant in Deleuze's philosophy – it simply does not appear as a relevant problem. In its place is the Spinozist provocation, of which Deleuze was so fond: we don't yet know what a body (image) can do. By this, we should understand that we don't know how an image might be able to combine (or not) with other images, so we don't know what power an image might have, and in this we find again hesitation and the zone of indeterminacy. Consequently, a powerful or perfect image is not one that has *more* being in it, but is instead one that is more intensely differentiated, not simply from other images, but from itself.

This differentiation means that an image cannot coincide entirely with itself. Every image passes through every other image, every image is perceived by every other image with greater or lesser clarity and obscurity (Deleuze 1994). If so, does this mean that any one image is capable of perceiving every other image for the purposes of action? The answer to this is no. The power an image has to act is dependent upon its composition with other images, which is not limited in the sense that it is possible to mark a cut-off point, beyond which an image would cease to be composed. In other words, there is no point at which an image ceases to differ from itself. Consequently, an image differs from itself without limit and, in this sense, contains within itself all other images. At the same time, an image is specific or singular – it cannot not be differentiated from all other images, otherwise all images would become indistinct, melting into a single, static image of being. The singularity of an image depends upon *how* it combines with other images: some images will be more relevant because they offer a more direct or immediate possibility of increasing (or decreasing) one's power, whilst other images will be seemingly more indifferent, and in this they will be less likely to be perceived, in the sense of offering a possibility for action.

This highlights that the perceptual relationship between images is not a necessarily benign, transparent, or well ordered one. Many images will be perceived in a weak and fuzzy manner. This fuzziness is not a degradation, nor an error, but a necessary consequence of the specificity of an image. For any image, there will be many more images that are less relevant than those that are. For any image, there will be more disorder than order, or, to employ a word from Deleuze that is relevant to this point, there will be more *stupidity*. For Deleuze, stupidity is not error or ignorance, meaning that it is not misrecognition or a lack of truth, nor is it what remains once 'rational' has been subtracted from 'rational animal' (Deleuze 1994: 148–53). Stupidity is the process by which images are individuated; that is, carved out, as the potential for action affects an image. In so doing, the acting image becomes insensitive to the elemental images that make up the image-to-be-acted-upon, in a process of becoming-imperceptible which is crucial to the potential for action becoming perceptible as such. If one imagines the elemental images as the numerous ripples moving out from the point at which a stone has been dropped in a pond, it is the outermost ripple that provides the shape of the process as a seeming whole, and it is this shape that is perceived for the purposes of action. The elemental images – that is, the ripples that constitute the process in movement and force – are imperceptible, so that a single image can be identified and combined with, to such a degree that the outermost limit seems to be defining of the process as a whole.

As it is not a matter of representing truth (Bergson 1991), it is not legitimate to consider the imperceptibility inside perception as an error or mistake. Stupidity is, rather, the zone of indeterminacy in which action occurs (i.e. in which images combine). Whilst any image is composed, to a greater or lesser extent, of all other images, action would be impossible if it were first necessary to survey all images, so that any action would be coextensive with the universe of images in its entirety. Because this universe differs from itself, any such action is impossible, and action is always then partial and *ad hoc*. In other words, action never begins from an origin in the sense of a cleared ground which could provide transparency to subsequent actions, but is always in the middle of things. Action, as the combination of images, always surprises, as those elemental images that were imperceptible begin to take effect in the combination. At this level, action is always a re-action to the affectation induced by the becoming perceptible of elemental images. This is not a process of enlightenment, but necessarily follows from the stupidity of action. Elemental images are not gradually uncovered and tabulated, meaning that individuation does not lead to good, clear images, but instead impacts upon the acting image in a formless and con-fused manner. In this process, the ground of action, along with the individual, rises to the surface yet assumes neither form nor figure. It is there, staring at us, but without eyes. The individual distinguishes itself from it, but it does not distinguish itself, continuing rather to cohabit with that which divorces itself from it. (Deleuze 1994: 152)

There is no clear image after the event of action, but rather action always extends beyond that which was intended, including beyond the acting image's own power of action. For this reason, there is the dreamlike encounter with images that are not fully individualised, and not fully within the action, but which nevertheless impact upon it. Action, in reacting to these eyeless gazes, must improvise, being forced into an on-the-hoof creativity in which the response is always provisional, and constant hesitation is internal to decisiveness. This hesitation is the consequence of what was not seen in advance: the future, as it affects the image now, in the present.

## Q. Decision: [1971] AC 424

Action proceeds from a composed ground, which is constituted by both the light of reason and, more profoundly, the structure of stupidity, making the ground rise up to the surface. When the problem of acting is posed, it is always as between two poles or faces. This is clearly illustrated in the problems constitutionalism sets itself. In his studies of Spinoza, Deleuze describes how the City appears to be formed by way of two contracts, being an initial contract whereby a whole is formed by individuals giving up some of their power in a very ambivalent situation, each being motivated by the fear of a possible future combination that might decompose them (and their hope of avoiding this); followed by a second contract where this 'whole' power is transferred to the State (see Deleuze 1988, 1992a).[2] In the first contract, we can see a confused response to the zone of indeterminacy, inasmuch as a joint effort is made to impose some order on the power of perception. At this point, we can still consider the contract to be marked by immanence, even though it follows from passion rather than reason in Spinoza's account. However, in the second, a properly transcendental function emerges, inasmuch as the indeterminate is now elevated to an objective principle of otherness, exclusion and institutionalised fear.[3] We might say that, in the first, *locus standi* is distributed whilst, in the second, it is allotted.

Are we then to take from this that, despite the universe of images, the State does, nevertheless, begin in an origin? To do so is to mistake the nature of the beginning, which functions not as a first principle, but rather as a constant intervention or repetition. The proper conclusion to be drawn is the one reached by Deleuze and Guattari: the State did not begin, but has always existed, fully formed (Deleuze and Guattari 1988: 360). In which case, what forces the constant repetition of the State? We have a sense of the answer already: it is the necessity of action that has both brought the State into existence and caused it to be repeated, continuously. The State arises at the point at which an image becomes sufficiently individualised that it can be acted upon. As such, it is a sort of doubling of action to the extent that it seeks to replace the consequent confusion and stupidity, resulting from the effect of the elemental images, with a regime of error – precisely, the power to exclude certain consequences as unimportant or non-existent. The operation through which this is achieved is the imposition, again and again, of a double contract or bind.

In *A Thousand Plateaus*, Deleuze and Guattari discuss the double bind with reference to Georges Dumézil's *Mitra-Varuna*. From this, they are able to show how the State always appears as double-headed, one side being the 'magician-emperor, operating by capture, bonds, knots, and nets', and, the other, 'the jurist-priest-king, proceeding by treaties, pacts, [and] contracts' (Deleuze and Guattari 1988: 424). First, there is a sort of bonding or congealing through individuation, and then an imposition of order and individualism. This order is not chronological, as both sides appear together, fully developed. State thought emerges dually in the sense of what it is able to think, along with the presuppositions which make that thought possible. However, there is also a third persona who is indifferent to the two-headed sovereign, whilst nevertheless being the condition of the latter. This is the warrior or nomad, the one who is unable to serve any one (or two images) because s/he is subject to too broad a range of affect or perception: one who bears too much. Throughout the 'Nomadology' and 'Apparatus of Capture' chapters of *A Thousand Plateaus*, Deleuze and Guattari are concerned to show how the double-headed sovereign draws its power from the nomad war machine, not by taming it or finally incorporating it, but by ensnaring some of its power or velocity between its (the sovereign's) two heads.

The nomad is the principle of differentiation, not in the sense of being able to incarnate difference as a substance, but rather of always differentiating so that, despite the proper order of things, other elemental images still rumble on, and questionable passions and affects continue to circulate. Despite what it might have claimed in the past, the double-headed sovereign cannot bring about the end of the nomad, because to do so would mean achieving the impossible: instituting an image equal to the universe of images itself. Instead, the sovereign can only ever act to draw off from nomad power, using this as a means to institute an order of good and common sense. For this reason, the distinction between idealism and materialism is always a secondary thought of the State, and the circle of presence and absence can only be forged and played out by continuously passing through each of the sovereign's two heads. Rather than the binary regime of error, the nomad opts for stupidity, causing the ground to rise up to the surface. This is not conditional upon the existence of the State – the nomad is not the antithesis of the sovereign, but is, rather, a force in his/her own right, coursing through the universe of images, constantly caught up in these latter's affects and becomings. Thus, the nomad does not move between the two heads as between two fixed points, but effects an absolute movement, one that does not pass across an extended space, but *distributes space through its movements*. Only then is it possible for the sovereign to use its two heads to divide up space.

Which is to say that the nomad is not an emancipator: s/he will not 'free' us from sovereignty, but will rather make us feel that sovereignty has not been able to do everything as it might claim. Nomadology provides the possibility of acting again and, even more crucially, insists upon the hesitation necessary to act. This underlines the emphasis Deleuze and Guattari give to the ambiguity of the nomad war machine: on the one hand, the nomad is indifferent to the two-headed sovereign, and deploys its own powers and affects so far as it can. On the other hand, this indifference inevitably brings the nomad into conflict with the sovereign, necessitating the waging of war if the nomad project is to be seen through to exhaustion. The nomad is first and foremost concerned to occupy a smooth space, meaning that the nomad takes up formless spaces, watching over them with an eyeless gaze. The nomad does not fall into an indistinct melange of images, but occupies the perceptual field of the fuzzy, of that which is anexact, or obscure in essence. The nomad is a singular process of individuation. Against this, the two-headed sovereign divides images up into specific, individualised units, which then function as simple and banal repetitions of one another. The danger is that the sovereign and the nomad can begin to operate as another double bind, with the particular threat of the war machine being reimparted by the sovereign state apparatus (Deleuze and Guattari 1988: 422). Consequently, it will be necessary to begin again, to find another combination that adds to one's power, rather than disassembling it.

If we consider a series of ripples once more, the nomad is the one

## The Perception of the Middle 141

who takes up the force and velocity of these ripples. In other words, the nomad does not divide the process up into individual ripples, but instead occupies the vectorial intensive space that the ripples constitute; not as so many parts of a whole, but as the absolute movement of their specific process. The singularity of this movement is ensured by the point of exhaustion – that is, the point at which the ripples cannot maintain themselves and their energy dissipates. On the other hand, the sovereign captures each ripple between his two heads, fixing them in place and ordering them relative to each other, as so many concentric circles. The outermost ripple is then taken to be defining of the set as a whole, and an identity is imposed in terms of this boundary. An alternative is to consider each ripple in itself, but to then find a way to connect the individualised ripple to the process in its entirety. This is a sort of middle way between the nomad and sovereign, not as a synthesis or reconciliation, but arising according to its own practices and logic. Here, it is a matter of experimenting to find out how each ripple might be extended, or connected to other ripples. So too with images: it is not necessary to prolong the indeterminacy of images, or to insist upon their ultimate individualisation. Rather, the indeterminacy can be grasped as something singular in its own right, as something that pertains to a specific zone. The problem is then not to occupy this indeterminacy as the nomad does, but rather to follow the elemental images constituting this zone so as to extract particular effects from them. It is to perceive images in a provisional and *ad hoc* way as the basis of an ongoing, and improvisatory, exploration of possible combinations. This third way is that taken up by the artisan or metallurgist.

If we think back to Bergson, it is perhaps useful to consider the nomad as occupying the points at which matter and memory pass into each other, as duration: the sovereign attempts to occupy memory to the exclusion of matter, in the hope of imposing a (representational) transcendental order that appears to emanate from him; and the artisan is on the other side, occupying matter or pure perception. However, s/he does not seek to exclude memory, but subordinates it to matter, calling upon it as technique in order to work with matter, whilst always being prepared to abandon memory, or representation, in order to follow the potentials of matter itself. For this reason, Deleuze and Guattari write, 'the artisan [is] one who is determined in such a way as to follow a flow of matter ... The artisan is *the itinerant, the ambulant*' (Deleuze and Guattari 1988: 409).

The exemplar of the artisan for Deleuze and Guattari is the blacksmith because s/he is a metallurgist. In working with metal it is necessary to activate the constant variations it contains, passing into the zone of indeterminacy that actually constitutes it, so as to find out what other images can be extracted from it. In this sense, the *form* and *matter* of metal are put into variation, making it impossible to say which determines the other, but thereby allowing for something previously unforeseen to emerge. It is as if the blacksmith discovered an eyeless gaze in metal that s/he was then able to combine with to increase his/her own power of perception and action.

> Matter and form have never seemed more rigid than in metallurgy; yet the succession of forms tends to be replaced by the form of a continuous development, and the variability of matters tends to be replaced by the matter of a continuous variation. If metallurgy has an essential relation with music, it is by virtue . . . of the tendency within both arts to bring into its own, beyond separate forms, a continuous development of form, and beyond variable matters, a continuous variation of matter: a widened chromaticism sustains both music and metallurgy; the musical smith was the first 'transformer.' (Deleuze and Guattari 1988: 411)

This reminds us that Deleuze and Guattari do not simply posit the smooth and the striated as the nomad and the sovereign. There is also another type of space, or perception of images: a holey one, and this is the realm of the artisan. In taking up such a space, the artisan is able to enter into relations with both nomads and the sovereign, whilst remaining independent of both. The relation with the artisan is, as Deleuze and Guattari maintain, a necessarily ambiguous one.

In Schmitt's formulation of sovereignty ('Sovereign is he who decides upon the exception') the significant element is that of the decision. The exception is not capable of generating a decision, but rather acts as a sort of break or limit upon the consequences of deciding. The exception is that which allows certain consequences of a decision to be refused. As such, the inadequacy of Schmitt's sovereign is underlined, and we understand him to make little sense without his other, Kelsenist, head. Sovereigns don't decide anything, they only capture. The realm of the decision is, properly, that of the artisan. Decisions are only ever possible in holey space, because the artisan must constantly decide which variations to follow, as well as knowing when to suspend technique so that something unforeseen might emerge. The artisan knows what is at stake in taking such decisions, inasmuch as the consequences of a decision cannot be avoided – there is no way to exclude some consequences as undesirable and unintended, whilst claiming others on the opposite basis. The artisan has to act on an *ad hoc* basis, responding to elemental images as they become perceptible, even if this perceptibility retains an essential becoming-imperceptible at its core. The artisan pursues this process for as long as s/he can, to the point at which his/her power is exhausted. We should consider law to be a product of holey space, as something that is taken up entirely by decisions.

The artisan must decide, and in so doing, creates a new consistency, not just in the matter under consideration, but also in themselves. We can get a clearer sense of this by considering the paper given by Deleuze for François Châtelet in 1987, *Pericles and Verdi*:

> It is neither 'lived experience,' which delights in singularities for their own sake and leaves them in isolation, nor is it the 'concept,' which drowns singularities in the universal and treats them as mere moments. Rather it is an operation that truly casts the dice, in order to produce the most consistent configuration, the curve that yields the most singularities within a given potential, an act of 'unfurling' that brings together various human relations in a weave. This is what it means to actualise a potential, or to *become active*: it is a matter of life and its prolongation, like reason and its process, a victory over death, since there is no other immortality than this history of the present, no other life than that which brings borders into closer proximity. Châtelet calls this a 'decision,' and his entire philosophy is a philosophy of the decision, of the singularity of the decision, as opposed to the universals of reflection or communication . . . (Deleuze 2006: 721)

The decision is the prolongation of a singularity, meaning the attempt to bring it into contact with other singularities. In the same way, the artisan must prolong the image, exploring its zone of indeterminacy to see how this might be activated to bring its specificity into contact with other images. Through this contact, this craft, a firmer consistency is established in the sense of an increase in power. An image still only perceives by narrowing, but in the decision, this narrowing is also an expansion in the special sense that it does not become quantitatively larger – it is not *more* being – but rather increases its power of differentiation, becoming capable of a broader, and ever more profound, hesitation. In which case, hesitation is not restricted to human images, but pertains to all images: what is the universe, if not the most powerful and differentiated of all hesitations?

However, the decision is not the product or end point of hesitation. In fact, they are the same, because one does not hesitate before, so much as after. It is in action that hesitation becomes obscurely apparent, as elemental images are encountered and their consequences played through. Hesitation is the process of deciding over and over again, as one realises that one's intentions and foresight have fallen short once more. However, the tragedy of this is superficial because it is always a secondary tragedy: the tragedy of the sovereign who is finally unable to capture everything between his two heads. The appeal to authority in law could then be considered likewise tragic, to the extent that it serves to sever and limit the consequences of a decision. The designation of a consequence as irrelevant or unimportant is the attempt to decide without deciding, or of instituting a decision after which no further decision is necessary. It is to claim for oneself God's decision, from which all else emanates. The figure of the lawyer should be transformed, so that s/he becomes more like an artisan of jurisprudence, crafting *locus standi* where before there were no grounds. Then, akin to Leibniz, we too can imagine a universal jurisprudence.

## R. Future: [2002] 4 All ER 689

Hesitation is coextensive with the act itself. Hesitating is not about trying to get a clearer picture, but of already being caught up in mixtures of clarity and obscurity, so that one is already reacting to the affects of elemental images. Equally, to react here does not mean to come second, or to be passive. The situation is more complicated, because one does not react to what *has* happened so much as react to what *will* happen, in the sense that this 'will happen' is happening now. There is, in the indeterminacy of the image, an unverifiable component that nevertheless reverberates in the present. It is not foreclosed or inaccessible to perception (although it might be better to say that perception is not foreclosed to it), but constantly differentiates or redistributes the present. In this light, we should understand the zone of indeterminacy to be *future* orientated. The future in this context is not messianic – it is not coming, nor is it ignorance – it is not what we don't yet know. It is not a content at all, but a form or structure of thought that provides the singularity of images, but without giving them an origin.

We should be clear that we cannot talk of *a* future in this regard, nor do we need to have recourse to theories of parallel universes. The future is the singularity of the image, effecting a crack in time that both individualises the image as such, *and* connects it to the universe of images as individuation. There is, then, no future common to all images, but a universe of futures acting always upon assemblages of matter and memory. The future does not progress, but rearranges. As such, stupidity is constantly rearticulated, and itself individuated as specific to a particular assemblage of images. Just as the nature of what is known changes from one era to the next, so too what is not-known (understood in the special sense of stupidity, rather than as error or a lack of knowledge) also changes. It is for this reason that action cannot occur in total clarity or transparency, and also indicates why we should consider intention to have less significance than has otherwise been generally allowed. The perception that allows for action is not the entirety of perception, because the latter also includes those formless perceptions and eyeless gazes that, whilst not always directly perceived as such, nevertheless condition what can be so directly perceived for the purpose of action whilst, in this process, ensuring a constant differentiation so that no number of actions can become *the* action of redemption, sentence, closure, restoration, forgiveness, etc. Instead, there are only decisions to be made, and this without end.

Unfortunately the tendency in legal thought is still to think in a quite linear way, using a simple model of cause and effect. Wherever the concern is for 'origins' or 'context', such thinking fails to escape the vicious circle it constructs for itself. For this reason, this thought works extremely well as a self-perpetuating mechanism, but its great shortcoming is the inability to think the future as anything more than a mechanical result. There has thus been a mass failure to understand how the future has become increasingly significant for *control* (Deleuze 1995), and how this impacts upon law. The exception to this is work by criminologists such as David Garland (2001) and Adam Crawford (2003), but their insights need to be combined with the legal assemblage more extensively.[4] Here, we can turn to the work of Jacques Donzelot (1988) and François Ewald (1991), as well as some of the writings of Paul Virilio (1986, 2000), to understand what the implications of a pre-emptive legal assemblage might be.

In the context of Deleuze's writing, we can of course turn to the well-known texts on control (see Moore 2007a, 2007b). Above, we referred to the double-headed sovereign attempting to locate the entirety of being in memory; we should now consider how, under control, the sovereign has grown a multitude of heads, all of them axiomatic (Deleuze and Guattari 1984) and attempting to sever images from their future dimension. We are familiar with this from theories of risk, but the more useful insight is that developed by Donzelot and Ewald in terms of insurance. It is not simply a question of trying to protect against the future by assessing risks in the present, but of making the process of that assessment profitable in every conceivable way. It is this profitability of the future that motivates control, extended to every image of the universe in the hope of replacing it with an ever modulating universe of data. Decisions become impossible because the construction of consequences, in the form of further decisions, is displaced by discrete, and isomorphic, choices, in which the aim is not to extend the consequence, but rather to limit it through new understandings of liability.[5]

It is significant that error is no longer taken seriously, and that politicians now seldom resign. The idea of error is becoming increasingly insignificant as control extends its grasp. What is on the rise is stupidity, but a degraded version that fails to understand the specificity of stupidity and attempts, instead, to extend it across the universe as a whole. Control institutes a *generalised* stupidity, and in this we see once more the old enemy, transcendence, return. In many ways, control seems to be a becoming-virtual of power, but it is not quite this. Rather, it is the further miniaturisation of interventions that seeks to create principles of transcendence, not applicable to a 'people' or a 'we', but instead applicable to each individual. For every individual image there should be a transcendental double, a representation that, crucially, the image cannot (and should not) coincide with. Every person their own norm, on condition that this norm is always the abstracted, non-liveable version of themselves[6] – the dream version, the version that one has a right to and that, in the frustration of this right, victimises one again and again. It is this abstraction that calls for explanation, yet the majority of legal academics seem content to accept it as such. For this reason, they have much trouble when trying to put these individuals together again as a society, group, or community, or when trying to place them in 'context'.

If the double-headed sovereign, as Deleuze suggests, made use of law, contracts and institutions in order to capture movement and harness the power of the nomad (Deleuze 2004: 253), today control utilises an intensification of contract to achieve this same end. Through contract an exchange is carried out, but no longer in the merchant's sense of buying goods and services. Instead, the contract allows for a never-ending debt to be imposed on the individual, who is now taken to have received something for which s/he will never be able to repay. Perhaps the best formulation of this comes from Tony Blair himself when, in 1997, he spoke of the need to

> re-create the bonds of civic society and community in a way compatible with the far more individualistic nature of modern, economic, social and cultural life . . . The basis of this modern civic society is an ethic of mutual responsibility or duty, something for something, a society where we play by the rules. You only take out if you put in. (Quoted in Collins and Cattermole 2006: 15)

Obviously, this 'taking out' extends as far as being able to depart from 'the rules', if it is made apparent that one has put sufficient 'in' – law is now a tactic, after all. In any case, the contract becomes the sovereign mechanism for normalising each individual because it rearticulates, in a highly fluid and transitory manner, the individual as the agent of a choice that has been made voluntarily, as the intention of free will. Through this tightly focused mechanism, the individual is responsibilised with its own self-management, a management that is primarily directed towards the data that the individual produces (Lyon 2003). The contract provides 'regulated self-regulation' (Crawford 2003) and an obligation to be free (Rose 1999), an obligation that cannot be met, since it is one's life that one owes for. With control, infinite debt (Deleuze and Guattari 1984) replaces both the sovereign function of tribute and taxation and the disciplinary function of investment and savings. No wonder we are now told that debt is productive! (Mellor 2010).

However, putting communities and the 'Big Society' together again is not really the problem. Rather, it is the problem of how to act, that is, how to narrow or subtract perception from the universe of images. Subtraction has nothing to do with essence – it is not a matter of trying to strip away the superfluous. Rather, it is a problem of assembling – how to assemble images so that the maximum power of differentiation is produced in each case? It is really the artisan who is prepared for the consequences of such a differentiation, as s/he is the one who is able to follow the elemental images and, by constantly deciding, extract new consistencies or assemblages. The point is well illustrated by Deleuze's discussion of Carmelo Bene's play *Romeo and Juliet*, in which the character of Romeo is subtracted from the production. Is the essence of the play lost? This is not really the question, the more interesting consideration being what happens to the body of the play if Romeo is removed?

> If you amputate Romeo, you will witness an astonishing development, the development of Mercutio, who was only a virtuality in the play by Shakespeare. In Shakespeare, Mercutio dies quickly. But, in Bene, he does not want to die, he cannot die, he does not manage to die since he will become the subject of the new play. (Deleuze 1997: 239)

Bene takes 'something out', but this is not the basis for a new debt. Precisely, Bene refuses to acknowledge that something is out of balance, and in need of restoration: there is no mania for 'community payback'. Instead, it is a matter of finding out what becomes possible, what elemental images will have to be followed, once a subtraction is made. This has a crucial political point inasmuch as the play refuses the 'representation of conflicts' (Deleuze 1997: 252) – it is not concerned to re-present the same idiotic disagreements, the same idiotic weapons, the same logic of conflict, nor provide a simple structure and narrative resolution. Rather, it is a matter of problematising in the sense that a zone of indeterminacy is opened out, and new actions, perceptions and affects become possible. Only by narrowing or subtracting can a zone of indeterminacy expand. Filmmaker Wim Wenders echoes this point when he says that to show scenes of violence, even as a critique of violence, is still to promote violence and thereby glorify it.

Perhaps the most appalling aspect of control is that it has reduced the City to nothing more than a representation of conflicts, and in this has sought to institute a new 'law of the jungle' to favour the survival of the fittest – but as Nietzsche pointed out, it is always the weakest who survive! Even so, the nomad refuses this conflict in favour of its own war machine, and the artisan continues to extract combinations that are not determined by the needs of conflict. This reminds us that decisions can still be made, and that the City remains. For Spinoza, the contract that institutes the City is not exteriorised for the benefit of a third-party sovereign, but rather forms a whole: 'the contract is made between individuals who transfer their rights to the whole they form by contracting' (Deleuze 1992a: 266), which is to say that the City has always existed, in the process of subtraction. This subtraction is the narrowing of perception by which one renounces 'being determined by *any personal affections whatever*' (Deleuze 1992a: 267). Rather than a world of choice, we should re-discover cities of decision.

## References

Ansell Pearson, K. (2002), *Philosophy and the Adventure of the Virtual: Bergson and the Time of Life*, London and New York: Routledge.
Bauman, Z. (1998), *Globalization: The Human Consequences*, Cambridge: Polity Press.
Bergson, H. (1991), *Matter and Memory*, trans. N. M. Paul and W. S. Palmer, New York: Zone Books.
Bergson, H. (2001), *Time and Free Will: An Essay on the Immediate Data of Consciousness*, trans. F. A. Pogson, Mineola: Dover Publications.
Bottomley, A. and N. Moore (forthcoming), *City, Cinema, Control*.
Collins, S. and R. Cattermole (2006), *Anti-Social Behaviour and Disorder: Powers and Remedies*, London: Sweet and Maxwell.
Crawford, A. (2003), '"Contractual Governance" of Deviant Behaviour', *Journal of Law and Society*, 30 (4): 479–505.
Deleuze, G. (1983), *Nietzsche and Philosophy*, trans. H. Tomlinson, London: Athlone Press.
Deleuze, G. (1988), *Spinoza: Practical Philosophy*, trans. R. Hurley, San Francisco: City Lights Books.
Deleuze, G. (1992a), *Expressionism in Philosophy: Spinoza*, trans. M. Joughin, New York: Zone Books.

Deleuze, G. (1992b), *Cinema 1: The Movement-Image*, trans. H. Tomlinson and B. Habberjam, London: Athlone Press.
Deleuze, G. (1994), *Difference and Repetition*, trans. P. Patton, New York: Columbia University Press.
Deleuze, G. (1995), *Negotiations 1972–1990*, trans. M. Joughin, New York: Columbia University Press.
Deleuze, G. (1997), 'One Less Manifesto', in T. Murray (ed.), *Mimesis, Masochism, and Mime: The Politics of Theatricality in Contemporary French Thought*, Ann Arbor: University of Michigan Press.
Deleuze, G. (2004), *Desert Islands and Other Texts, 1953–1974*, trans. M. Taormina, New York: Semiotext(e).
Deleuze, G. (2006), 'Pericles and Verdi: The Philosophy of François Châtelet', trans. C. T. Wolfe, *The Opera Quarterly*, 21 (4): 713–24.
Deleuze, G. and F. Guattari (1984), *Anti-Oedipus*, trans. R. Hurley, M. Seem and H. R. Lane, London: Athlone Press.
Deleuze, G. and F. Guattari (1988), *A Thousand Plateaus*, trans. B. Massumi, London: Athlone Press.
Donzelot, J., (1998), 'The Promotion of the Social', *Economy and Society*, 17 (3): 395–427.
Ewald, F. (1991), 'Norms, Discipline, and the Law', in R. Post (ed.), *Law and the Order of Culture*, Berkeley: University of California Press.
Foucault, M. (2008), *The Birth of Biopolitics: Lectures at the Collège de France 1978–1979*, trans. G. Burchell, Basingstoke: Palgrave Macmillan.
Garland, D. (2001), *The Culture of Control*, Oxford: Oxford University Press.
Guerlac, S. (2006), *Thinking in Time: An Introduction to Henri Bergson*, Ithaca and London: Cornell University Press.
Lindhal, H. (2007), 'Constituent Power and Reflexive Identity: Towards an Ontology of Collective Selfhood', in M. Loughlin and N. Walker (eds), *The Paradox of Constitutionalism: Constituent Power and Constitutional Form*, Oxford: Oxford University Press.
Loughlin, M. and N. Walker (eds) (2007), *The Paradox of Constitutionalism: Constituent Power and Constitutional Form*, Oxford: Oxford University Press.
Lyon, D. (ed.) (2003), *Surveillance as Social Sorting: Privacy, Risk and Digital Discrimination*, London and New York: Routledge.
Mellor, M. (2010), *The Future of Money: From Financial Crisis to Public Resource*, London: Pluto Press.
Moore, N. (2007a), 'Icons of Control: Deleuze, Signs, and Law', *International Journal of Semiotics and Law*, 20 (1): 33–54.
Moore, N. (2007b), 'Nova Law: William S. Burroughs and the Logic of Control', *Law and Literature*, 19 (3): 435–70.
Rose, N. (1999), *Governing the Soul: The Shaping of the Private*, London and New York: Free Association Books.
Virilio, P. (1986), *Speed and Politics*, trans. M. Polizzotti, New York: Semiotext(e).
Virilio, P. (2000), *A Landscape of Events*, trans. J. Rose, Cambridge: MIT Press.

# Notes

1. For example, see Lindhal 2007. It is possible to have some sympathy with Lindhal's proposed solution to these double circles, inasmuch as he posits a collective selfhood that responds to problems as they occur, in the middle of things. However, the form of this response, encapsulated in the question 'Who are we?' (or even 'What are we?'), is untenable, depending as it does upon a 'we' that,

however tentatively, reflexively and problematically, nevertheless must first recognise itself as such in order to pose that question. This means that Lindhal himself remains in the circle of secularised theology.
2. It is interesting to note ambivalence between the two texts. In the earlier *Expressionism in Philosophy*, Deleuze is undecided as to whether there are two contracts or a single contract that doubles itself retroactively (Deleuze 1992a: 390, fn. 29). In the later *Practical Philosophy* he refers only to there being two contracts (Deleuze 1988: 108).
3. It is worth noting that the other and the excluded pose no threat or disruption to the second contract, but rather result from it.
4. See also Bottomley and Moore (forthcoming).
5. As Zygmunt Bauman's work shows (1998), globalisation should be understood as nothing more, nor less, than a complex set of processes for limiting liability. See also Donzelot's argument of how sovereign-juridical reasoning is displaced by insurance assessments.
6. See Donzelot 1998 and Ewald 1991 on the abstract nature of the norm.

Chapter 8

# Rhizomatics, the Becoming of Law, and Legal Institutions

*James MacLean*

## Defining the Problem: An Illustration

The story is told of a little girl in a West Highland village who, every week as she watched her mother preparing the Sunday roast, began to wonder why it was that her mother always prepared it in the same way. 'Mummy, Mummy', she asked, 'why is it that every week, when you prepare the Sunday roast, before you put it in the oven you first of all cut about an inch off the end of it?' 'Oh', replied her mother, 'that's the way you do it. That's how it's done! That's the way my mother did it and that's the way her mother did it before her. That's the way you do it. Every week, when you prepare the Sunday roast, before you put it in the oven you first of all cut about an inch off the end of it. That's just how it's done!' The little girl thought for a moment but didn't feel her question had really been answered. Not entirely satisfied with her mother's response, she decided she would go and ask Grandma. So, off she went to Grandma's house.

'Grandma', she enquired, 'can you tell me? I've asked Mummy but, to be honest, she was no help. Why is it that every week, when you prepare the Sunday roast, before you put it in the oven you first of all cut about an inch off the end of it?' 'Oh', replied Grandma, 'that's the way you do it. That's how it's done! That's how your mother does it, that's the way I do it, and that's the way my mother did it before me. That's how you do it. Every week, when you prepare the Sunday roast, before you put it in the oven you first of all cut about an inch off the end of it. That's just how it's done!' At this point the little girl felt like she was getting nowhere with her enquiry. Nonetheless, undeterred, she determined to make one last attempt to find an answer. She decided to go to ask Great-grandma. So, off she went to Great-grandma's house.

'Great-grandma', she asked, 'can you tell me? I've asked Mummy but she was no help. And I've asked Grandma but she was no better. Why is it that every week, when you prepare the Sunday roast, before you put it in the oven you first of all cut about an inch off the end of it?' 'Oh', replied Great-grandma, 'that's easy. I don't know why Mummy does it, and I don't know why Grandma does it, but I always did it because my oven was too small!'

I sympathise with that little girl and I recognise her frustrations . . .

## Locating the Problem in Law: Rules and Facts

Traditional understandings of law are, to a large extent, dualistic and rely on familiar dichotomies; for example, between thought and action, meaning and application, rule and fact. Central to this way of thinking about law is the dialectical relationship of correspondence between universals and particulars, in which the legal task is conceived in terms of negotiating the gap that opens up between two, essentially separate but connectable, domains. Here, legal reasoning becomes a matter of managing the flow of knowledge and securing the delivery of communications between these two points. An important challenge for theorists and decision makers alike, as they engage in this practice and reflect upon it, is that of maintaining the integrity of legal knowledge as it is 'transferred' from one domain to the other. That the judicial role in decision making is often understood in precisely this way is implicit in the descriptions of it offered by decision makers as they reflect on the enormity of their professional task. For example, Lord Justice Ward, giving judgment in *Re A (Children) (Conjoined Twins: Surgical Separation)* ([2000] 4 All ER 961), outlines the court's responsibilities thus:

> This court is a court of law, not of morals, and our task has been to find, and our duty is then to apply the relevant principles of law to the situation before us – a situation which is quite unique. (*Re A* at 968)

Similarly, Lord Wheatley, in the much earlier case of *MacLennan v MacLennan* ([1958] SLT 12), asserts that 'this problem which I am called upon to solve must be decided by the objective standard of legal principles as these have been developed . . . in the eyes of the law'. Likewise, Lord Mustil, in *R v Monopolies and Mergers Commission, ex parte South Yorkshire Transport* ([1993] 1 WLR 23), comments on how,

> once the criterion for a judgement has been properly understood, the fact that it was formerly part of a range of possible criteria from which it was difficult to choose and on which opinions might legitimately differ

becomes a matter of history. The judgement now proceeds unequivocally on the basis of the criterion as ascertained. (*R v Monopolies and Mergers Commission* at 32)

In this way, a justifying relationship between reason and decision is woven into the fabric of legal doctrine, which helps to close the gap and secure and seal the seamless web of law. In so-called 'easy' cases, where it seems that a judicial decision can be deduced unproblematically from a general rule and relevant facts, this appears relatively straightforward; indeed, it is often assumed that all that a judge has to do in order to justify a decision is merely to identify the rule that applies to the situation and outline the relevant facts of the case. But in 'hard' cases, where it might seem like the rules have 'run out' or where a judge must choose between competing rules or rival interpretations of a rule, and where any decision at all might well be controversial, a judge is expected to give written reasons and arguments to support her decision and to demonstrate how her choice of rule and its application are legally justified. It is here that deeper, more theoretical, questions about the nature of the justifying relationship between reason and decision begin to surface more clearly; in particular, concerning the criteria that will be used to evaluate the adequacy of the reasons and arguments used by the judge to defend her decision. Precisely because of this, a major part of the legal theoretical task in this area has been directed towards the development of a more refined understanding of the justifying relationship between rules and facts, universals and particulars.

Neil MacCormick stresses that for a judicial decision to be justified this must be done on specifically legal grounds as well as on general rational grounds. So, for example, he argues that what Ward LJ's ruling in *Re A* demonstrates conclusively is that this case must be understood in law as a 'type-case, as a universally stated situation' (MacCormick 2006: 16). The point is that, whatever the approach adopted, the decision must make clear exactly what it is that justifies it as a *legal* decision. Now, in the real world, 'particular reasons must always exist for particular decisions' but the central point here is 'the significance of the justifying relationship between reason and decision, and whether or not this involves the universalisability of grounds of decision' (MacCormick 2006: 3). It is 'an important aspect of the rule of law', argues MacCormick, 'that courts and judges take seriously the established rules of the institutional normative order' and, precisely because of this, the whole business of the justification of legal decisions will 'focus on a syllogistic element, showing what rule is being applied, and how' (MacCormick 2006: 5).

What this means is that for any reason to be a justifying reason it must indicate 'the generic nature of the act and the generic circumstances of the action' and, as soon as this is provided, 'an implicit principle – universal in terms – is revealed'. There can be 'no justification without universalisation. For particular facts ... to be *justifying reasons* they have to be subsumable under a relevant principle of action universally stated' (MacCormick 2006: 21).

Contrarily, Bernard Jackson (2009) argues that a major difficulty facing any approach such as MacCormick's attempt to articulate the significance of the justifying relationship in terms of the universalisability of grounds of decision is the unquestioning way in which it embraces an assumption about the essential calculability of law and the relative ease with which this then effects a separation between the analysis of law and the facts in order to construct the syllogism. Jackson points to what he describes as a conflict between the temporal aspect of the past tense in the minor premise that appears in the process of adjudication and the atemporality of the major premise enacted in legislation. This presents a problem; not least, in terms of the value we attach to the prospectivity of laws in terms of the Rule of Law. If a rule is enacted before the events to which it refers occur then adjudication becomes impossible (because a rule can refer only to those acts that precede it) and if a rule is enacted after the events to which it refers the result will be retrospective application of law: both situations amount to a denial of the Rule of Law. Clearly, the prospectivity of the Rule of Law and the atemporality of the deductive syllogism reveal an internal inconsistency that is problematic: the rule simply cannot cover the instant case. Jackson's response to this is to propose an alternative theory, based not on correspondence but on coherence. For him, because reality is always filtered through the frameworks that we impose on it, our only way of making sense of it is 'mediated through significatory systems'. Thus, for Jackson, the real point is that in decision making both premises are reduced to the level of 'narrative structures' and meaning is constructed through relations within systems of signification (Jackson 1991: 179). In this sense, what otherwise seemed like a striving in vain after the necessary correspondence to close the gap in the law–fact relation now gives way to a form of 'pattern matching'. On Jackson's account, law and fact are both reduced to the level of claims constructed within language: a fact is a truth-claim concerning an actual state of affairs in the real world; a law is a validity-claim with respect to the normative significance of a particular form of conduct or behaviour. But, in one sense at least, the difference might make little difference, for matching patterns might be seen as not dissimilar to seeking correspondence of an actual pattern with the master pattern; namely, that a particular account of 'facts', or story, corresponds with, or matches, the 'controlling' master pattern. In this sense, it may be claimed that coherence ultimately dissolves into correspondence.

In a variety of different ways, legal scholars sometimes mark a distinction between different contexts; for example, between the processes engaged with by a judge in the making of her decision (the 'context of discovery') and her later public demonstration of that decision as legally justified (the 'context of justification'); for example, MacCormick argues that the latter context serves to provide a test as to whether the procedures and outcomes of the former are legally justified. Here, the relevant question is whether a particular judicial decision, as presented, meets the requirements of rationality and objectivity demanded by the legal system.

Michael Detmold (2006) has further elaborated on the problems of particularity in adjudication, identifying two problems: the 'in-tray' and the 'out-tray'. The 'in-tray' is the matter of what it is that informs a decision, how it will be justified and the extent to which the informing thing is particular or universal; the 'out-tray' is the making of the decision and deciding to whom or to what it applies, the particular or the universal. All practical judgements are of the out-tray and are radically particular, because it is always a particular person and a particular history that form the basis of the law's judgment. According to Detmold (1989), there will always be particular situations, practical questions that universal reasoning simply cannot answer; indeed, part of the meaning of universality, the idea that a rule is always applied whenever the conditions of its application are met, furnishes us with this problem. Detmold points to a gap, between a rule and its application, which he calls the 'particularity void'. It is not so much that we cannot use a rule in deciding a case, more a recognition of the fact that rules are not self-applying: there is a difference between asking whether a rule is reasonable and whether it is reasonable to apply it. Effectively, this means that an assessment has to be made every time a decision is taken as to whether or not the conditions of its application are met. In other words, we cannot simply evade responsibility for our decisions by hiding behind the rules: the particularity void becomes the place where I must take responsibility for my decisions. For Detmold legal reasoning is practical in so far as it is 'reasoning towards a decision for or against action' and his primary concern is with a 'judge's practical reasoning towards the action of giving judgement' (Detmold 1989: 436), what he calls '[t]he particularity of adjudication'. To illustrate, he gives the example of someone striving to accede to 'judicial office' through examination:

> I am given a problem to solve consisting of facts A B and C. I work it out and conclude, the defendant must pay damages. My conclusion is universal: *a* defendant in circumstances A B and C must pay damages. But am I right? I check my reasoning and conclude I am right. I finish the exam, content. But being rather introspective, I go to my books after the exam to make sure. Yes . . . I am sure. I am now sure that I have the answer to the (universal) question: where A B C must the defendant pay damages? (Detmold 1989: 455)

But this answer is still not 'a practical answer', he argues, and it 'will become practical [only] when it becomes particular'. In due course I am appointed and my first case replicates the case of my exam. As I sit alone in my chambers contemplating judgement, why does my will not unleash itself? It is not that I doubt my conclusion: 'I remember my reasoning very clearly.' However, 'I now have a radically different problem', a problem that 'universal (hypothetical) reasoning does not solve'; indeed, 'no reasoning can solve it. It is particular.' It is something of which 'nothing can be said (anything I *say* will be universal)' (Detmold 1989: 455–6). In this sense, theorists who, like MacCormick, seek to find through 'the progressive refinement of the categories of law according to experience' a means by which to settle these issues are mistaken. On this basis, no matter how 'highly defined A B and C are . . . [the] problem [is] exactly the same . . . A judgement in respect of A B and C . . . cannot cross the void . . . [I]t can justify *a* judgement . . . a theoretical/hypothetical [one] . . . right up to the void. But the final rationality of practical judgement [always] seems in doubt' (Detmold 1989: 458). For Detmold, this 'act of justification is incapable of solving the problem for it immediately raises the question, why justify?; and the answer . . . will be ultimately particular, not universal; so it will have its own particularity void' (Detmold 1989: 459). On this view, the gap may be seen to have at least two aspects: first, in terms of the potential asymmetry between addressor and addressee; second, in terms of the void between determination and application. In general, judges only tend to make law conservatively, says Detmold, but 'the fullness of law as practical reason is achieved when the law that judges apply is law that has crossed the citizen subject void; when law is in a true sense the citizen's law, when law is common law' (Detmold 1989: 467).

We can develop this question concerning the bridging of the gap between facts and norms a little further by looking at 'discourse theory', which suggests that legal reasoning should be understood as a form of rational communication designed to achieve consensus through dialogue. Jürgen Habermas claims that the answer to the question of how a judgment is reached in respect of the issues arising for determination in a case can be realised through anticipating the response that participants in a democratic discourse would have made if they had considered these issues. What this means is that we conceive of a decision as having been achieved through a process of communication by hypothesising a temporal continuity between legislation and adjudication that operates retrospectively. Effectively, a relationship is constructed between two discourses – justification and application – such that the decisions arrived at in adjudication are already provided for in legislation. Habermas adopts and adapts the Kantian principle of universalisability to formulate the 'discourse principle' (Habermas 1996: 107), which 'assume[s] the shape of a principle of democracy ... by way of legal institutionalisation' (Habermas 1996: 121–2). Vis-à-vis Kant, a correspondence is communicatively achieved such that the addressor of the law becomes and is, really and simultaneously (not counterfactually), the addressee of the law. This provides law with its strongest possible basis for legitimacy: 'only those statutes may claim legitimacy that can meet with the assent of all citizens in a discursive process of legislation that in turn has been legally constituted' (Habermas 1996: 110). But the question still arises as to how any particular, determinate fact circumstance might be held to have been in the contemplation of those who agree upon any law so that an abstract legal norm can be understood to cover a particular, determinate fact? Klaus Günther argues that a 'perfect' norm must be understood to include, from its beginning, all the possible future instances of its application: a perfect norm is perfectly particular since, in each case, 'every particular situation can be anticipated by everyone' (Günther 1993: 33). Only in this way can participants in a discourse 'be certain that there will be no situation where observance of a norm will violate a universalised interest' (Günther 1989: 156). Günther suggests, and Habermas agrees, that a distinction must be drawn between these two types of discourse: justification and application. Thus, while novel and unexpected cases may arise that remain unaccounted for in the justification discourse, because they could not have been foreseen or otherwise included under norms that pick out only a limited series of typical fact circumstances, nonetheless, they can be accounted for within the application discourse: 'we apply a valid norm *as if* we could have foreseen this situation under the conditions of unlimited knowledge and time' (Günther 1989: 163, emphasis added).

In this sense, what discourse theory provides is a way of obtaining the full, universally agreed content of a norm from contemplation of the contingent, concrete fact circumstances of an individual case through positing the latter as always already included in the former. Everything hinges on this sense of 'appropriateness' that does all the work here to distinguish between and reconnect the two discourses and enable the construction of a coherent and consistent body of 'perfect norms'. In this way, for discourse theory, the gap between fact and norm is closed through the relatively straightforward application of a relevant norm whose essential content remains unaltered throughout the transitional process. The transfer of knowledge effected in this way is entire and complete, but it occurs only at the expense of ensuring that nothing significantly new enters the process of its communication from one pole to the other.

## Reconfiguring a Response: Bergson and Deleuze

In legal reasoning, as we have seen, commonly accepted understandings of the relationship between rule determination and rule application have given rise to a number of important questions; not least, that of how to 'bridge' properly the gap that opens up in decision making between fact and law. The difficulties involved in articulating the decision-making task in this way are well described in the literature, as are the various theories of practical judgment that have been employed to meet them, whether this is thought to be problematic (Detmold) or not (MacCormick, Habermas). One feature common of all of these 'solutions' is the view of legal knowledge as something to be passed on, expanded and applied to meet the practical requirements of daily life. Here, in the main, the central challenge facing decision makers is how to preserve the correspondence of law to fact, theory to practice, thereby confirming and maintaining the legal status quo. Put differently, the aim of the process is to facilitate the transition, or transmission, of legal norms from one point to another, from the locus of creation to their locus of application, without diminution, dissolution or corruption.

In a number of recent contributions to organisation studies, Martin Wood and others have sought to present a radical challenge to the idea that any adequate understanding of the dynamic of organisational change can ever be built on the basis of punctuated equilibria. Wood, employing a process metaphysics informed by the work of Henri Bergson and Gilles Deleuze, proposes the adoption of 'an alternative *becoming* ontology' and argues that our understanding of the production and use of knowledge must be reconceived as dynamic movements of enfolded meaning: 'the production-use relationship is . . . not one of integration between extrinsically distinct entities, but one of *internal difference* with a focus on differentiation and division' (Wood 2002: 157). In this sense, 'information and communication do not merely convey representational contents that bridge the various stages of an evolutionary process'; rather, they must be seen as 'contribut[ing] to the fabrication of new *assemblages* of movement, flows . . . and connections that cannot be simply located' (Wood 2002: 159). Here, Deleuze and Guattari's notion of 'creative involution' (Deleuze and Guattari 1988) helps to provide a way of expressing how the 'relaxation of natural, obvious and reified forms, and the creation . . . of heterogeneous combinations and novel alliances . . . cut across and beneath . . . assignable relations . . . and break out across closed thresholds and species' to form '"unnatural" combinations', with 'communications that cut across distinct lineages' and 'break out of fixed or stable determinations'. In this sense, 'its inventions do not exist in advance but involve rhizomic modes of becoming' (Wood 2002: 160).

Clearly, it is only on the basis of an assumption favouring the simple location of essentially separate, substantial and stable 'things' and their causal mechanisms that any correspondence theory of truth between linguistic terms and the external world of objects they are used to represent is possible. Without this assumption any correspondence theory of truth falls and, with it, the whole edifice of causal and explanatory types and relations upon which it is built. It is precisely this assumption that underlies, for example, the notion of the 'particularity void' as a troublesome gap between rule creation and rule application: the 'bridging' of this gap only makes sense on the basis of an assumption about the possibility of transferring knowledge between its abstracted ends. In other words, the 'gap' emerges only if we first of all focus on the abstracted 'ends' of the processes of creating, communicating and applying legal knowledge ahead of any analysis regarding the nature of such knowledge, and the problem with this is that it prevents us from seeing the degree to which rule creation and rule application, universals and particulars, legal categories and living experience, are not actually separate but, indeed, already and actually permeate each other, profiting from this interpenetrative difference.

Taking a cue from organisation studies and employing a process metaphysics informed by the work of Henri Bergson and Gilles Deleuze, I will argue that such an ontology of being involves a counterfeit movement. Terms like rule and fact, universal and particular, theory and practice are really only convenient labels, images extracted from heterogeneous continuity and movement that we exploit in order to describe and illustrate interpenetration in terms of side-by-side representation. Alternatively, I will argue that we ought not to say that rules as universals are applied to facts as particulars, neither should we talk of legal practitioners as somehow reflecting upon theory to justify their practice (contexts of 'justification' and 'discovery'), as if these were somehow essentially separate but connectable entities or activities. Taking the cue from Bergson and Deleuze, we should not say that law is a system of rules applied to facts or, indeed, any form of reflection on this. Our 'systems' of laws and our 'processes' of decision making are mere snapshots of reality, images that we have extracted from an otherwise continuously moving and changing flow, merely a reflection of our attempt to break into it, and to halt, hold and handle what we abstract, in an effort to make sense of its otherwise elusive, enigmatic and inexpressible quality. We can understand this as we realise that even our attempts to ground the act of giving justifying reasons for a legal decision in the particulars of the lived situation to which that decision refers is already something beyond the decision itself. Clearly, there is a flow of knowledge but, on Bergson's view, not in the sense of some derived relationship connecting discrete spatial positions. Rather, utilising Deleuze and Guattari's concept of the rhizome to illuminate the decision-making process can help us to see how the movement or spread of information in law is best described as a forever jumbling up of distinct phases, stages and patterns, a complex form of growth like that associated with the roots of certain plants.

Elizabeth Grosz (1993) identifies five features of Deleuzian 'rhizomatics' that are relevant for this way of thinking about legal knowledge. First, the rhizome involves a way of bringing together diverse elements. Second, those elements that are brought together are not usually thought of as belonging together: the rhizome is founded on heterogeneity. Third, the rhizome is not reducible to a series of points or individual parts: it is neither singular nor multiple. Fourth, the rhizome is liable to unspecified and ubiquitous fractures, tears and interruptions whilst always retaining its essential self-configuring composition. Fifth, it is never possible to trace the rhizome back to a principal root or source: it is nomadic (Deleuze and Guattari 1988: 380ff), forever traversing the landscape without encircling the land. In this way, rhizomes always appear in-between, without beginnings or ends, always permitting the continual participation of all points within each other; albeit, one point never becomes the other or achieves correspondence with it. Employing a Deleuzian metaphor of rhizomic communication, we can begin to see how the perception about the apparent stabilities of universals and particulars, rules and facts, might be exchanged for an awareness that, although we dwell in a world of continual change, the continuous processes of change are actually imperceptible to us.

Put differently, the relations between universals and particulars, contexts of discovery and contexts of justification, rule creation and rule application, are not simply connective but involve the becoming of law through a development that neither contains nor instantiates but is always a middle, an in-between. To be sure, to function properly law depends on explicitly formulated rules, but legal expertise and the law-specific distinctions that judges internalise in and through their socialisation in the institutional practice of judging is something that is learned within the context of this discursive practice. This is what forms the tacit dimension (Polanyi 1966), the unarticulated and inarticulable background that undergirds a judge's representation of her decisions. In this sense, judicial decision making derives essentially not from rules, and rules about rules, but from meanings that are shared collectively within a network of relations; that is, rhizomic systems of communication. This type of continual movement already permeates the practice of law, at all levels.

The proposal that law has always operated rhizomatically (MacLean 2011) might seem like a bitter pill to swallow, for it presents a challenge both to the dominant theories of law as institutional and also to the traditional understandings of law as a cumulative flow of information between the areas of production and use. Law, as commonly observed, functions as a hierarchical institution, with normative procedures organising and shaping all its constituent parts: formal and substantive rules, rules of evidence and procedure, requirements of coherence and consistency, customs and practices, principles and values, are all carefully arranged from the top down. Against this institutional background, legal professionals strive to find the best possible fit, and to bridge the gap, between rules to facts, always under the supervision and direction of peers and contemporaries whose power is exercised through the procedural techniques of precedent, *ratio decidendi*, *stare decisis*, and so on. The more impressive an individual judge's justification of her decisions, the greater the impact and the more authority her reputation acquires. But, abstracted from this institutional structuring and ordering of decisions, or looked at in isolation, a particular judge's decisions will reveal very little. The full appreciation of law as an institution demands a correct understanding of its hierarchical arrangement and ordering of decisions.

Inevitably, though, decision making takes place in real time and is constrained by lack of resources and evaluative (rules of evidence, burdens of proof) and subjective (peer scrutiny and public acceptability of decision) elements that provide continual sources of frustration. Therefore, in the real world of decision making judges tend to cut their suits 'according to their cloth'. So much so that, as such frustrations appear, over and again we find that a decision is 'justified' where the facts and the rules do not overlap but where, nonetheless, public opinion or social mores have moved on so far that the reasons advanced are deemed sufficient for believing that the decision is acceptable because it is in line with modern understanding, even if it cannot be justified purely on legal grounds. What this means is that a large part of the judicial task in decision making involves developing new lines of precedent that cut across recognised borders, reasoning beyond accepted, and sometimes acceptable, boundaries. Is a new decision a new line of thought or a development of an old one? Rule creation and rule application, theory and practice, universals and particulars are perhaps not always as far removed from each other as they are often thought to be:

> There is always a host of new ideas galloping around the outskirts of a society's thought. All of them seek admission but each must first win its spurs; the law at first resists, but will submit to a conqueror and become his servant. In a changing society (and free societies that are composed of two or more generations are always changing because it is in their nature to do so) the law acts as a valve. New policies must gather strength before they can force an entry; when they are admitted and absorbed into the consensus, the legal system should expand to hold them, as also it should contract to squeeze out old policies which have lost the consensus they once obtained. (Devlin 1979: 1)

We can begin to observe the possibility of presenting a challenge to traditional understandings of law by revisiting Edward Levi's (1948) study of judicial decision making. According to Levi, it is nothing more than pretence to assert that 'the law is a system of known rules applied by a judge'; rather, 'the basic pattern of legal reasoning is by example. It is reasoning from case to case.' Levi demonstrates how this pattern progresses by means of a 'three-step process', whereby 'a proposition descriptive of the first case is made into a rule of law and then applied to a next similar situation' (Levi 1948: 501). In truth, then, the type of reasoning that actually occurs in the legal process is one in which 'the classification changes as the classification is made'; in other words, '[t]he rules change as the rules are applied'. That is, 'the rules arise out of a process which, while comparing fact situations, creates the rules and then applies them' (Levi 1948: 503). And yet, although 'it cannot be said that the legal process is the application of known rules to diverse facts', nonetheless 'it is a system of rules; the rules are discovered in the process of determining similarity or difference', and 'the existence of some facts in common brings into play the general rule' even though 'no such fixed prior rule exists'. Furthermore, 'there is an additional requirement which compels the legal process to be this way . . . The categories used . . . must be left ambiguous in order to permit the infusion of new ideas.' In precisely this way, these 'laws come to express the ideas of the community . . . molded for the specific case' (Levi 1948: 502–3). Crucially, this method of reasoning discloses 'characteristics which under other circumstances might be considered imperfections', in particular, it affirms that 'change in the rules is the indispensable dynamic quality of law' (Levi 1948: 502).

To press this home, Levi outlines the development of danger as a legal category, describing how, as it progresses, ideas and definitions appear to flow in and out of the legal system. First, a distinction is drawn, observed (but not articulated), and then refined. Afterwards, in a later case, the distinction finally achieves code value within the system. As Sean Smith (1995) observes, Levi reveals that

> patent dangers are illegal: they give rise to liability. Latent dangers are legal: they give rise to no liability. The one distinction is superimposed on the other . . . the distinction between patent and latent re-enters the legal system. It now has orientation value [and] can be used to guide further operations of the system. (Smith 1995: 195)

However, although the concept is now 'treated as fixed and unchanging . . . the context or precise nature of the distinction is constantly shifting'. Smith notes how Levi teaches us how to see what is really going on by encouraging us to 'reconstruct the history of these cases'. In this way, we find that 'the "authority" is Dixon. The "development" is Winterbottom' and 'the Longmeid case . . . represents the re-entry of the distinction between patent and latent dangers in the legal system'. Then, in the following phase, the distinction 'becomes condensed and confirmed . . . Not only are different cases treated as identical, but the same distinction gains in authority from its repeated application in . . . new contexts and acquires additional meaning.' Eventually, 'even the confirmations . . . get condensed', the distinction is 'turned . . . into a contradiction', and there is 'a crossing of the code values themselves'. Or, more simply, what was once the exception has now become the rule (Smith 1995: 195–6).

Levi claims that it is the process going on here to which we must pay particular attention. The important thing is the mechanism of transformation. We see the law as both certain and uncertain, changing and unchanging: 'the law forum is the most explicit demonstration of the mechanism required for a moving classification system' based on 'the presentation of competing examples' (Levi 1948: 503–4). Therefore, while it may indeed be true to say that, 'in case law, when a judge determines what the controlling similarity between the present and prior case is, the case is decided', nonetheless, it is with 'a set of . . . satellite concepts that reasoning by example must work'. Moreover, 'no satellite concept, no matter how well developed, can prevent the court from shifting its course, not only by realigning cases, but by going beyond realignment back to the overall ambiguous category written into the document'. In other words, what we have is a procedure that 'permits the court to be inconsistent' (Levi 1948: 505–6).

What we observe here is a continuous 'movement of concepts into and out of the law'. It begins with recognition of similarities and differences, out of which there emerges a word or a phrase that, once recognised, 'becomes a legal concept'. But such a concept is unstable because its meaning is always subject to change as it is continually brought out for comparison, 'not only between the instances which have been included under it and the actual case at hand, but also in terms of hypothetical instances which the word by itself suggests'. At this point, reasoning might 'appear to be simply deductive', says Levi, but in fact it is a 'circular motion' that is to be observed, as concepts are built up and fixed before finally breaking down once more. Then, during breakdown, there is an inevitable 'attempt to escape to some overall rule which can be said to have always operated and which will make the reasoning look deductive'. But this identification of the rule can be very misleading:

> Particularly when a concept has broken down and reasoning by example is about to build another, textbook writers, well aware of the unreal aspect of old rules, will announce new ones, equally ambiguous and meaningless, forgetting that the legal process does not work with the rule but on a much lower level. (Levi 1948: 506–7)

For Levi, this attempt to 'soar above the cases and find some great overall rule which can classify the cases as though the pattern were not really a changing one' (Levi 1948: 510) is 'mere window-dressing' (Levi 1948: 507). Throughout this analysis and his exposure of these 'lower level' operations of the Common Law, Levi strives continually to stress the contingent character of change. As Smith observes, what we see is a legal system that 'fumbles its way in an environment which is in principle inaccessible to it and can only be reconstructed using its own categories, its own distinctions' (Smith 1995: 192). Here, with the construction of trends and patterns, as cases are ruled in and out as authority, history is effectively rewritten. 'This is redundancy', says Smith. It is 'the attempt to reduce the element of surprise in the system . . . to convince that a particular decision is compelled by the history of the system' (Smith 1995: 197). What Levi shows us, concludes Smith, is that 'legitimation does not come through legal reasoning but through the legal process. It is law as system . . . that legitimises itself.' And what this suggests is that

> there is no simple exchange of ideas between law and its environment. Any idea has to be read together with the past and the future decisions of the system which gives it is legal sense . . . What is important is not so much the substantive values of the ideas themselves, but the institution of a procedure of revisability . . . a procedure [that] provides the forum for the making and the unmaking of ideas . . . (Smith 1995: 203)

## Rhizomatics, the Becoming of Law, and Legal Institutions

Revisiting Levi's analysis, we can see how the actual experience of decision making better resembles a Deleuzian rhizomic web than a hierarchically ordered structure of linear progression. The natural tendency is to resist systematisation and to spread out, not top-down but bottom-up, extending, integrating and incorporating in every direction, gathering together elements not normally considered as belonging together. In the same way, just as a rhizome does not appear to have any identifiable starting point, so, according to Levi, concepts, definitions and lines of reasoning seem to move freely across the judicial landscape without identifiable start or end points. And perhaps this helps to provide us with a way of understanding the often paradoxical nature of the judicial task, how it seems that so much of a judge's work in decision making actually involves introducing and developing lines of thought that cut across recognised boundaries, and how, in constructing their opinions, judges can be seen to use deliberate engagement strategies to achieve this. For example, a point of view is expressed that does not contribute to the overall ratio of the case but which is nonetheless intended to set out an alternative strategy. While it might not impact on the case at hand in any significant way it may nonetheless be picked up later in support of a future decision. In this way, although it does not have the force of a ratio in terms of the doctrine of precedent, it is accorded informally and assumed unofficially to have some credible force simply by way of the reputation of the judge, and, by extension, the status of the court in which it was delivered. Thus, for example, on 28 October 1931, six weeks before legal argument began in *Donoghue v Stevenson* ([1932] AC 562), Lord Atkin delivered a lecture at King's College, London, on the subject of 'Law as an Educational Subject'. Here, he declared:

> It is quite true that law and morality do not cover identical fields. No doubt morality extends beyond the more limited range in which you can lay down the definite prohibitions of law; but, apart from that, the British law has always necessarily ingrained in it moral teaching in this sense: that it lays down standards of honesty and plain dealing between man and man . . . He is not to injure his neighbour by acts of negligence; and that certainly covers a very large field of the law. I doubt whether the whole of the law of tort could not be comprised in the golden maxim to do unto your neighbour as you would that he should do unto you. (Atkin 1932: 30)

Four months later, on 22 January 1932, he delivered his opinion in *Fardon v Harcourt-Rivington* ([1932] All ER Rep 81), drawing attention to 'the ordinary duty of a person to take care either that his animal or his chattel is not put to such a use as is likely to injure his neighbour – the ordinary duty to take care in the cases put upon negligence' ([1932] All ER Rep 81 at 83). Another four months after this, on 26 May 1932, Lord Atkin rose in the House of Lords to deliver his immortal speech in *Donoghue v Stevenson*, introducing the 'neighbour principle' into British law.

The process of judicial decision making as a whole is perhaps more accurately described under the metaphor of the rhizome. It is simply not possible to reduce the organisation of legal knowledge to a single source. Just like the analogue of the rhizome, it appears as an assemblage of incongruent parts, irreducible to any ordered sequencing of its parts but, instead, always 'a no man's land, a non-localisable relation sweeping up the two distant or contiguous points, carrying one into the proximity of the other' (Deleuze and Guattari 1988: 293). Always creating, combining and integrating, inherently vulnerable to irruption, disruption or interruption, always without fatally undermining its continuing capacity for self-organisation. Under traditional models, legal reasoning is understood in terms of the connecting of two or more separate points, facts and law. Yet, as Bergson states, and as Levi has shown, we *cannot* say that legal knowledge progresses along any pre-arranged pathway. Rather, there is a continuity of becoming from rules to decision, which is realised through engagement with particular, local fact situations. Why? Because reasons need to be accessible and meaningful for law's audience, its end users. The development of law and legal change does not occur in abstraction, but in and through the real world where men and women live and work: rule and fact, universal and particular, 'melt into and permeate one another, without precise outlines' (Bergson 1911: 104).

So, perhaps we need to reassess our fidelity to the logic of institutionalisation that segments legal knowledge into separate stages. There is a good argument to be made for an account of law and legal decision making that cuts across our often arbitrary divisions and focuses more on their immanent relations. Because while it is true that we do often act and think as if we owned a storeroom of convenient and clearly defined legal rules pending application and implementation, nonetheless, as we have seen, the demarcation of legal knowledge is not always as obvious as it would appear.

# References

Atkin, Lord (1932), 'Law as an Educational Subject', *Journal of the Society of Public Teachers of the Law*, 27 (also in G. Lewis, *Lord Atkin*, London: Butterworths, 1983).
Bergson, H. (1911), *Creative Evolution*, trans. A. Mitchell, London: Macmillan.
Deleuze, G. and F. Guattari (1988), *A Thousand Plateaus: Capitalism and Schizophrenia*, trans. B. Massumi, London: Athlone Press.
Detmold, M. J. (1989), 'Law as Practical Reason', *Cambridge Law Journal*, 48: 436–71.
Detmold, M. J. (2006), 'The End of Morality: Radical and Descriptive Particularity', in Z. Bańkowski and J. MacLean (eds), *The Universal and the Particular in Legal Reasoning*, Aldershot: Ashgate.
Devlin, P. (1979), *The Judge*, Oxford: Oxford University Press.
Grosz, E. (1994), 'A Thousand Tiny Sexes: Feminism and Rhizomatics', in C. V. Boundas and D. Olkowski (eds), *Gilles Deleuze and the Theater of Philosophy*, London: Routledge.
Günther K. (1989), 'A Normative Conception of Coherence for a Discourse Theory of Legal Justification', *Ratio Juris*, 2 (2): 155–66.
Günther, K. (1993), *The Sense of Appropriateness*, trans. J. Farrell, Albany, NY: SUNY Press.
Habermas J. (1996), *Between Facts and Norms: Contributions to a Discourse Theory of Law and Democracy*, trans. W. Rehg, Cambridge, MA: MIT Press.
Jackson, B. (1991), 'Semiotic Scepticism: A Response to Neil MacCormick', *International Journal for the Semiotics of Law*, IV (11): 175–90.
Jackson, B. (2009), 'Structuralist Semiotics of Law', <http://ivr-enc.info/index.php?title=Structuralist_Semiotics_of_Law> (accessed 6 Feb 2012).
Levi, E. H. (1948), 'An Introduction to Legal Reasoning', *The University of Chicago Law Review*, 15 (3): 501–74.
MacCormick, D. N. (1978), *Legal Reasoning and Legal Theory*, Oxford: Clarendon Press.
MacCormick, D. N. (2006), 'Particulars and Universals', in Z. Bańkowski and J. MacLean (eds), *The Universal and the Particular in Legal Reasoning*, Aldershot: Ashgate.

MacLean, J. B. (2011), *Rethinking Law as Process: Creativity, Novelty, Change*, Abingdon: Routledge.
Polanyi, M. (1966), *The Tacit Dimension*, London: Routledge and Kegan Paul.
Smith, S. C. (1995), 'The Redundancy of Reasoning', in Z. Bańkowski (ed.), *Informatics and the Foundations of Legal Reasoning*, Dordrecht: Kluwer.
Wood, M. (2002), '"Mind the Gap?" A Processual Reconsideration of Organizational Knowledge', *Organization*, 9 (1): 151–71.
Wood, M. (2003), 'Journeying from Hippocrates with Bergson and Deleuze', in *Organization Studies*, 24 (1): 47–68.

# Chapter 9
# Deleuze and Camus: Strange Encounters

*Lissa Lincoln*

> The primacy of writing signifies only one thing: not a form of literature alone, the enunciation forms a unity with desire, beyond laws, states, regimes. Yet the enunciation is always historical, political and social. A micropolitics of desire that questions all situations. (Deleuze and Guattari 1986: 41)

## Deleuze and Camus

'Why Deleuze and Law?' Thus opens Alexandre Lefebvre's work on *The Image of Law*. Why indeed? After all, as Lefebvre reminds us, 'few philosophers have so systematically criticized and rejected the concepts of law and judgment as Deleuze has' (Lefebvre 2008: xi), and since there is certainly no shortage of articles – whether or not explicitly from a Deleuzian perspective – criticising and rejecting the concepts of law and judgment, adding to the collection is perhaps not the most pressing of tasks for Deleuze scholarship. Why deepen the pile? More curious yet, perhaps, is an article on Deleuze and Camus. Or, in a word, 'Why Deleuze and Camus?' For – it has to be said – despite the philosopher's obvious and well-known interest in literature, Albert Camus was decidedly not one of the writers that interested Gilles Deleuze. One of the reasons for this is no doubt the fact that Camus represented the reprehensible sort of humanism that Michel Foucault held in such contempt: 'the little prostitute of all thought, of all culture, of all morality and of all politics for the last 20 years'.[1] In the case of Deleuze, this was also the reflection of the way in which philosophers in general,[2] and Sartreans in particular,[3] perceive Camus' work – and let's not forget that Deleuze was himself at first a Sartrean:

> In those days, who except Sartre knew how to say anything new? Who taught us new ways to think? As brilliant and profound as the work of

Merleau-Ponty was, it was professorial and depended in many respects on Sartre's work. (Sartre readily likened the existence of human beings to the non-being of a 'hole' in the world: little lakes of nothingness, he called them. But Merleau-Ponty took them to be folds, simple folds and pleats. In this way, one can distinguish a tough, penetrating existentialism from a more tender and reserved existentialism.) As for Camus – alas! Either it was inflated heroism, or it was second-hand absurdity; Camus claimed descent from a line of cursed thinkers, but his whole philosophy just led us back to Lalande and Meyerson, writers well-known to any undergraduate. (Deleuze 2004: 76)

On a broader scale, Camus' work is habitually associated with a very specific or, more precisely, very moral conception of literature. Generally speaking, this perspective can be divided into two categories. On the one hand, we have the positive image of Camus the literary genius whose creative work brilliantly reflects the rigorous (moral) philosophical system laid out in his theoretical thought, the latter being expressed, for the most part, through his nonfiction writing (namely, *The Myth of Sisyphus* and *The Rebel*). This viewpoint is usually associated with the image of Camus the eminent (as opposed to soft!) humanist. On the other, he is seen as a very unoriginal or even weak thinker philosophically speaking, whose theoretical writings lack both intellectual rigour and integrity; at best a hasty and less than accurate revision of Nietzsche, and at worst a dangerous strain of the armchair humanism evoked by Foucault above. This viewpoint, while still generally according the status of brilliance to Camus' literary work, sees within it a subjacent drive to promote the philosophical ideas, or 'theses', conveyed in the author's non-literary essays. In both cases his work is reduced, on a theoretical level, to series of *romans à thèses*.

Indeed, it would seem Camus was a representative of a kind of literature that might appear to be in direct opposition to Deleuze's literary tastes, or at the very least one that he considered outdated – a literature centred on subjects in opposition and the torments of decision; a kind of obsolescent existentialist writing, with its 'characters' and 'dramatic circumstances'. In short, a literature based on 'the idea of the tragic, of the internal drama, of the intimate tribunal, and so on' (Deleuze and Guattari 1986: 45).[4] Associated as it is with existentialist '*roman à thèses*' Camus' work would seem to be the direct antithesis of what interested Deleuze in literature. The paradigm of 'major' (representational) literature, it incarnated as such one of these literary styles, genres or movements that 'have only one single dream: to assume a major function in language, to offer themselves as a sort of state language', that he opposes to minor literature, one which 'create[s] the opposite dream: know[ing] how to create a becoming-minor' (Deleuze and Guattari 1986: 27). Deleuze's interest in literature lay in the direction of writing that proposed an alternative to the concept of the self-conscious subject as a pivoting point for the coordination/organisation of experience; one that expressed a non-anthropocentric or anti-humanist point of view. A view point which 'corresponds not only to a "logic of sense" but also to Deleuze's own conceptions of time, life and destiny in which the time of an individual life is not seen as a linear, progressive sequence, but as a structure of repetition and variation' (Due 2007: 58). At the same time he did not see a literature based on positivism (i.e. one based on a scientific explanatory model, that would reduce experience, knowledge, culture and so on, to 'underlying material causes') as a viable alternative to the subjective point of view, since subjectivity and positivism were, in his eyes, just two sides of the same (representational) coin. As such, Deleuze's interest lies in a form of literature that functions as what Reidar Due has called a 'double attack' on these two levels of representation: 'the subject [as] the self-conscious centre of representation; and positivism [as] the view that reality can be represented as a totality of so-called facts' (Due 2007: 59).

To sum up, it is difficult to imagine an author further removed from the philosophical ideas and literary tastes of Gilles Deleuze than Albert Camus.

However (and at the same time), it is important to remember that Camus was *also* (and contrary to Sartre) one of the forerunners of the New Literature. He was held in the highest esteem by some of the most innovative thinkers of his time, notably Blanchot,[5] who is quoted extensively throughout Deleuze's work and by whom, it is well known, both Deleuze and Foucault were tremendously influenced.[6] Admittedly, and, in the eyes of the intellectual elite, problematically, Camus was not a representative of the political *avant garde* of the 1950s – especially as this was the period of the Nobel Prize and the Algerian War. But in many respects, this position of indecision and 'non-critique' is much closer to Blanchot and Deleuze's style than that of a Sartre. Undeniably, the literature of Camus is not that of Sartrean commitment. But this is not, as is generally thought, due to an incapacity in Camus to think through thoroughly and live without contradiction his so-called 'moralism'. It is, rather, because Camus' was a different project entirely – a project, I will argue, of a dismantling of power. What is particularly interesting, as we will see, is the fact that this dismantling is done from within a machine of power itself – the 'literary machine, an assemblage of enunciation or expression' (Deleuze and Guattari 1986: 88). Camus' literature, I would suggest, *mimics* the project of 'assuming a major function in language' and of offering itself 'as a sort of state language', but, precisely, it is not. If he resembles a 'totalising intellectual', let's not forget that Camus is not Sartre. He did not want to be labelled as an existentialist. He did not call for a 'new humanism'.

But the proximity between the two thinkers is in fact much greater than this. In his relation with literature, Deleuze gives tremendous importance to the framework of law. Questions of judgment and the juridical permeate the pages of his oeuvre.[7] However, and perhaps curiously, although there is much questioning around Deleuze and law, it would seem that there is considerably less interest aroused by the fact that the majority of his philosophy of law lies *within* his philosophy of literature.[8] Likewise, there has been enormous interest generated around the ideas of law and judgment in Camus, but very little attention paid to the *use* of them in his writing. To put it in more Deleuzian terms, critics show a keen interest in the *themes* of law and judgment in Camus, but have neglected the only thing that can make such an interest pertinent, namely their *function*.[9] The intent of this chapter, then, is to probe this proximity – the thematic *function* of law (and not its *sense*) in literature for both Camus and Deleuze.

In a passage that uncannily echoes conventional interpretations of Camus' chef d'oeuvre *The Fall* Deleuze asks: 'Can we conclude that not being a critic of his time Kafka turned his criticism "against himself" and had no other tribunal than an "internal tribunal"?' Deleuze pinpoints the insufficiency of this approach, one which blinds us to the real goal of the author's non-critique:

> This would be grotesque, since it would turn criticism into a dimension of representation. If representation is not external, it can be only internal from here on. But it's really something else in Kafka: Kafka attempts to extract from social representations assemblages of enunciation and machinic assemblages and to dismantle these assemblages ... Kafka was drawing lines of escape; but he didn't 'flee the world'. Rather it was the world and its representations that he made take flight and that he made follow these lines. ... in the novels, the dismantling of the assemblages makes the social representation take flight in a much more effective way than a critique would have done and brings about a deterritorialization of the world that is itself political and that has nothing to do with an activity of intimacy. (Deleuze and Guattari 1986: 46–7)[10]

Thus, far from providing a means for its author to 'flee the world' Deleuze sees in Kafka's literature – by virtue of its very refusal of (representational) criticism – a much more radical approach to both creation and critique. I will argue that for Camus, like for Kafka, 'it's really something else' than representational literature, and that it is this 'something else' that perplexed critics, causing them to underestimate his thought.

Interestingly, Camus was criticised in intellectual circles for very similar reasons to those underlying the Communists' opposition to Kafka; that is, the absence of any (sufficiently consistent/constant) voice of social criticism. Indeed, it was this very absence that provoked Camus' highly publicised rupture with Sartre,[11] despite the fact that Camus' work is still widely associated with committed existentialist literature. However, the goal of Camus' 'non-critique', was not to 'flee the world', any more than it was for Kafka. In fact, and despite the apparently opposed visions of Deleuze and Camus, what emerges when we consider their work outside of the philosophical categories and presuppositions that are normally superimposed on the latter (that is, looked at from a literary perspective), is that Camus is not so far removed from Deleuze. For both, literature is a question of dismantling, and not representing (whether positively or negatively) mechanisms of power and their transcendental justifications (Deleuze and Guattari 1986: 51).

## Camus and the Abstract Machine

Camus was highly suspicious of the discourses of justification that are traditionally used to explain (and justify) existence. Indeed, he saw this determination to justify oneself in all of one's actions as being that which distinguishes modern man from his predecessors. Our criminals are no longer helpless children who could plead love as their excuse. On the contrary, they are adults and they have a perfect alibi: philosophy, which can be used for any purpose – even for transforming murderers into judges. Heathcliff, in *Wuthering Heights*, would kill everybody on earth in order to possess Cathy, but it would never occur to him to say that murder is reasonable or theoretically defensible. He would commit it, and there his convictions end. This implies the power of love, and also strength of character. Since intense love is rare, murder remains an exception and preserves its aspect of infraction. But as soon as a man, through lack of character, takes refuge in doctrine, as soon as crime reasons about itself, it multiplies like reason itself and assumes all the aspects of the syllogism. Once crime was as solitary as a cry of protest; now it is as universal as science. Yesterday it was put on trial; today it determines the law (Camus 1991: 6).

Hence, whether it be in his literary works or in his philosophical essays, the author's project was 'to face the reality of the present, which is logical crime, and to examine meticulously the arguments by which it is justified' (Camus 1991: 6).

A rapid glance at his oeuvre shows that one theme predominates: it is neither the Absurd, nor Revolt but the question of justice, or rather how what is just is determined in a given situation. One has simply to evoke a few of Camus' major works to highlight his preoccupation with this problematic: *The Outsider*, in which the intrigue centres around a murder and the almost burlesque trial of the taciturn misfit who committed it, incapable of defending himself against a justice system founded upon the primacy of self-justification; or *The Plague*, where an entire population finds itself under the yoke of an invading enemy whose assault is as unjust as it is merciless, bringing to the forefront the question of the death of the innocent; or, again, *Caligula*, which describes a universe of terror in which absolute power reigns, founded on a monstrously logical conception of justice. One work in particular indicates with exceptional clarity the very specific interest Camus has in this question, Camus' chef d'oeuvre, *The Fall*. Almost all of the aspects usually associated with the theme of law seem to converge here: its central concern is the problem of judgment as revealed at the crossroads of confession and guilt; the exquisitely rhetorical monologue of its sole character, an ex-lawyer become 'judge penitent', is the exemplification of both an inquisition and artful self-defence.

What renders Camus' suspicion of these discourses of justification particularly interesting is that he was well aware of the fact that literature itself is, of course, a justificatory discourse, and as such not incapable of justifying (as well as committing) its own 'logical crimes'. What was Camus' reaction faced with such a paradox? How to examine the justifications of logical crime, when one's tool of analysis (language and thus rhetoric) is haunted by and indeed dependent on logic itself?

French political philosopher Emmanuel Renault, in his book entitled *L'Experience de l'injustice*, talks about the particular power with which poetry can destabilise discourses of justification, due to its capacity to observe the world through a language of description rather than judging it through a language of prescription: 'The destabilization of the modes of justification of the social order is precisely what [the poet] attempts to do. Not to denounce nor to demystify but to subvert from the bottom up through a cancellation of the established logical forms' (Renault 2004). What Renault is suggesting is that poetry is possibly a more effective model for social change than the more theoretical discourses typically associated with it, because, rather than engaging with its object through a discourse of prescription (and hence via a language of judgment) as theoretical discourses do, the poet engages with his object through observation via a language of description. The poet, then, by his very relation to language, deliberately distances himself from the ever present danger of any theoretical approach – that of falling into judgment and consequently collaboration with and/or perpetuation of the very social orders they are looking to challenge. It is precisely here that the work of Camus finds its power and its capacity to destabilise; that is, in his refusal of judgment.

This may seem paradoxical given the proliferation of the theme of justice in Camus, for how can justice be separated from judgment? It is here that Deleuze's warning about 'themes' finds its place. For it is true that Camus has a great need for the themes of justice, but only in the sense of 'the superficial movement of his work'. And Deleuze reminds us that here,

> superficial movement doesn't mean a mask underneath which something else would be hidden. The superficial movement indicates points of undoing, of dismantling, that must guide the experimentation to show the molecular movements and the machinic assemblages of which the superficial movement is a global result. (Deleuze and Guattari 1986: 45)

What then is Camus' particular interest in justice? Or, rather, what is this theme's function in his work?

More than the simple defence of one notion (i.e. justice) with regards to another, opposite notion (which would then be injustice), or an attempt to justify his ideas about what is just (and, in consequence, what is not), Camus' interest appears to stem from a much more nuanced objective. He is, in fact, interested not so much in transmitting (whether through promotion or denunciation) an idea/ideal of justice but rather in questioning how it is we come to decide *what is just* in a given situation (not, to use a paradigmatic example, whether Meursault, the central character of *The Outsider*, is guilty or innocent of killing an Arab on the beach, but rather how his innocence or guilt is decided). Looked at from this angle, Camus' interest would seem to be less related to a paradoxical desire to *judge* different aspects of justice, than to understand the mechanisms upon which any system of judgment depends. Camus would not, then, seem to be looking to convince the reader that a given system of justice is right or wrong, good or bad, moral or immoral. Nor does his interest lie in unmasking a hidden underside to universal justice *per se*. He is looking, rather, to examine and to describe the *function* of the different strategies of power which are inherent to all systems of judgment and, consequently, to all prescriptive or, in its largest sense, legal discourses (discourses that prescribe and/or legislate laws, rules and codes of conduct in domains that exceed and indeed subsume the purely juridical). Thus the theme of law, both in its strict and in its broader sense, permits Camus to indicate the points of unravelling, of undoing in these discourses – allowing him to trace the minute movements of judgment of which justice is simply a result. In this sense, for Camus, justice as a 'universal value' doesn't exist. It is, rather, what Deleuze calls an 'abstract machine'.

Camus' dismantling of this machine takes its form in the numerous figures through which he undertakes an interrogation of 'discourses of judgment', the most vertiginous of which being that of Clamence, our judge-penitent of *The Fall*. In this novel we have a particularly enlightening example of the machinations of judgment, because Clamence incites the reader to insert himself in the question of judgment and succeeds in ensnaring him in its nets. Thus, not only does the text illustrate the problem of judgment for the reader; it subjects him to it directly.

Despite a growing resistance to Clamence's discourse, who proves himself increasingly less reliable as a narrator as the story progresses, the reader persists in following him, spurred on by his hope of being led to the 'real' or 'true' perspective that would allow him to interpret objectively everything that he is being told. However, what he discovers at the end of the story is that this longed-for perspective simply does not exist. There is no 'true' or 'false' existing outside of Clamence's discourse, that would allow the reader to judge it 'objectively', for it is Clamence's discourse itself which creates these impressions within the reader, according to the interpretation that the narrator wishes to produce. And in the case of Clamence, it is a discourse with a very clear goal: to make the reader guilty in order to make himself innocent. In the end, Clamence's 'solution' for escaping judgment consists, finally, of establishing himself as the supreme judge by means of first fabricating a sense of guilt in, then extracting a confession from, his interlocutor.

We begin to see, then, how this work indicates the particularity of Camus' interest in the mechanics that support the system of judgment. He has no interest in convincing the reader that Clamence is in the right or in the wrong, that he's good or bad, moral or immoral, guilty or innocent. Rather, he is interested in tracing, examining and describing the functioning of different strategies of power.

Where Clamence possesses total power in his interlocutor's conception of reality, the author, indeed any author, has this same role with regards to his readers. Likewise, on a larger scale, whoever holds the dominant discourse (the narrator in the register of the story, the author in the register of literature, the judge in the register of law, etc.) will always be the one who creates 'truth' through the imposition of his interpretation of reality in order to assure the reinforcement and perpetuation of his own value system. Hence, the possibility of justifying a prescriptive (whether judicial or literary) discourse is shaken in its foundations. Once truth is revealed to be nothing but a construction which serves to perpetuate a value system, there is no longer any point in justifying it, nor, for that matter, in condemning it. What becomes important to observe is how the system works ('How it works is the sole question' [Deleuze and Guattari 1977: 180]). In this sense, rather than appearing to be a text of cynical moralism, *The Fall* becomes a sort of instruction manual.

We encounter this same configuration in what is possibly one of Camus' most disturbing pieces, the short story *The Renegade*. It also provides us with one of the most vivid examples of how the author uses law – this time in its broader, moral sense, through the theme of religion[12] – to indicate points of unravelling and dismantling of discourses of judgment.

Indeed the discourse of judgment appears here to be 'subverted from the bottom up' from the onset, reduced to a delirious diatribe of revenge. The sole character, the renegade himself – a heretic Catholic missionary, imprisoned and tortured by the population he set out to convert – recounts his trajectory to himself in a state of utter delirium, a delirium into which the reader is plunged from the opening words of the monologue. In his efforts to reinterpret the events that led to his current demise, he presents the reader with explicitly prescriptive discourses rooted in diametrically opposed value systems: Good and Evil. Despite his obsession for order, the inner contradictions manifest in his adherence to first one then the other of these value systems creates a certain resistance in the reader, impelling him to look for alternative interpretations of the events than those provided by a narrator who seems less than reliable. As a result, the reader becomes aware that far from adhering to a given truth supporting the authority of these discourses, the renegade's interest in them is linked uniquely to power. The 'truth' of a discourse is determinable only in so far as it proves itself stronger than the others; i.e. when it 'wins'. As such the madness of the renegade might be seen as not only that of a tortured individual, but also that of justificatory discourse in all of its implacable logic.

One could multiply the examples here: in *The Plague* for instance, one is confronted with the debilitating effect that occurs when judgment encounters that which is irreducible to the values (or Truths) that supposedly underlie its authority. No longer able to maintain his (abstract) detached perspective on the plague once faced with the concrete reality of the anguished death of an innocent child, the character of the priest (up to this point an embodiment of absolute certainty in a transcendental justice) begins to doubt the possibility of justifying his value system to the point of his own psychological paralysis and eventual annihilation. In *Caligula*, we encounter the at once bizarre and terrorising relationship that exists between the arbitrary and the absolute in judicial institutions. The central character of the play, Caligula, a young emperor invested with complete power, is an image of authority untethered from any need for justification. In *The Just Assassins*, we see the tendency in any prescriptive discourse, be it political, judicial or ideological (and regardless of the altruism of the ideas behind it), to slide into tyranny as soon as it begins to establish itself as a 'solution' to moral problems. One could cite further examples, encompassing even the author's more obscure works (*L'Hôte*, *Jonas*, *Le Malentendu*, etc.), to indicate the extent to which the problem of judgment and its underlying dogmatism permeates Camus' *oeuvre*.[13]

It is here that Deleuze's concept of dogmatic thought (recognition, categorisation) versus creative thought is very helpful. For what, if not dogmatic thought, is Camus identifying and dismantling in his dissection of the mechanisms of power? How not to see, in the examples above, evidence of Camus' resistance to a kind of thought that has as its (implicit or explicit) goal the *prevention* of a genuine engagement with an 'outside' thought, with encounters irreducible to itself? Whether it be on the register of literature, in the reader's encounter with the magisterial manipulations of a narrator who adroitly side-steps and exploits to his own ends our dogmatic attempts to recognise or categorise the truth of his discourse, or, on the level of the story, the discursive dementia of an agonising 'renegade' spewing vitriolic attacks against a reality that denies the possibility of absolute truth (or interpretation), or the slow inner implosion that eventually shatters the world of a priest unable to accept the cracks – and ensuing ambiguity – in the edifice of absolute certainty upon which his faith depends, Camus' *oeuvre* would seem to bring to the forefront constructions of resistance. On the one hand, it throws into relief dogmatic thought's resistance to (or, more precisely, suppression of) encounters irreducible to itself, and on the other, highlights a kind of counter-resistance, that of 'outside thought' to its assimilation (recognition, categorisation) by dogmatism. Hence the renegade's rage and ultimate defeat faced with reality's refusal to cooperate with his demands for absolutes, the priest's bafflement and consequent disintegration when his value system encounters something irreducible to itself or, on another level, the reader's confusion faced with Clamence's refusal to provide a trustworthy (i.e. identifiable) narrative. Hence also, it might be suggested, the perplexity of conventional critics faced with the resistance of Camus' *oeuvre* to their attempts to classify it according to preexisting categories (moralist, humanist, existentialist) or even to Camus' own preexisting work. In this sense, we might say that for Camus, as for Deleuze, what makes thought dogmatic is the fact that it in effect suppresses encounters (through recognition and categorisation) and as such chokes off all possibility of real creation.

This brings us back to what Deleuze identifies as the 'supreme instance' of dogmatic thought: transcendental judgment. It is in its assumption that everything encountered can be recognised that thought demonstrates its dogmatic quality (Deleuze 1994: Chapter 3). The problem, of course, with this kind of dogmatism, is that it in effect prevents the occurrence of 'real', i.e. creative, thought. Precisely because thought, in order to be creative (to 'think' as opposed to 'recognise'), must be impacted by an external encounter, one that it can neither engender nor anticipate (Lefebvre 2008: 59):

> Concepts only ever designate possibilities. They lack the claws of absolute necessity – in other words, of an original violence done to thought; the claws of a strangeness or an enmity which alone would awaken thought from its natural stupor or eternal possibility: there is only involuntary thought, aroused but constrained within thought, and all the more absolutely necessary for being born, illegitimately, of fortuitousness in the world. Thought is primarily trespass and violence, the enemy, and nothing presupposes philosophy: everything begins with misosophy. Do not count on thought to ensure the relative necessity of what it thinks. Rather, count upon the contingency of an encounter with that which forces thought to raise up and educate the absolute necessity of an act of thought or a passion to think. The conditions of a true critique and a true creation are the same: the destruction of an image of thought which presupposes itself and the genesis of the act of thinking in thought itself. Something in the world forces us to think. This something is an object not of recognition but of a fundamental encounter. (Deleuze 1994: 139)

## Concluding Remarks: An Encounter

We are now in a better position to answer our initial question: why Deleuze and Camus? First, on the most obvious level, Deleuze's thought allows us to free Camus from the clutches of 'dogmatic thought'.

Camus's literary work has been so deeply entangled with the fact that *The Outsider* is one of any high school student's 'rites of passage' and his non-fiction work used as a preparation, or an appetiser, for serious philosophy classes, that it is today almost impossible to *encounter* it (as opposed to *recognising* it). Deleuze allows us to see a much more interesting facet of Camus: that of a writer actively dismantling the very 'mechanisms' he is typically considered to be 'representing'. Thus we see that in the case of literary criticism (critique), as in the case of literature itself (creation) 'this method of active dismantling [that] doesn't make use of criticism that is still part of representation ... is much more intense than any critique' (Deleuze and Guattari 1986: 48).

Literature, like philosophy, being dependent on 'established logical forms' (even when it sets out to expose them) is inherently plagued by the danger of transcendental judgment and, consequently, of being rendered sterile through the blockage of real creative thought (as opposed to mere identification or recognition, as in the case of literature rooted in representation). It is precisely this problematic rapport with his own role as a writer that preoccupied Camus. The power of language is not that of preventing us from attaining the real, it is that of forcing us to assume, despite ourselves, its normative power. Escape via pure creation is for Camus an illusion, and produces what he refers to as 'salon nihilists' (Camus 1991: 46). The reason is simple: all discourse, whether it wants to or not, exercises a form of power. However strong the revolt that incites it, it will invariably degenerate into terror and tyranny if it doesn't turn against its own power. Any creation of values is a seizing of power, and any power that enstates itself slides into tyranny. Deleuze reminds us of this in terms of the literary machine:

> Let no one say that this line [of escape] is present only in spirit, as though writing isn't also a machine, as though it isn't also an act, even when it is independent of publication. As though the machine of writing isn't also a machine ... sometimes taken up by capitalist, fascist or bureaucratic machines, sometimes tracing a modest revolutionary line. Let us note Kafka's constant idea: even with a solitary mechanic, the literary machine of expression is capable of anticipating or precipitating contents into conditions that, for better or worse, concern an entire collectivity. (Deleuze and Guattari 1986: 59–60)

Hence the 'particular power' of 'poetry' (as opposed to creation based on representation) to destabilise 'established logical forms' (of power). It is the poet who provides a response to the 'logical crime'. Precisely *not* through a language of judgment (identification, recognition) that will either denounce or demystify (and in so doing run the risk of degenerating into the very established logic it sets out to denounce) or flight ('fleeing the world') but rather by a movement of *subversion*, an act of playful sabotage of the very rules that bind and define it; once again, 'to subvert from the bottom up through a cancellation of the established logical forms'.

This is also interesting for understanding *why* Deleuze passes through literature in his critique of law. The voice of the poet is indeed the royal road to dismantling transcendental judgment through the destabilisation of its discourses of justification, notably law. Because of their common trait, rhetoric (whose judiciary and literary roots can be traced back to Ancient Greece [Barthes 1985: 85–164]), literature and law are both pervaded with the need to propose alternatives to pure rhetoric within their respective discourses. That is, to establish that their discourses cannot be reduced to *just* rhetoric, but rather are rooted in something else. In both cases it's a matter of calling into question discursive norms. A juxtaposition of the two discourses thus provides fertile ground for examining their (respective and reflective) internal tension; that between 'good discourse' and rhetoric. It is this relation of tension between the two domains that emerges in the questioning of the act of writing through legal discourse.

But there is also another (and symmetrical) interest in studying both Camus and Deleuze – or to provoke an encounter, so to speak, that did not occur. In fact, as alluded to in the first part of this chapter, Camus appears by all accounts to be a paradigm of 'major literature'. Of course, one could certainly try to argue that he was not: he was part of a minority (the 'Pieds Noirs' from Algeria) and, more than this, his first study on poverty among the Kabyle population in Northern Algeria, that had a deep influence on his work, would seem to point to a typical process of 'becoming minor'; his first published work, *The Outsider*, is commonly taken as a dismantling not only of the representation of justice, but also of the 'state language'; he created the 'blank writing' (*l'écriture blanche*) that so impressed Barthes and Blanchot and which was so influential on the French 'Nouveau Roman'; finally, it cannot be stressed enough, Camus was not Sartre: he loved football and the beach of Tipaza more than the smoky Cafés of Saint-Germain des Près; he did not want to launch a 'school of thought', nor even to belong to one; he had no romantic entreaty to revolutionary ideals concealing sheer desire for the appropriation of power. But still, we cannot escape the evidence: Camus is not the first example that comes to mind when speaking of 'minor literature' and there are good reasons for this.

In identifying the various factors that could have led him towards a 'becoming minor', one cannot help but see that he seems, in reality, to have cautiously (and deliberately) avoided moving in such a direction. This fact, I would like to suggest, could lead to a very interesting interrogation around Deleuze's philosophy of law, in so far as it belongs to a philosophy of literature. If I am indeed correct and Camus' work does offer a parallel to Deleuze's analyses of the 'dismantling of transcendental justifications', this would mean that many features that were correlated with 'minor literature' belong in fact to something deeper, namely an intimate connection between literature and the figures of law which is independent of the former's 'becoming minor' or not.

Now, one might argue that this is an innocuous remark and that distinguishing between what belongs to the 'becoming minor' and what to the 'dismantling of transcendental justifications' is inconsequential. But this is not entirely true. As greatly emphasised by Jacques Rancière, Deleuze's aesthetic carries its own danger: although it is directed against the representational model of literature and the figure of the almighty Subject, it relies heavily on representations and classical figures of subjectivity to conduct its demonstration (see Rancière 2009). What interests Deleuze in the case of Kafka is how literature reflects something of 'world history' and how it is 'traversed' by political and social microdeterminations, but when one looks closely at this relationship, this way of 'reflecting' is a kind of second level representation; moreover, it relies heavily on a very classical figure of the 'subject' (in this case Kafka 'the writer' in the grips of political and cultural oppression). In this sense, and on a different plane, Deleuze himself might be seen as guilty of the very representation he set out to undermine and this representation would be a very important factor in the allegorical process[14] which grounds the characterisation of a 'minor literature'.

This is perhaps – is most likely – a misunderstanding in the reading of Deleuze, but it is a misunderstanding that is persistent, and which threatens 'Deleuzianism' in its risk of becoming, itself, 'dogmatic thought' – as opposed to a 'toolbox'. If its encounter with Camus could help liberate us from this misunderstanding, this encounter would be, in and of itself, far from minor.

> Camus: il a souvent éprouvé une sorte de malaise, parfois de l'impatience, à se voir immobilisé par ses livres; non seulement à cause de l'éclat de leur succès, mais par le caractère d'achèvement qu'il travaillait à leur donner et contre lequel il se retournait, dès qu'au nom de cette perfection l'on prétendait le juger prématurément accompli. Puis, au jour de sa mort, la brusque, la décisive immobilité: elle a cessé alors de le menacer. C'est

chacun de nous qu'elle risque d'atteindre, nous obligeant à nous arrêter auprès de l'oeuvre désormais trop calme que nous nous sentons cependant tenus de préserver, pour que ne se fige pas en évidence le sens secret qui lui est propre. Car c'est une oeuvre secrète. (Blanchot 1971: 215)[15]

# References

Barthes, R. (1985), 'L'Ancienne rhétorique, aide-mémoire', in *L'Aventure sémiologique*, Paris: Seuil.
Bergen, V. (2009), 'Visages de l'esthétique chez Jacques Rancière et Gilles Deleuze', in J. Game and A. Wald Lasowski (eds), *Jacques Rancière et la politique de l'esthétique*, Paris: Editions des archives contemporaines.
Blanchot, M. (1971), 'Le détour vers la simplicité', in *L'Amitié*, Paris: Gallimard.
Blanchot, M. (1997), *Friendship*, trans. E. Rottenberg, Stanford: Stanford University Press.
Brochier, J-J. (1979), *Albert Camus: philosophe pour classes terminales*, Paris: Balland.
Camus, A. (1991), *The Rebel*, New York: First Vintage International Edition.
de Sutter, L. (2009), *Deleuze La pratique du droit*, Paris: Michalon.
Deleuze, G. (1989), *Cinema 2: The Time-Image*, trans. H. Tomlinson and R. Galeta, London: Athlone.
Deleuze, G. (1994), *Difference and Repetition*, trans. P. Patton, New York: Columbia University Press.
Deleuze G. (2004), 'He Was My Teacher', in *Desert Islands and Other Texts*, trans. M. Taormina, Los Angeles: Semiotext(e).
Deleuze G. and F. Guattari (1977), *Anti-Oedipus*, trans. R, Hurley, M. Seem and H. R. Lance, Minneapolis: University of Minnesota Press.
Deleuze G. and F. Guattari (1986), *Kafka: Toward a Minor Literature*, Minneapolis: University of Minnesota Press.
Due, R. (2007), *Deleuze*, Cambridge: Polity.
Foucault, M. (1966), 'La pensée du dehors', *Critique*, 229.
Foucault M. (2001), *Dits et écrits*, vol. 1, Paris: Gallimard.
Lefebvre, A. (2008), *The Image of Law: Deleuze, Bergson, Spinoza*, Stanford: Stanford University Press.
Lincoln, L. (2002), *Albert Camus et la question du juste*, thesis, McGill University.
Rancière, J. (2009), 'Deleuze accomplit le destin de l'esthétique', in *Et tant pis pour les gens fatigués*, Paris: Les Editions Amsterdam.
Renault, E. (2004), *L'Experience de l'injustice: Reconnaissance et clinique de l'injustice*, Paris: La Decouverte.
Sloterdijk, P. (2009), *Theory of the Post-War Periods*, Vienna: Springer-Verlag.

# Notes

1. Indeed, Foucault went so far as to classify Camus amongst the 'pale figures of our Culture' and cites him as an example of the 'totalising intellectual' – the epitome of what he called 'soft humanism': 'I adopted the expression "soft humanism" . . . but on second thought, I'd have to say that it's a purely redundant formula, and that in any case, humanism necessarily implies softness . . . It is precisely this humanism that served in 1948 to justify Stalinism and the hegemony of Christian democracy . . . it is the very humanism that we find in

Camus or in the existentialism of Sartre. At the end of the day this humanism has been the little prostitute of all thought, of all culture, of all morality and of all politics for the last 20 years' (Foucault 2001 [1967]: 615–16, my translation).
2. For a notable exception to this rule, see Sloterdijk 2009: 32–5.
3. See, for example, Brochier 1979.
4. Though I will be henceforth referring to the author of this text in the body of my paper as 'Deleuze', it is understood that this is only a manner of speaking.
5. See, for example, Blanchot 1971.
6. One has only to think of the role played by the Blanchotian notion of '*Dehors*' in Deleuze's thought (see, for example, Deleuze 1989: 178–80), or the development on 'powerlessness' in thought in Deleuze 1994: 199–200. See also Foucault 1966.
7. It suffices to read *Critique et Clinique* to be convinced by the intimate connection between literature and the question of judgment in Deleuze's thought.
8. In his influential studies on Kafka, Melville's *Bartleby*, Sacher-Masoch, etc. A notable exception to this rule can be found in de Sutter 2009.
9. 'It is absolutely useless to look for a theme in a writer if one hasn't asked exactly what its importance is in the work – that is, how it functions (and not what its "sense" is)' (Deleuze and Guattari 1986: 45).
10. As Deleuze specifies: 'petit-bourgeois intimacy and the absence of any sort of social criticism will be the primary themes in the opposition of the communists to Kafka' (Deleuze and Guattari 1986: 96 fn 3).
11. More interestingly yet, it was Sartre, as Deleuze points out, who, despite his scathing criticisms of Camus for his political irresponsibility as an artist, took the defence of Kafka in this regard: 'Sartre intervened in the Moscow Peace Conference in 1962 to call for a better analysis of the connections between art and politics and of Kafka in particular' (Deleuze and Guattari 1986: 96 fn 3).
12. Thus demonstrating law as a structure of prescription that traverses different themes (justice, religion, politics, etc.).
13. As documented at length in my thesis. See Lincoln 2002.
14. As Véronique Bergen points out: 'Rancière's point can be condensed into one word –"allegory". Every time Deleuze exhibited buttresses, where thought would break out of its ordinary regime of the peaceful circle of recognition (where subject and object shoulder one another in their harmonious correspondence), he would rely on allegories and transfer what the characters accomplish to what is being played out on the level of the phrase or the image, extrapolating to the form of expression that which comes from the form of content, from narration. The rupture of sensory-motor coordination, the throwing off balance of a language carried off into stuttering, would simply not figure in the materiality of the works, but would be the object of the sole Deleuzian proposition of a new image of thought' (Bergen 2009: 25, my translation).
15. 'Camus: he often experienced a feeling of discomfort, at times impatience, to see himself immobilized by his books; not only because of their resounding success, but by the finished quality he worked to give them and against which he turned, as soon as, in the name of this perfection, one wanted to judge him prematurely accomplished. Then, on the day of his death, the abrupt, decisive immobility: it ceased then to threaten him. It risks overtaking each of us, forcing us to stop beside a work henceforth too calm, which we nevertheless feel called upon to preserve, in order that the secret meaning that is specific to it not become frozen in the obvious. For it is a secret work' (Blanchot 1997: 189).

Chapter 10

# Cases Against Transcendence: Gilles Deleuze and Bruno Latour in Defence of Law

*David Saunders*

When philosophers and social theorists address positive law, we've come to expect them – in their programmatic intellectual roles and in their particular departments of existence – to favour some overarching, transcendental stance. A disjunctive and superior intellectual relation towards law, then, be it to redirect or rectify, to reform or even to redeem.[1] Gilles Deleuze and Bruno Latour, intriguingly, seem not to have satisfied this conventional but rather constant expectation for supremacist voicings of a universal perspective or cosmopolitan principle. To the contrary, these noted figures – one philosopher, the other social theorist – surprisingly furnish defences of positive law. Is their defensive stance faulty? Or might such leaning against the wind become the new model stance, your counter-current pathway to tomorrow?

The surprise is compounded if you have a certain expectation of these two figures as intellectual personae. Suppose you expect only the 'metaphysical' Latour of 'cosmopolitics', 'assemblies of assemblages' and – most recently – 'plasma'.[2] How surprising, then, a Latour who will praise a disposition '*superficial enough*' to recognise the force of law as irreducible in its positivity. In this latter persona, though, Latour observes the same protocol of irreduction of the object as distinguishes his studies of science practice. As for the Deleuze who will defend the practice of case-law as a cardinal instance of creativity, finding in its adjudicative processes the very model for a renovated philosophy, this lawyerly persona must surprise those expecting the unambiguously antinomian Deleuze, so well known and publicised since *Différence et répétition* (1968) as the remorseless scourge of judgment. In his antipathy to a philosophical reprise of law, though, the antinomian persona remains active. When Latour and Deleuze surprise us with a defence of law . . . what should we make of this?

Latour's 2002 ethnography of the Conseil d'Etat de France, *La fabrique du droit*, offers a gentle satire on the theme that social-theoretic structural explanations of law or philosophical ideas of universal judgment are rightly matters of indifference to the lawyers.[3] The satire inverts a classical model. Rather than setting an innocent among the refined so as to illuminate the latter's absurd excess, Latour places a seriously but excessively knowing persona with an overly developed capacity for abstraction – termed the 'philosophically-minded' one – into the mundane setting of the court. Here the lawyers adjudicate cases *via* an 'attitude of indifference' (Latour 2002: 250) to higher-order determinations, philosophical or social-theoretic. The satire offers would-be hyper-intellectuals a conduct guide on self-de-transcendentalising.

Law's capacity for indifference to 'transcendental nonsense' underpins Gilles Deleuze's positive disposition towards the *pratique du droit*.[4] With the indifference comes a capacity for invention. To give an immediate instance of legal inventiveness, here is Deleuze – filmed in a smoke-wreathed interview with Claire Parnet – recalling how, before smoking in taxis was made illegal, a client had sued the driver who had not let him smoke.[5] The court found for the customer: taxi hire was a private rental. The taxi was – legally speaking – an *'apartement roulant'* in which by his *'droit d'usage'* the client was free to smoke his Gauloise as if *chez lui*. A decade later, though, another court reinvented the taxi's wheeled space. Taxi hire was now assimilated to accessing a public service where individual conduct could be regulated and thus smoking banned. Deleuze welcomes such innovation. As he observes, it's precisely why we should 'fight for *jurisprudence*'. This positive embrace of law as innovation leads a recent scholar to an 'astonishing proposition': for Deleuze, 'law is the future of philosophy' (de Sutter 2009: 105).

Before elaborating this defence of law's inventiveness and outlining the serial distinctions in which Deleuze frames his account of the *pratique du droit*, let's return to Latour's satire. The lawyers of the Conseil, as noted, adjudicate *via* an 'attitude of indifference' that keeps them centred on the operations of law to the exclusion of other determinations, whether political, economic or social-theoretic. The aim is to describe law at work as it is, not as what social theorists say it should be or must become. Being himself a social theorist, Latour as narrator here performs a self-purgation, deploying a mask or persona quite at odds with the context in which the narrator finds himself. In the juridically-minded context of the court, the 'philosophically-minded' one's initial all-knowingness will be decanted into perplexity.

He soon admits to uncertainty: among the lawyers, he encounters a 'subtlety without need of foundations – even doctrinal – entirely typical of

## Cases Against Transcendence: Deleuze and Latour

law yet capable of constantly surprising the philosophically-minded ethnographer' (Latour 2002: 26). By one-third distance, he is distressed that his high-sighted gaze is sighting nothing up there: 'How is it possible? Is there really nothing higher than these infinitesimal discussions on words and texts in this so-called "supreme" court?', the ethnographer asks himself . . . 'Is there really nothing higher than the laws?' (Latour 2002: 79). For the 'philosophically-minded' one, the answer hurts. 'Beyond this rather derisory institution, [there's] nothing that is better, quicker, more effective, more economic – in particular, nothing that is more just' (Latour 2002: 80). Transcendence, it seems, is not the lawyers' game.

By the mid-point of his research, the narrator is ready to jettison the two established intellectual perspectives that had promised to uncover deep structures of normativity underlying law (Latour 2002: 152–4). The first is socio-theoretic – associated with Pierre Bourdieu – and sees law only as an armature of the structure of power in society. In this light, the juridical order is nothing more than an 'elaborate camouflage for relations of power that we must learn to overturn'. The second perspective is philosophical but no less reductive. It treats the work of law as the application of a rule in a formal system of *a priori* master norms – epistemic or moral – whose practical realisation the legal order serves to secure. Either way, law becomes a secondary or derivative reality, stripped of its positivity

Still 'philosophically-minded' although now less so, the observer faces a dilemma. To embrace these two 'philosophical' perspectives – sociologism and formalism – would entail 'abandoning the sinuous pathways of [juridical] practice to follow a different reality, invisible to the eyes of the [legal] actors yet offering the explanation of their conduct: that of society and its violences; that of the rule and its own logic' (Latour 2002: 153). The satire's tipping point comes when the narrator himself abandons his theorist's quest for a transcendental X that the lawyers do not see:

> Far from following the sociologists' and epistemologists' contradictory advice to recover the deep reality of law, we're choosing to *remain on the surface*, doggedly following the uncertain trail of the judgments in the course of which judges openly admit their prejudices while affirming that these don't furnish the solution, or attach themselves passionately to the forms while constantly guarding against a fall into what they call 'juridism' or 'formalism'. (Latour 2002: 154)

Resolved to 'remain on the surface', the observer can describe the working of the Conseil positively, that is, in its own terms as a *mise en droit*. Only now is it possible 'to make description of the law compatible with the practice of the judges' (Latour 2002: 204).

With this hard-won embrace of 'superficiality', I'll leave Latour for the moment and return to Deleuze's recommendation for an inventive *jurisprudence*. Importantly, *jurisprudence* in the sense of legal science or doctrine is not Deleuze's concern. His enthusiasm for law's inventiveness lies with *jurisprudence* in the more current sense of judicial decisions rendered in courts by way of resolving given issues. French law does not observe a doctrine of precedent and *stare decisis* in the manner of a common-law jurisdiction. Article 5 of the Code Civil rejects 'government by judges' by precluding judge-made law.[6] Yet, the familiar locution – *le cas fait jurisprudence* or 'the case makes law' – confirms that French judges can make original decisions when confronted by novel problems. Such decisions may become generally adopted. Deleuze makes this zone of judicial action on singular cases an exemplary zone of invention. Hence his essential formulation: '*Ce qui est créateur de droit, ce ne sont pas les codes ou les déclarations, c'est la jurisprudence. La jurisprudence est la philosophie du droit, et procède par singularités, prolongement de singularités*' ('What creates law is not codes or declarations, it's jurisprudence. Jurisprudence is the philosophy of law, and proceeds by singularities, extension of singularities') (Deleuze 1990: 209–10).[7]

To get to our topic – Deleuze's defence of law in its capacity for invention – involves traversing his quartet of conceptual distinctions: *critique/clinique*, *pensée/pratique*, *loi/droit*, and *axiomatique/topique*. *Critique/clinique* distinguishes between an abstract theorisation and a descriptive project.[8] *Critique* operates in a philosophical register, positing some higher-order norm that projects an idea (*pensée*) of what law should be or must become. *Clinique* entails describing and assessing the lower-order practice (*pratique*) of the law as it has been and now happens to be.

Now to superimpose the distinction *loi/droit*.[9] Deleuze unmakes *la pensée de la loi* to diminish the prestige enjoyed by ideas of a higher law. In Nietzschean style, he deflates programmatic notions of a law above the laws, a *pensée de la loi* on which any *pratique du droit* would depend for its legitimacy. It's a pity passing quickly over this deflationary work. Suffice it to cite the memorable reading of Kafka as a great ironic recipient of Kant's moral law, a dogmatic *loi* that might be accessible in the transcendental realm of universal human reason yet which – in Kafka's picture of things – remains unknowable by men and women in this present world. Down here among us, *la loi* 'is always in the next office, or behind the door, for ever' (Deleuze and Guattari 1975: 93). However, our concern is not with what Deleuze deflates but with what he defends.

The defence *of jurisprudence* crystallises as ideas of a higher law are displaced by a 'clinical' description of the *pratique du droit*. Now law's workings emerge from the shadows of the 'critical' philosophising to which normative Kantianism stands as an enduring carceral monument. Carceral, because non-malleable *a priori* norms entail repetition, not invention. They thus relegate an inventive *jurisprudence* in which outcomes of cases might be novel, unforeseen, or even unforeseeable.

With the fourth conceptual distinction, we close in on Deleuze's unexpected embrace of *la pratique du droit*. The distinction between *axiomatique* and *topique* – axiomatic and topical – demarcates between two styles of thought. It appears in *Mille plateaux* (Deleuze and Guattari 1980: 563) and in *Qu'est-ce que la philosophie?* In the latter, it allows a schematic comparison of legal systems – English, German and French – that illustrates Nietzsche's 'geo-philosophical' take on German, French and English thought as unsurpassably 'national, or better nationalitarian' in character. In this 'territorialisation' of thought according to the 'trinity Founding-Building-Inhabiting', it is 'the French who build, the Germans who lay down foundations, but the English inhabit. All they [the English] need is a tent' (Deleuze and Guattari 1991: 101).

After such bravura – 'One can't even say [the English] have concepts, like the French and the Germans' – the allusion to the three countries' legal systems is brief, just a lightning bonus. The relations between the three jurisdictions mirror those between the three territorialised philosophies, with English law – like English philosophy – being 'a question of pragmatism': 'English law is a law of custom and convention, as French law is a law of contract (deductive system), and the German a law of institution (organic totality)' (Deleuze and Guattari 1991: 101). The comparison turns on the varying degree to which – in English, German and French systems – *le droit* remains bound to *la loi*.[10] English common law, we could say, is the least bound to *la loi* and – being satisfied like English thinkers with mere tent-occupation – the least codified or, indeed, codifiable. Remaining closest to custom and centred on cases, the English system is the most pragmatic, the most casuistical and thus the most open to particular cases.[11] Above all, it is least concerned with unifying itself into a coherent, inward-looking system of pre-ordained axioms.

In this schematic comparison, English common law approximates a *pratique topique du droit* while French law tends towards a *pratique axiomatique du droit*. Deleuze's target, though, is not French law but the philosophical tradition that conceptualises law's practice as necessarily devolved from a prior system of predetermining axioms.[12] The sociologism and epistemological 'formalism' from which Latour's 'philosophically-minded' observer finally turns are precisely of this axiomatic species. To defend *jurisprudence*, Deleuze like Latour will first reject the notion that outcomes of concrete cases are prescribed in higher-order precepts, theological, moral, epistemological, socio-economic, *la loi*. Then he moves to restore a sense of why the *pratique topique du droit* matters.

Mention of restoration carries a historical charge. In footnotes to *Mille plateaux*, *axiomatique* and *topique* are distinguished by contrasting two historical forms of law (Deleuze and Guattari 1980: 564, fn. 39; 566, fn. 45). On one side there is a *pratique topique du droit*; on the other, a *pratique axiomatique du droit*. With Paul Veyne's *Le pain et le cirque* cited as authority, Roman law is taken to exemplify the former, operating as a 'law without concepts that proceeds by topics'. By contrast and as exemplified by the French *Code civil*, modern law operates as a *pratique axiomatique du droit*. Unlike this modern, concept-bound and codified form, the *pratique topique du droit* works through 'topics' or cases, that is, in casuistical mode. The Latin *casus*, we recall, refers to an unanticipated happening, a fortuitous event. In Deleuze's perspective on law, it is the specificity of the *pratique topique du droit* to create the possibility of unforeseen outcomes.

In *Mille plateaux*, classical Roman law exemplifies the *pratique topique du droit*. It's better, though, to read Deleuze's note on anti-speculative Romanism as expressing his anti-Platonist Nietzschean disposition, rather than as the considered judgment of a legal historian in the style of Aldo Schiavone. Still, in *Ius: l'invention du droit en occident*, Schiavone too recognises that what we ordinarily designate as 'Roman law' is a work of *jurisprudence*:

> A 'living customary law', casuistically organised (*à dispositif casuistique*), directed by experts: [Roman law is] much closer in resemblance, in its concrete configuration, to modern English and (in some respects) American law – which nonetheless developed outside any romanist tradition comparable to that of continental Europe – than to French law subsequent to the Code Napoléon. (Schiavone 2008: 42–3)

However, Schiavone's focus is less on Roman law as case-based practice than on its 'codificatory trend that must be considered the most important innovation in the juridical experience of Late Antiquity' (Schiavone 2008: 15), a trend embodied in Justinian's *Corpus Iuris*. Hence his characterisation of Roman law's function as a 'disciplinary machine . . . capable of a total formalisation of life' as 'the hard centre (*noyau dur*) of the ancient heritage' (Schiavone 2008: 49). This is, to say the least, most un-Deleuzian!

Can we pursue Deleuze's take on the non-systemic spirit of the *pratique topique du droit* with a glance in the direction of the English common law? That the common law remains largely 'topical' and casuistical is a proposition that its historian, Brian Simpson, endorses: 'Life might be much simpler if the common law consisted of a code of rules, identifiable by reference to source rules' (Simpson 1987: 368). Indeed, but Simpson quickly precludes such wishful thinking: 'the only way to make the common law conform to the ideal would be to codify the system, which would then cease to be the common law at all'. Indeed, as the historian puts it, to tie the common law to some higher-order rules or a priori principles would be 'surely a programme, or an ideal, and not a description of the *status quo*' (Simpson 1987: 381).

To concretise the sense of the common law as a *pratique topique*, let's take a case in point. On 19 March 2009, Lord Hoffmann delivered the Annual Lecture of the English Judicial Studies Board. His topic: 'The Universality of Human Rights'. Confrontation could not be more clearly staged between the transcendental value of a universal principle and the historical singularity of a national *jurisprudence* in its national setting. The battle line is drawn where abstract principle confronts concrete enforcement. Having cited the US Bill of Rights and the French Declaration of the Rights of Man and the Citizen as expressing a certain moral and political philosophy of man, Hoffmann pursues:

> At the level of application, however, the messy detail of concrete problems, the human rights which these abstractions have generated are national. Their application requires trade-offs and compromises, exercises of judgment which can be made only in the context of a given society and its legal system. (Hoffmann 2009: §15)

In short, 'human rights are universal in abstraction but national in application' (Hoffmann 2009: §23).

Problems start, though, at the point where what might be valid as principles in moral philosophy or axioms in political theory threaten to override the historical processes of *jurisprudence*. Here Hoffmann gets down to the 'messy detail'. An abstract doctrine – human rights – is being treated as if it were universally applicable. Under the terms of the European Convention for the Protection of Human Rights and Fundamental Freedoms, adopted as a United Kingdom constitutional instrument in the Human Rights Act 1998, the doctrine now seeks application in the English courts. Pressure to this end is exerted by 'the Strasbourg court' – Hoffmann does not once give the European Court of Human Rights its full title – as the final court of appeal for citizens of the United Kingdom. For Hoffmann – and this might be closer than expected to what Deleuze might also argue – the problem is that 'the Strasbourg court . . . has no mandate to unify the laws of Europe on the many subjects which may arguably touch upon human rights'. Hoffmann continues: 'Because, for example, there is a human right to a fair trial, it does not follow that all the countries of the Council of Europe must have the same trial procedure. Criminal procedures in different countries may differ widely without any of them being unfair' (Hoffmann 2009: §24). At stake is the future of the particular English mode of adjudication. A historically grounded *pratique topique du droit* is threatened with supercession by an abstract principle – protection of human rights – driven by a would-be isonomic European law.

Among instances of inappropriate intervention by 'the Strasbourg court', Hoffmann cites the case of *Al-Khawaja and Tahery v UK* (20 January 2009). The problem, he writes, lies with 'the Strasbourg court's enthusiasm for the hearsay rule'. Finding the English decision in breach of article 6 (the 'fair trial' provision) of the Convention, the Strasbourg court asserted a fundamental human right as a universally applicable principle: that a trial has not been fair if conviction rested 'solely or to a decisive degree' on a statement by a person whom the accused has had no opportunity to examine. Hoffmann outlines the case:

> Dr Al-Khawaja was a doctor charged with indecent assault on two of his patients. One of them, after making a statement to the police, committed suicide. The judge admitted her statement under the provisions of the [Criminal Justice Act 2003] but warned the jury that they had not seen the complainant or heard her cross-examined. But her story was supported by strong similar fact evidence, not only from the other complainant but from two other witnesses who had had similar experiences. The jury convicted unanimously and the doctor was given a custodial sentence. The Court of Appeal said that the overall case against the appellant was very strong and they were wholly unpersuaded that the verdicts were unsafe. (Hoffmann 2009: §31)

The Court of Appeal had in fact checked procedure for compliance with article 6. Singularities, however, were being overridden by an abstraction.

I'll return to human rights.[13] For now, Hoffmann's lecture can serve to illustrate the tensions between a concrete practice of *jurisprudence* and an abstract *a priori* principle that Deleuze would identify as *la pensée de la loi*. Of course Hoffmann risks dismissal as a voice of reactive conservatism. Yet, this risk might be lessened if he had underscored the common law's capacity for invention that – for Deleuze – distinguishes the *pratique topique du droit*. At this point, though, we need an extended concrete illustration of what such legal inventiveness might look like. Despite Schiavone's comment on the *Code Napoléon*, nineteenth-century French *jurisprudence* was to prove more than capable of invention. Ample supporting evidence is provided in Marcela Iacub's recent history of the *outrage public à la pudeur* (Public Offence Against Decency). With article 330 of the *Code pénal* 1810, *outrage public à la pudeur* was created as an infraction under French law. The new crime embodied the Revolution's anti-clerical heritage, being 'the solution found by the Napoleonic State for definitively separating penal law from religion, so that criminal penalties should no longer be used as a tool of purification or salvation' (Iacub 2008: 14). In a striking act of liberal self-restriction, the Bonapartist State resiled from spiritual regulation. Because the eye of God would no longer exercise coercive civil powers, citizens would no longer be at risk of clerical-penal sanction for those ecclesiastical 'crimes against nature' that had long come with the charge of heresy:

> their law, unlike that of the Ancien Régime, had freed itself from religion . . . it had distinguished sin from crime, and . . . it limited itself to punishing acts contrary to social order. No more pyres to burn the homosexual, the incestuous or those who had sexual relations with animals. No more commissions appointed to measure the erections of impotent husbands. Non-violent sexuality that took place in the secrecy of private life was no longer a State concern (*question d'Etat*). (Iacub 2008: 28)

Under a less secularised English criminal law and in the absence of such a bifurcation, we might recall, homosexuality remained a capital offence into the 1860s.

In classic liberal mode, the State had withdrawn from regulating sexuality 'in the secrecy of private life'. Viewed in a post-Revolutionary perspective, this initiative was an appropriate stance against old-style clerical unreason. It would remove from public space and view any sexual action that – by provoking popular scandal – might risk reactivating clerical purchase over the public life of citizens. French citizens would thus enjoy an 'unprecedented' freedom of private conduct in the first half of the nineteenth century. But how would the courts deploy their inventive power when it came to regulating sexuality in public places? Iacub reconstructs the building of a 'wall of decency' (*mur de pudeur*). Under article 330, the wall rose and rose as judges demonstrated a capacity for inventive *jurisprudence*. Iacub (2008: 15) recognises 'an intense jurisprudential history' as the spaces in which men and women played out their sexual scenes were brought into the ambit of article 330. If not the earth, the 'wall of decency' certainly moved, impelled by judges. Was it not, asks Iacub (2008: 23), 'a task for titans' that in the course of the nineteenth century French judges would assimilate an act in a locked bedroom to an act on the corner of a public street? Her interrogative does not imply her approval. Indeed, her history is all the more persuasive as an illustration of legal inventiveness to the extent that she regrets its direction. The new freedom of privacy, she writes, would prove 'without posterity' (Iacub 2008: 120).

For the judges, issues of visibility and accessibility proved levers of invention. I'll select five indicative instances of inventiveness from the many. With the very first case brought under article 330, in 1813 night was made day. In a darkened street and hidden from view, a man and a woman made love. Accused of having committed an *outrage public*, at trial they were found not guilty. She was consenting and thus no act of violence had occurred. More important, because whatever they had done, they had done it in the depth of the night, their action was invisible. No private passer-by had seen them. Yet, the Cour de cassation annulled the trial judgment, arguing that the lovers' action met the criterion of article 330 that such *outrages* 'must have occasioned a public scandal for the honesty and decency of those who, fortuitously, might have been witnesses'. The court found that a place in darkness was a place of *publicité*, as if at high noon ... because 'anyone might use a public street, day or night' (Iacub 2008: 70). There will be no lovemaking in the public street, even if the street is empty and it's the dead of night. You and your scandal could have been seen by someone, indeed all the world might have happened to pass by – 'fortuitously' – at that moment of *jouissance*.

Regarding visibility, not everywhere is as accessible to all comers and as open to view as the public street. What, then, was the status of such private places as are visible from the street or from some other public place? For inventive judges, it was a matter of your being seen – or seeable – through an open door or window that could let a passer-by catch you in erotic action. Given your visibility, your private place became a public place ... and therefore not beyond the reach of criminal prosecution. Adjudicating the question of lines of sight between two private places entailed further invention. Given a glance across the street from one apartment to another, a space that had been private now became public for the purposes of article 330. *Jurisprudence* created a new space in which your loving activity became eminently justiciable.

Regarding accessibility: how closed should a closed door be . . . if you want to be safe in your sex? For an inventive *jurisprudence*, degrees of closure now became preconditions for defending a charge of *outrage public*. A door that was closed but not actually locked did not cover the contingency whereby someone might chance to enter and to see you both at that beautiful moment. By dint of your negligence in not turning the key in the lock, your private space was now so public that you were vulnerable to being charged with the scandalous offence.

But you can never be too careful, given so inventive a *jurisprudence*. In 1858, the Cour de cassation faced a new question: had those who had indeed locked the door behind them – and thus established the privacy of their private place – taken the further precaution of blocking the keyhole?[14] At trial, the lovers were found to have been negligent, leaving the keyhole unblocked. In consequence, the court assimilated a locked private interior space to a public exterior space where a keyhole-viewing passer-by might have been exposed to the *outrage public à la pudeur*. At cassation, defence for the accused persons presented new material evidence: the morally *outragés* keyhole-viewers who had suffered the scandalous sight – as if on behalf of the whole community – had in fact removed a paper plug from the keyhole. Precautions had been taken. This time the private remained private.

With the *affaire Armand* (1869), the *arrêt Salmon* (1872) and the *arrêt Ponce* (1877), conceptual invention then created *publicité intérieure*.[15] No longer an oxymoron, *publicité intérieure* installed a juridical division within what had been a single private space. Your bedroom – given your negligence with keys and the co-presence of three persons – was assimilated to the public square. Potential problems arise, as Iacub (2008: 115) observes, for the *colocataires* of a single apartment and, more sharply still, where the single space of a studio has no internal doors to lock and therefore no keyholes to block. This stunning de-reification of inside/outside and private/public was the accomplishment of an inventive *jurisprudence*.

At one point, Iacub (2008: 78) observes that 'article 330 did not aim to sound out the morality of human conduct, but its visibility'. Elsewhere, though, she wholly regrets the judges' creativity, terming it a 'grand moral crusade' (*grande croisade morale*) and denouncing the 'remorselessness' (*acharnement*) with which they pursued this 'purifying' campaign (Iacub 2008: 29, 88). Without insisting to the contrary that the courts' decisions were entirely random, it has to be said that her view reduces this remarkable nineteenth-century episode of legal inventiveness to the pre-ordained outcome of some unifying higher power. The historical *jurisprudence* loses its unpredictability and positivity, becoming a merely symptomatic expression of the will of a repressive State 'to open closed spaces to its control' (Iacub 2008: 132). The lawyers and the law become its pliant instrument: 'If this State was liberal in that it did not watch people at home, and only on this condition, the fact of extending its field of vision enabled it to demonstrate the truly restrictive ideas that it held concerning sexuality' (Iacub 2008: 120). But isn't this to frame the legal history of inventive singularities in an overarching dialectic of repression and de-repression? If the first part of *Par le trou de la serrure* addresses the rise of a repressive law, the second part – 'The visual liberation of public places' – welcomes a twentieth-century falling away of old restrictions on the public world.[16] Does such neatly dialectical clamping impose – retrospectively – an 'axiomatic' coherence on a *pratique topique du droit*, a coherence that makes the paths of *jurisprudence* seem inevitable?

Yet, the historical evidence is less of unity than of disagreement between the different tribunals, the Cour de cassation in particular being notably reluctant to go down the 'repressive' path. Not the least conflictual aspect of the history, as Iacub herself observes, is the distance travelled from the Code's original conception of *outrage public*: 'In fact, the usage that the judges made of article 330 in the final quarter of the nineteenth century implied the abolition of the wall of decency such as it had been conceived by the imperial legislator' (Iacub 2008: 119).

She might regret the outcomes but Marcela Iacub in effect recognises the courts' capacity for inventive self-extension as judges 'deployed comparisons, analogies and fictions, which became stabilised, generalised and standardised' (Iacub 2008: 24). When Deleuze recalled the smoking ban in taxis to illustrate this same inventiveness, the matter in question was more mundane. In the philosopher's conversation with Claire Parnet, though, a most substantial issue arose: was inventive *jurisprudence* a positive antidote to human rights talk?

In that part of the video entitled '*G comme Gauche*', Parnet asks Deleuze to comment on 'human rights which are so *à la mode*'. Citing the situation of the Armenians, he responds on human rights in general. These he denounces as 'pure abstraction, empty', as 'discourses for intellectuals, and for odious intellectuals at that, for intellectuals who have no ideas'. What 'such hypocrites' advocate is worth 'zero, philosophically it's zero'. Conversely, *jurisprudence* provides the counterpart to human rights, concrete where the latter are abstract. The Armenians' situation constitutes a 'complex problem of jurisprudence', 'a question of organisation of territory not of human rights, not a question of justice, it's a question of jurisprudence'. It's a matter of 'cases'. Invention is the crucial theme: 'It is a question of inventing the jurisprudence for each case . . . Creation in law (*droit*), it's *jurisprudence*. Only that exists. So, fight for *jurisprudence*.' The topic also draws an autobiographical reflection from Deleuze: 'I've always been excited (*passionné*) by jurisprudence, by law. If I hadn't done philosophy, I'd have done law but precisely not human rights. I would have done *jurisprudence*.'

It would be amusing to know how the English Law Lord might respond to the French philosopher who repudiated human rights universalism as pure abstraction and who defended *jurisprudence* in terms of concrete cases, situations and definite territorial arrangements. That conversation, though, must remain a work of the imagination . . . although we can easily imagine a Lord Hoffmann not entirely in dissent. Instead, in ending, it's not to him but to Latour's satirical ethnography that I now return.

In the final chapter of *La fabrique du droit* Latour turns positive: the Conseil has afforded 'an occasion to study "pure" law' (Latour 2002: 271).[17] It has been a case of uncovering the specific character of legal enunciation as a *vinculum juris* (Latour 2002: 273), a legal concatenation:

> in a few moves, by means of a few translations, an obscure matter concerning expulsion of an alien, or dustbins, or a mayor, finds itself linked, hooked up, attached to the ensemble of administrative law, to the Constitution, to general principles of law, to the European Convention on human rights, as well as to edicts of François I or letters patent of Louis, fourteenth of that name. (Latour 2002: 276)

No matter how extensive, the linkages do not bind law into some higher order or deeper structure of being. Given this exemplary irreduction of the law as object, Latour draws his lesson: 'there is no metalanguage stronger to explain law than the language of law itself. Or, more exactly, law is itself its own metalanguage' (*Il n'y a pas de métalangage plus fort pour expliquer le droit que le langage du droit lui-même. Ou, plus exactement, le droit est à lui-même son propre métalangage*) (Latour 2002: 278–9).

The transcendental turn is set aside: 'There is no point', Latour concludes, 'in being profound in studying the law' (Latour 2002: 284). He has found in the lawyers' work:

> nothing strong, nothing true, nothing sensational, nothing sentimental, nothing – in fact – just: instead, [there is] recall of a basic principle of non-contradiction, delicate and loose, always liable to review and reinterpretation, that avoids – 'in the present state of the texts' – leaving too much incoherence in the scattered actions of humans. Nothing but surface . . . (Latour 2002: 286)

With this clinical assessment, the satire completes the un-making of the 'philosophically-minded' one: 'the ethnographer despairs: will he ever be *superficial enough* to grasp the force of the law?' (Latour 2002: 286). The challenge of mundanity is to embrace a *pratique topique du droit* that is not 'overloaded' with 'impossible virtues'. These transcendental 'virtues', writes Latour, include sovereignty, morality, justice, politics 'and even religion' (Latour 2002: 287). Deleuze would term them instances of *la pensée de la loi*.

This is the light in which to view Deleuze's key formulation: '*La jurisprudence est la philosophie du droit, et procède par singularités, prolongement de singularités*' ('Jurisprudence is the philosophy of law, and proceeds by singularities, extension of singularities.') With Latour's account of legal enunciation, we can better see why viewing law's practice as an 'extension of singularities' in an ongoing relay of cases provides a basic defence against transcendental capture. At the most general level, this answers the question posed at the outset: if Deleuze and Latour defend law, what should we make of this? Given these two exercises in un-making intellectual pretention regarding law in practice, exercises probably pursued independently of one another, a number of more specific observations now follow.

First, despite all that has been said regarding Deleuze's defence of the *pratique topique du droit* and his recognition of case-law judgments as the model for a renovated philosophy, we still hesitate. In *Le pli: Leibniz et le baroque*, Deleuze conjures the prospect of '*une transformation du Droit en Jurisprudence universelle*' (Deleuze 1988: 91). Does a 'transformation of law into universal jurisprudence' once more subordinate law – *le droit* – to the empire of a would-be transcendent *loi*? The early modern apostle of a new *ecclesia* to replace a fractured Christianity, Leibniz projected a natural law of reason as foundation for the positive laws of territorial States. The theo-rational Leibnizian project echoes in advocacy of universal human rights as necessary principles of human reason. Having hesitated, though, we see that Deleuze conceives this transformation of law into a 'universal jurisprudence' as inverting the subordination of legal case to philosophical principle. Rather than the case providing a contingent occasion to apply the necessary principle,

## Cases Against Transcendence: Deleuze and Latour

'the principle will be invented, the case being given: it's the transformation of law into universal jurisprudence. It is the marriage of the concept and the singularity' (Deleuze 1988: 91). Case is not subordinated to principle, nor positive law returned to natural law.[18]

Second, at this point a caveat must be posited. Beyond doubt, the particular inverting of case and principle and, more generally, the recommendation of the *pratique topique du droit*, are distinctive components in Deleuze's project for a practical philosophy re-modelled in light of case law practice. Likewise, his impressive resistance to giving law (*le droit*) foundations in the would-be master discipline of philosophy (*la loi*). Notwithstanding this, as to Deleuze's contribution in the context of mainstream jurisprudential studies, a caveat is appropriate. Concerning the distinction between philosophical habits of mind and legal ones, it is difficult to claim that he significantly or surprisingly augments understandings already available in common law and comparative law perspectives. On the distinction between principles and precedents, for instance, the well-known work of Atiyah can be signaled, as indeed can Hart's now classic demarcation between settled law and its shifting penumbra. This is a matter of proportion, not critique.

Third, a question concerning the concept that distinguishes Deleuze's defence of *jurisprudence*: law's creative capacity for innovation. As he envisages this, the contingent intersection of empirical factors in a given case allows the possibility that a new and unforeseen, even unforeseeable outcome may emerge. It was not always already known that a hired taxi would transmute – legally speaking – from a private apartment on wheels to a place of public service access. The question is: does Deleuze's account of legal 'innovation' diverge from invocations of the 'event'?[19] The question is non-trivial: absent such divergence, the crucial distinction between legal habits of mind (*le droit*) and philosophical ones (*la loi*) would be levelled. The 'extension of singularities' would lose the positivity that secures it against the threat of reprise by philosophy. Law's 'innovation' would pale in the face of the 'breakthrough' experienced when an epiphanic 'event' allows the suitably groomed and faithful – as if freed from the shackles of the empirical world – a moment of unconditioned possibility to enjoy a prophetic glimpse into unthought being. Worse, positive law would be returned to a philosophical foundation. Conversely, if Deleuze understands law's 'innovation' as its front of resistance to philosophical capture, this marks a definitive divergence from such notions of 'event'. His point, I would argue, is absolutely not to reduce the law as 'extension of singularities' to a series of 'breakthrough' moments. Rather, it is to appreciate the inventiveness of the historically mutable and wholly immanent juridical order of *le droit*. The courts innovate, but that does not make them the setting for staging a philosophical 'event'. That said, the relation of Deleuze's notion of legal 'innovation' and 'event' remains contentious enough to provoke further argument.[20]

A fourth and final observation is properly 'clinical'. The dual defences of law that we have been considering invite a historical-juridical observation: modern western law does not adjudicate on actions of persons natural or moral in the name of a universally true judgment, be this judgment philosophical or theological, epistemological or moral. There is a political history to this. If legal judgments are binding and have social finality – if we now accept the law as final court of appeal – this is because in pluralist liberal States the law has come to stay within its own quite narrow set of procedures, categories and purposes.

Legal relations in the liberal State, Latour writes, 'hold and protect us – on condition that they remain on the surface, that they do not engage deeply, and that we too remain on the surface, not too deeply engaged, in order to follow and interpret them' (Latour 2002: 286). Hence the requisite 'attitude of indifference' that distinguishes the persona of the Conseil lawyers, allowing them to administer the particular cases that come before the court. Deleuze might not have explicitly characterised lawyers' enabling disposition as one of 'indifference'. Addressing the Armenians' case, though, his outrage at the practical ineffectivity of human rights as universalistic principle was immediately counterbalanced by his recommending a *jurisprudence* better able to deal with the concrete circumstances of their case. A *jurisprudence* of this sort comports an ethic that is situational. Its disposition is particularist and eminently casuistical, adjusting principle to case. Given such a disposition, can we take Deleuze's positive recommendation as extending to legal relations – prudent relations that 'do not engage deeply' – as these operate in the historical setting of the liberal State? Given his 'transgressive' philosophical reputation, this might seem a paradox too far. Yet, at stake are survival, sociability, *le vivre ensemble*.

## References

Badiou, A. (2007), 'The Event in Deleuze', *Parrhesia*, 2: 37–44.
Caenegem, R. C. van (1993), *Judges, Legislators and Professors. Chapters in European Legal History*, Cambridge: Cambridge University Press.
Cohen, F. S. (1935), 'Transcendental Nonsense and the Functional Approach', *Columbia Law Review*, 35.
de Sutter, L. (2009), *Deleuze: La pratique du droit*, Paris: Editions Michalon.

Deleuze, G. (1980), 'Spinoza. La puissance, le droit natural classique', 09/12/1980, available at www.deleuze.com
Deleuze, G. (1988), *Le pli: Leibniz et le baroque*, Paris: Minuit.
Deleuze, G. (1990), *Pourparlers. 1972–1990*, Paris: Minuit.
Deleuze, G. (2004), 'G comme Gauche', *L'Abécédaire de Gilles Deleuze*, DVD2, Montparnasse.
Deleuze, G. and Guattari, F. (1975), *Kafka: Pour une littérature mineure*, Paris: Minuit.
Deleuze, G. and F. Guattari (1980), *Mille plateaux : Capitalisme et schizophrénie 2*, Paris: Minuit.
Deleuze, G. and F. Guattari (1991), *Qu'est-ce que la philosophie?*, Paris: Minuit.
Derrida, J. (1992), 'Force of Law: The "Mystical Foundations of Authority"', in D. Cornell, M. Rosenfeld and D. G. Carslon (eds), *Deconstruction and the Possibility of Justice*, New York: Routledge.
Dworkin, R. (1986), *Law's Empire*, London: Fontana.
Dyzenhaus, D. (2006), *The Constitution of Law: Legality in a Time of Emergency*, Cambridge: Cambridge University Press.
Goodrich, P. (2004), 'Satirical Legal Studies: From the Legists to the *Lizard*', *Michigan Law Review*, 103 (3): 397–517.
Harman, G. (2009), *Prince of Networks: Bruno Latour and Metaphysics*, Melbourne: Re-Press.
Hoffmann, L. H., Lord (2009), 'The Universality of Human Rights', UK Judicial Studies Board Annual Lecture, <http://www.judiciary.gov.uk/media/speeches/2009/speech-lord-hoffman-19032009> (accessed 6 Feb 2012).
Iacub, M. (2008), *Par le trou de la serrure: Une histoire de la pudeur publique (XIXe-XXIe siècle)*, Paris: Fayard.
Latour, B. (2002), *La fabrique du droit: Une ethnographie du Conseil d'Etat*, Paris: Editions La Découverte.
Lefebvre, A. (2008), *The Image of Law: Deleuze, Bergson, Spinoza*, Stanford: Stanford University Press.
Schiavone, A. (2008), *Ius: L'invention du droit en Occident*, Paris: Belin.
Schlag, P. (1996), *Laying Down the Law: Mysticism, Fetishism, and the American Legal Mind*, New York: NYU Press.
Simpson, A. W. B. (1987), *Legal Theory and Legal History: Essays on the Common Law*, London: Hambledon Press.
Zourabichvili, F. (1996), 'Six Notes on the Percept: On the Relation Between the Critical and the Clinical', in P. Patton (ed.), *Deleuze: A Critical Reader*, Oxford: Blackwell.

# Notes

1. For a properly ironic view of claims to 'redeem' American law through 'perfectionist jurisprudences', see Schlag 1996: 10.
2. For a comprehensive exposition of Latour as metaphysician, see Harman 2009.
3. Goodrich (2004) offers an endearing scan of 'satirical legal studies', but makes no mention of Latour's ethnography.
4. 'Transcendental nonsense' is the title term in a famously parodic article in which Felix Cohen, a leading presence among the American Legal Realists, satirises the elevation of law into the abstractions of 'langdellian' legal science. See Cohen 1935.
5. The interview, conducted by Claire Parnet, is available on three DVDs. Topics are organised by letters of the alphabet, beginning with 'A for Animal'. The

comment on smoking in taxis occurs in '*G comme Gauche*' (see Deleuze 2004). Deleuze died in 1995.
6. Article 5 of the *Code civil* reads: 'Il est défendu aux juges de prononcer par voie de disposition générale et réglementaire sur les causes qui leur sont soumises.'
7. Deleuze pronounced these words when challenged by François Ewald and Raymond Bellour over his relative political quiescence after 1968 and regarding the role of human rights. In response, Deleuze (1990: 209–10) indicated that the French legal codes – civil and penal – were in crisis. He then offered these lapidary words on *jurisprudence*. Perhaps because his interlocutors evinced no reaction whatsoever, Deleuze makes no attempt to further gloss his statement.
8. On the 'critical' and the 'clinical', see Zourabichvili 1996.
9. This is not the place to attempt to resolve once and for all the problem of uncovering the English equivalents of *loi* and *droit*. So I'll persist with using the French terms. Simply to translate both terms by 'law' risks obliterating their crucial difference. Thus Lefebvre can write – misleadingly – of 'the negative and abstract structures of law and rights', even while correctly recognising that the 'concepts of institution and jurisprudence consistently appear as concrete and positive' in Deleuze's writings (Lefebvre 2008: 55).
10. The social relations of judges, legislators and law professors are not Deleuze's concern. Conversely, Raoul van Caenegem (1993) offers a neo-Weberian historical-sociological perspective on the three-way comparison between English, French and German systems of law. He characterises them as driven respectively by judges and case law, legislators and statute, and professors and 'book law'. Van Caenegem's account of codification as a 'weapon' against the judiciary is pertinent to Deleuze's stance towards the French system.
11. The idea of the common law as pragmatically proof against dogma invites a caution. Its most celebrated historical voice, the early modern jurist Sir Edward Coke, believed the law of England to be infallible because founded in godliness. More recently, its enthusiasts accord the common law a truly moral capacity as historical protector of essential liberties. See, for instance, Dyzenhaus 2006.
12. Seen in an 'axiomatic' perspective, a *pratique topique du droit* relates to a *pratique axiomatique du droit* in the manner that positive law might be conceived as incorporated in a higher or natural law of which it provides a more or less faithfully devolved actualisation. In an unpublished lecture on Spinoza – the key argument defined 'being' not in terms of 'essence' but as 'mode of existence' and '*puissance*' – Deleuze (1980) unmade the 'axiomatic' by means of 'a long parenthesis' on the variability of norms of natural law. Citing 'a precise moment in the history of thought' to show the historicity of would-be universal norms – the point of confrontation of Christianity and the traditions of Antiquity, he signalled Hobbes's radical inversion of 'classical' Ciceronian-Thomist natural law. The latter had identified law with *essence* – in the nature of things humans were rational – such that society was the realisation of this rational nature. Conversely, seeing the nature of things as a matter of rival *puissances*, Hobbes viewed society as that which came into being (*le devenir*) only when men's natural forces were constrained by a greater active force. He thus sectioned positive law from natural essence. Of course, Hobbes's axiom still grounds law in a higher power. However, this is no longer that of human rationality as universal law of nature; it is the will of the civil sovereign.
13. There is no consensus on the relations of human rights and common-law values. Against an 'antagonist' position in Hoffmann's style, for example, Dyzenhaus (2006) argues for a 'rule of law project' which perfectly harmonises a historical 'common-law constitutionalism' and a more recent international human rights law.

14. See Cass, 11 mars 1859, Dalloz 1959.1.626.
15. On these cases, see Iacub 2008: 95–114.
16. This 'liberation' is described in terms of artistic nude display, topless bathing and a restriction of legal constraint to the matter of exhibitionism. We might sum these repressive gestures up as a display of private parts in public places.
17. This 'purity' relates to the autonomy or 'autocthony' of the legal work. As such it is not to be equated either with Kelsen's normative 'pure theory' of law or with the axiomatic moral 'purity' envisioned by Dworkin: 'It falls to philosophers, if they are willing, to work out law's ambitions for itself, the purer form of law within and beyond the law we have' (Dworkin 1986: 407).
18. In relation to this non-subordination of 'singularity' to 'concept', and to Deleuze's observations on the historicity of would-be universal natural law, see note 9 above.
19. See, for instance, Jacques Derrida's celebrated lecture, 'Force of Law', in which he depicts the work of law in terms of an 'interruption' of the established legal order by an 'event', a 'moment of decision': 'And even if [the law] ... did give itself the time, all the time and the necessary facts about the matter, the moment of *decision as such*, always remains a finite moment of urgency and precipitation, since it must not be the consequence or the effect of this deliberation, since it always marks the interruption of the juridico- or ethico- or politico-cognitive deliberation that precedes it, that *must* precede it' (Derrida 1992: 26). Derrida then invites his audience to commune in recognising this 'event', this 'interruption', as the moment when a perpetually unrealised 'justice' that is always 'to come' (*à venir*) fleetingly intrudes into the temporality of mere historical law. The 'event', we could say, is made for this: a recapture of law by philosophy.
20. See, for a start, how Alain Badiou differentiates his own understanding of 'event' from that which he attributes to Deleuze.

# Postscript: A Brief Reflection on the Universality of Jurisprudence

*Laurent de Sutter and Kyle McGee*

Of all the paradoxes invented or seized upon by Gilles Deleuze as stimulants to thought – from the nonlinear temporality of eternal recurrence in Nietzsche and the linguistricks of Lewis Carroll to the very idea of constructing a metaphysics whose first principle is *becoming* – it is perhaps his partial appropriation of G. W. Leibniz's project of a universal jurisprudence that is the most important, most revealing, and even, perhaps, most shocking. The contours of the Deleuze/Leibniz relation remain fuzzy and underdetermined, and this essay harbours no pretension of having resolved this question. Rather than undertake to determine it once and for all, here, we would like to explore the relation – more from the vantage point of Deleuze's thought than that of Leibniz – along the three axes described above: importance, revelation and unlikelihood.

Has Deleuze 'appropriated' the Leibnizian fantasy of a universal science of law? As is customary in matters of paradox, the answer is: yes and no. Yes, in so far as Deleuze builds a vast conceptual matrix premised on the idea that, as we explain in this volume's introduction, *philosophy* needs to learn from *law*. In this sense, the universality of jurisprudence describes the need for philosophy to take seriously the unprecedented, the radically unique, the non-generalisable, or, more accurately, the singular case. All of that which escapes the logics of generality and particularity or model and instance must no longer suffer banishment from the halls of philosophy. This is the anti-Platonic gesture par excellence, and one that is, now as in the 1960s when it first found its way into the elite universities of postwar Europe, hotly contested (see Badiou 2009: 381–7). Let us interrogate this gesture more closely, hoping, if faintly, that doing so will offer grounds for negotiation with the militant (some would rather say: dogmatic) philosophy of the Idea that, together with Deleuze's metaphysics, composes the heart of the contemporary situation of thought.

In *Qu'est-ce que la philosophie?* Deleuze and Félix Guattari claim that the highest exercise of philosophical invention can be captured in a few words: wedding concept to singularity.[1] We will suggest that this – a claim finally given rigour and clarity in that final collaborative text but apparent in Deleuze's early studies of Hume and especially Bergson, in the ontology of difference, and throughout *Capitalisme et schizophrénie* – is a fundamentally *juridical*, even *lawyerly* kind of exercise. How so? To craft a concept tailored to a singularity entails that that concept will be no larger or more extensive than that singularity, and will not be transportable, will not speak to problems outwith the narrow confines of the irreducibly singular case before the philosopher. To every event its unique concept. The most that can be said is that concepts created in other contexts can guide, in an ad hoc fashion, the development of new ones. As a philosopher, you will never encounter the same singularity again, thus you will never subsume the new case under the rule of the old; instead, you will chart a new path into the problem, you will codify the singularity before you with its own philosophical construction (or you will propagate *doxa*, hatred of thought). As Philippe Pignarre and Isabelle Stengers argue, 'An event is not reproducible, but it is possible to explore the possibilities of bringing about its repetition, which is risky and different every time' (Pigarre and Stengers 2011: 133). They thus speak of 'recipes' in politics and law rather than strategies or theories. And this is precisely the practice of the advocate: the case before her calls for its own 'recipe', and while bits of argument are constantly recycled and prior cases repeated in citation, the singular kernel of the case is not compromised as long as the lawyer's recipe, what practitioners call a 'theory of the case' (*theory*, here having a distinctively pragmatic charge), clasps tightly to it. Taken to its limits, this proposition operates a becoming: philosophy soon finds itself practising a kind of case-law. In this way, *universal jurisprudence* competes with *transcendental empiricism* as the best descriptor of Deleuze's philosophy as a whole, prompting a serious revaluation of the relation between metaphysics and law as well as Deleuze and Leibniz. (Take note, however, that philosophy constructs concepts while law constructs principles; the wrinkle, the fold introduced by rethinking the vector of becoming between law and philosophy is that, as universal jurisprudence, philosophy learns to use the principle to create conceptual assemblages.)

How is this appropriation of Leibniz's universal jurisprudence arguably the most important paradox grasped by Deleuze, more important than even Nietzsche's eternal return? First, how is it paradoxical? It is in so far as Leibniz envisioned the universality of jurisprudence to consist in a calculative apparatus of moral thought together with a theory of universal justice as unconditional benevolence,[2] but when recruited by Deleuze, it becomes something decidedly different and even contradictory vis-à-vis Leibniz's formula. If the universality of jurisprudence masquerades as a cover for the illegitimate extension and decontextualisation of localised rationalities (like that of modern legal reasoning) or principles (like conventional moral and legal precepts, such as the inviolability of property), Leibniz's fantastic and hegemonic project is well and truly done for – and quite rightly. (And this is the 'no' component of our answer.) For Deleuze, universal jurisprudence describes the philosophical exercise of tailoring concepts to events as they emerge, which is precisely *not* what Leibniz's jurisprudence seeks to do – yet Leibniz himself made this move possible. Crucial to this formulation is the *lawyerly*, as distinguished from the *judicial*, practice of philosophy. Deleuze envisions the philosopher not as judge, but as lawyer – which is to say, as *advocate*. And here Deleuze aligns with Leibniz, who similarly thought himself always engaged in advocacy, taking sides and making a case – thus the importance, in Leibniz, of the diplomatic rhetoric of harmony. Deleuze's friend Michel Serres expresses the point well: 'The philosopher is not a judge; if he is a judge, a critic, he never produces anything, he only kills' (Serres 1995: 98). The expression 'making a case' is apropos: *La pratique du droit* is launched by the making, the fabrication, of a case. Too often, legal philosophy imagines that a case is something transparent, given and unproblematic. Instead, Deleuze challenges legal philosophy to shed this judicial prejudice and attend to the element of advocacy through which cases are shaped and constructed. We admit to a certain partiality in this question because we are lawyers, but this particular gesture seems to us more important than the others in understanding and thus in working with Deleuze's thought.

What does this reveal about Deleuze's thinking? By foregrounding the jurisprudential dimension of Deleuze's thought, what obscure areas become illumined? Naturally a longer study would be more appropriate for this question, and several essays collected in this volume have responded in their own ways, but we can offer the outlines of our own perspective. One difficult area that becomes more tractable by this gesture is mentioned in this volume's introduction: the movement from *critique* to *clinique*, and the subservience of the former to the latter. As François Zourabichvili suggested, the clinical irrefragably takes on an evaluative posture – and this has always been the alternative way forward proposed in Deleuze's polemics against judgment (Zourabichvili 1996). Though Deleuze summons examples from medical practice to illustrate the nature of *clinique* in his study of Sacher-Masoch and the later essays in *Critique et clinique*, lawyers too work in this way: presented with a set of facts offered by a subjectively invested source (symptoms) and a store of legal texts (practical knowledge), the lawyer is tasked to construct a theory for the just disposition of the case (diagnosis) and to argue its merits (treatment). There is no judgment at work here, only careful evaluation. The resulting ethical framework is fluid instead of rigid, situational rather than doctrinaire, embedded and affective rather than a priori and intellectualist. The ethics of *clinique*, however, is no longer the most pertinent question in this connection. Instead, we can take things in a new direction by advancing this hypothesis: having arrived at the point where philosophy has convincingly learned from law (having become a universal jurisprudence), it is time that the question is made to shift about and turn over on itself. That is to say, that universal jurisprudence offers something new to law.

Philosophy can offer only philosophical somethings, of course, and law, ever intolerant of pure theory, will have to make do with that. On the question of *clinique*, however, philosophy has a particularly valuable something to offer law. We must recall first that Deleuze never abandoned, and indeed fought for, *truth*; what he rejected, in good pragmatist fashion, was *the True*. The True would be a final state or completed Form and so also a condition of utter closure. The being of the True is that of a problem finally solved, a dried-up flow, a matter, thus, of no concern. The question of truth in Deleuze is problematic and we do not intend to weigh in on its concrete content at present.[3] Only note that, orientated as a universal practice of jurisprudence, philosophy can finally grasp law as something other than a handmaiden to politics or economy, namely, as a site for the materialisation of truths. We must recall that little phrase of Deleuze and Guattari's that has been so very important for Isabelle Stengers, among others: 'Not a relativity of truth but, on the contrary, a truth of the relative' (Deleuze and Guattari 1994: 130). To play interpreter, what this means in the present case, we may suggest, is that the interiority of a practice – of the sciences, of philosophy, of art, yes, but also of law, of medicine, of politics – comprises the only resources needed to carry out its projects, its applications, its inventions. It is not necessary – it is in fact misleading – to have recourse to explanatory principles that have taken root and matured under the auspices of other practices, which subject themselves to other constraints, than the one at hand. We have already heard in this volume David Saunders's impassioned cry against appeals to extralegal transcendences, 'external profundities' – religious and moral axioms, for instance – as means of justifying or rationalising or explaining legalities, and here we amplify it. The truth of the relative specifies, to invoke Bruno Latour's lexicon, the differences in and indeed the incommensurability of the unique sets of felicity conditions that distinct practices have progressively engendered. Translations between orders of practice are not outlawed – on the contrary, such transversal communications are the lifeblood of a practice – but explanation by appeal to another Court certainly is. In this way Deleuze can be seen to offer space for specifically juridical truths – and this reopens the question of *lex contra jus*. Let's briefly unpack how this occurs before taking up the third axis mentioned at the outset.

Philosophy as universal jurisprudence, practised in the mode of *clinique*, presupposes or enacts a bi-directional relationship of becoming between law and philosophy. We have seen the outlines of the becoming-law of philosophy, and the becoming-philosophy of law is now before us. Returning to the crucial disjunction between judgment and evaluation, we can say that the natural law tradition in jurisprudence and moral theory, for all its faults, got at least one thing right: *law is always at least two*. No unimpeachable, unintelligible and excessive standard (*jus*) stands above *lex*, to be sure: among other objections, it is difficult to conjure a more offensive exercise of judgment in law than this – one that is, moreover, heavily dependent on such 'external profundities' as Nature's moral code! The relation is of an altogether different nature. Schematically, we should say that *jus* inhabits or insists in the laws and in legal processes, legal history, and concrete cases. *Jus* or *droit* connotes this force or this structure of force, making the philosophical basis for any embedded evaluative (clinical) study of legality as well as the very stuff of legal practice in the service of justice. In this way, *lex* (or *loi*) itself becomes a site or a platform for the truths of *jus* (or *droit*) to materialise. (Its intelligibility remains uncertain, but the logic of sense, which is not exactly a linguistic trajectory as some have suggested [Badiou 2009: 386], may be a good point of entry to determine this, especially if *lex* is taken for the legal text.) No longer set in contraposition, *lex* and *jus* are thus freed to entertain a more productive relation, one of inhabitancy, envelopment and impulsion, rather than externality, vain approximation and condemnation. The legal text – judicial opinion, legislative memorandum, administrative policy proposal – may be a dissimulative purification meant to obscure or shield from view the practical invention at the heart of *vincula juris*, but this exercise in saying the law is also just as much a part of the *doing* of law as the argument and advocacy, or the slow rhythms of deliberation and hesitation, or again the gradual composition of the principle out of the matter of the event-become-case. What should not be missed in the reopening of the *lex/jus* problem is that *jus* comes to signify not a juridico-normative view from nowhere but a principle of variation situated at the heart of what we register as legality.

After the revelation comes the shockwave. In what sense is this particular philosophical deterritorialisation unlikely, upsetting, maybe, for some, astonishing? For one thing, Deleuze is often portrayed as a Spinozist, and any historian of ideas knows that Leibniz and Spinoza come together as harmoniously as oil and water. Spinoza – that prince of philosophers, that necessitarian moralist, that demagogue of might[4] – would have nothing to do with a universal jurisprudence. To describe Deleuze's philosophy as *primarily* that should thus evoke some consternation on the part of readers that have become comfortable with the image of Deleuze as a neo-Spinozist of sorts. But there is a more profound sense in which a Deleuzian universal jurisprudence may overturn or shatter ossified images of this philosopher and of philosophy more generally.

Let us return to Leibniz. We said above that Leibniz's idea of the universality of jurisprudence consists partly in the distillation of moral propositions – such as 'live honourably' – that would govern the right conduct of any divine or mortal being endowed with reason (Leibniz 1969: 421–4). This is one basis on which Leibniz calls his jurisprudence universal, often thought to be the sole or primary one. But Leibniz writes the following: 'As we are divinely taught by Christ, all our hairs are numbered, and not even a drink of water is given to the thirsty in vain; thus nothing is neglected in the commonwealth of the universe. It is on this ground that *justice* is called *universal*' (Leibniz 1969: 423). What should not be missed in this declaration is the implicit reference to Leibniz's metaphysics of substance, according to which every distinct substance is defined by a complete concept from which all that has or will ever be attributable to that substance can be derived (Leibniz 1969: 303–30): hence 'nothing is neglected in the commonwealth of the universe' inasmuch as all things embody a complete individual concept. The complete concept of a substance unites its past and its future and captures, in the language of *The Logic of Sense*, the Event of all the events it suffers, encompassing a space of virtuality (Leibniz 1969: 307) sufficient to render implicit the contingency of all that happens. Leibniz never claims that the vocation of the philosopher is to formulate complete concepts for individual substances; rather, these concepts serve as explanatory principles in Leibniz's ontology, epistemology and theodicy.

Deleuze seizes a line of flight in this logico-metaphysical articulation and radicalises the complete concept doctrine. Specifically, he abandons the substantialism that characterises Leibniz's approach and opts for a processual account of the doctrine. In Leibniz, of course, events qualify substances and shape their individuality in accordance with a complete concept – this is why Leibniz is 'the first great theoretician of the event' (Deleuze 1990: 196). For Deleuze, events are primary and generative: there is no substance taking shape in events, only states of relative stability through which events pass. An individual is a slice or phase of becoming, not a composed unity. In this connection Deleuze's innovation amounts to granting full-fledged conceptuality to events, similar to the way in which Leibniz grants conceptuality to individual substances.

The event – and the Event – is a subject of dispute in the relation between Deleuze and Badiou, and in ongoing debates about the very nature of speculative philosophy. The only point we want to make in this connection has to do with the contemporary image of Deleuze as furnished by Badiou; it is here that Deleuze's appropriation of Leibniz's universal jurisprudence may appear particularly unlikely, as this is inconsistent with that image, which is quickly becoming the conventional and uncritical adjudication on the Deleuze case. How so? Badiou objects to the transitivity and the ontological univocity of difference found in the theory of the Event, according to which all localisable events are shards of the cosmic Event determined as the intensity cutting between affirmation and negation, being and nothing, *de facto* and *de jure*, posteriority and priority, body and language. This Event is a One, on Badiou's reading, which is to say an illegitimate conjuration of the Undifferentiated under the guise of the permanence of becoming. However, as we have seen, the universality of jurisprudence, the practice of *clinique*, does not admit into conceptual construction anything beyond the elements of the singular case. While a fuller answer to Badiou's objection than can be advanced here is needed, the starting point for such an answer surely lies in the idea of universality informing Deleuze's jurisprudence. It is a peculiar and paradoxical universality: that of the event itself in all its inconsistency and its adventurousness.

A further question attendant to this one is that of the *relationality* of the event. For Deleuze, as for Whitehead before him, the event is at once radically discrete and fully relational. Its singularity, its discontinuity and its unforeseeability are as insistent as its connection, extension and prolongation into the localities and vicinities of other events. Stengers' point about the extension of the event in Whitehead is just as pertinent to the event in Deleuze: 'A discerned event always has an extension because it includes or comprises others, and it testifies to the extension of other events that include or comprise it' (Stengers 2011: 45). Events continuously enter into and transform the continuum of the Event, the 'structure' or virtual 'Whole' that resists totalisation and finality. The Event is an Adventure. The insertion of an event into this relational Whole, its inscription on this immanent plane, endows it with its unique principle. A case for a universal jurisprudence is nothing but an event endowed with a principle, a principle derived only from the extension of the event, a principle of mobility impelling the Adventure. This is a further meaning of universality, one which moreover frees Deleuze's universal jurisprudence from the clutches of parochialism that has compromised the concept of the case in other quarters.

In summary, Deleuze's universal jurisprudence contains two irreducible vectors: philosophy learns from law to take the case seriously, to tailor or 'wed' concept to singularity; and correlatively, law appears, under its aegis, as a locus for the materialisation of truths, specifically juridical truths, and this reopens the question of *jus* in relation to *lex*. By taking Deleuze's Leibnizian heritage as our principle, moreover, it becomes possible to problematise contemporary thought's reception of Deleuze and to invent once more an essential untimeliness for a new time and a new generation.

# References

Badiou, A. (2000), *Deleuze: The Clamor of Being*, trans. L. Burchill, Minneapolis: University of Minnesota Press.
Badiou, A. (2009), *Logics of Worlds: Being and Event II*, trans. A. Toscano, New York: Continuum.
Deleuze, G. (1990), *The Logic of Sense*, trans. M. Laster, ed. C. Boundas, New York: Columbia University Press.
Deleuze, G. (1993), *The Fold: Leibniz and the Baroque*, trans. T. Conley, Minneapolis: University of Minnesota Press.
Deleuze, G. and F. Guattari (1994), *What is Philosophy?*, trans. H. Tomlinson and G. Burchell, New York: Columbia University Press.
Grua, G. (1953), *Jurisprudence universelle et théodicée selon Leibniz*, Paris: PUF.
Leibniz, G.W. (1969), *Philosophical Papers and Letters*, 2nd edn, trans. and ed. L. Loemker, Dordrecht: Reidel.
Leibniz, G.W. (1985), *Theodicy: Essays on the Goodness of God, the Freedom of Man, and the Origin of Evil*, trans. E. M. Huggard, ed. A. M. Farrer, La Salle: Open Court.
Leibniz, G.W. (2006), *The Shorter Leibniz Texts: A Collection of New Translations*, trans. L. Strickland, New York: Continuum.
Pignarre, P. and I. Stengers (2011), *Capitalist Sorcery: Breaking the Spell*, trans. Andrew Goffey, New York: Palgrave Macmillan.
Riley, P. (1996), *Leibniz' Universal Jurisprudence: Justice as the Charity of the Wise*, Cambridge, MA: Harvard University Press.

Serres, M. (1995), *Genesis*, trans. G. James and J. Nielson, Ann Arbor: University of Michigan Press.
Stengers, I. (2011), *Thinking with Whitehead: A Free and Wild Creation of Concepts*, trans. M. Chase, Cambridge, MA: Harvard University Press.
Zourabichvili, F. (1996), 'Six Notes on the Percept (On the Relation between the Critical and the Clinical)', trans. I. H. Grant, in P. Patton (ed.), *Deleuze: A Critical Reader*, Oxford: Blackwell.

# Notes

1. See Deleuze and Guattari 1994. In *Le pli*, Deleuze had spoken of a 'honeymoon' of concept and singularity, which he dubs 'the Leibnizian revolution' (Deleuze 1993: 67).
2. Key texts in which Leibniz develops his *jurisprudence universelle* include his famous 'Preface to the "Codex Iuris Gentium Diplomaticus"', in Leibniz 1969: 421–4; Leibniz 1985; and 'The True Piety' in Leibniz 2006: 164–5. (The preface to the *Codex* is also retranslated in Strickland's volume, but we continue to prefer Loemker's.) In France, this trajectory in Leibniz is given an authoritative interpretation, with which Deleuze was familiar (having cited it in *Le pli*), in Grua 1953. In English, Patrick Riley has recently treated the subject with scholarly precision and an elegant eclecticism worthy of Leibniz himself in Riley 1996. Both Grua's and Riley's interpretative grids differ rather dramatically from our own, of course, and so we object to much in these books (e.g., their theism, Grua's moral mathesis, Riley's amplification of Platonic elements). But we cannot recommend them enough to the jurisprude of either Leibnizian or Deleuzian universality.
3. Some of Badiou's most forceful criticisms of Deleuze emerge in this context (see Badiou 2000: 54–66). However, Badiou's primary criticism on this front – namely, that Deleuze's only notion of truth is the power of the false as detailed in *Cinema 2* – rings hollow. Badiou confuses cinematic truth, which does indeed take the form of the narrative power of the false, with truth 'in general'. Deleuze does not deploy a general idea of truth (and, rejecting the Platonic form of the True, how could he?) but, consistent with his universal jurisprudence of the case, sets up a frame of reference in which local elements of production, cancelled in the process of actualisation, can be recovered in their singular truths. There is not, then, a general idea of truth, but a philosophical practice of truth whose compass extends only to the circumference of the case. In ethics, this is called counter-actualisation; in politics, it is the analysis of collective cohesion or consistency (stratification, striation, miraculation, etc.); in ontology, the procedure of dramatisation; and so on. Hence the truth of the relative that we encounter in *What is Philosophy?*.
4. Actually, we quite like Spinoza. The rhetoric is for a contrastive effect.

# Notes on Contributors

**Laurent de Sutter**
Laurent de Sutter is FWO Senior Researcher in Legal Theory at Vrije Universiteit Brussel. He also teaches at Facultés Universitaires Saint-Louis (Brussels) and has been Visiting Honorary Research Fellow at Benjamin N. Cardozo School of Law (New York). He is the author of four books, including *Deleuze: La pratique du droit* (Deleuze: The Practice of Law) (Michalon, 2009) and *Contre l'érotisme* (Against Eroticism) (La Musardine, 2011). He is the editor of the 'Travaux Pratiques' series at Presses Universitaires de France.

**Peter Goodrich**
Peter Goodrich is Professor of Law and Director of Law and Humanities at the Benjamin N. Cardozo School of Law, New York. He is the managing editor of *Law and Literature* and serves on the editorial board of *Law and Critique*. Recent books include (with Mariana Valverde) *Nietzsche and Legal Theory: Half-Written Laws* (Routledge, 2006); and (with Lior Barshack and Anton Schutz) *Law, Text, Terror* (Routledge, 2006). His most recent book is *Laws of Love: A Brief Historical and Practical Manual* (Palgrave-Macmillan, 2006).

**Alexandre Lefebvre**
Alexandre Lefebvre is Lecturer in the School of Philosophical and Historical Inquiry (SOPHI) and the School of Social and Political Sciences (SSPS) at the University of Sydney. He is the author of *The Image of Law: Deleuze, Bergson, Spinoza* (Stanford University Press, 2008), and the editor, with Melanie White, of *Bergson, Politics, and Religion* (Duke University Press, forthcoming). He is Associate Editor of *Contemporary Political Theory*.

### Lissa Lincoln
Lissa Lincoln is Lecturer in Law and Literature, critical legal theory, literary scandal and censorship, critical theory, French literature, and composition at the American University of Paris. She has published numerous papers on these topics, and co-edited (with Mark Orme and Christine Margerisson) *Camus in the Twenty-first Century: A Collection of Critical Essays* (Rodopi Press, 2006). Her first book, *Albert Camus: Legal Discourse and the Problem of Judgment*, is forthcoming.

### Kyle McGee
Kyle McGee practises law in the US and has published articles in law and philosophy in several journals. His first book, *The Normativity of Networks: Bruno Latour*, is forthcoming.

### James MacLean
James MacLean is Lecturer in Law at the University of Southampton, England. His writings have appeared in the *International Journal for the Semiotics of Law* and the *Journal of the China University of Political Science and Law*. His first book, *Rethinking Law as Process: Creativity, Novelty, Change* (Taylor & Francis 2011), was recently published.

### Nathan Moore
Nathan Moore is Lecturer in Law at Birkbeck College, University of London, England. He has published numerous articles on Law and Literature, Law and Film, and Gilles Deleuze's theory of law in *Cardozo Law Review*, *Griffith Law Review*, *Law and Literature*, *Law and Critique*, amongst others. He recently passed his doctorate, the thesis of which focuses upon the interrelation of property and subjectivity through the lens of the work of Deleuze.

### Paul Patton
Paul Patton is Professor of Philosophy in the School of History and Philosophy at the University of New South Wales, Sydney, Australia. One of the most distinguished Deleuze scholars in the world, he has published numerous books, including *Deleuze: A Critical Reader* (Blackwell Publishing, 1996); *Deleuze and the Political* (Routledge, 2000); and *Deleuzian Concepts: Philosophy, Colonization, Politics* (Stanford University Press, 2010).

### Penelope Pether
Penelope Pether is Professor of Law at the Villanova University School of Law, Pennsylvania. She is a general editor of *Law and Literature* and

serves on the editorial boards of *Law and Critique* and *Social Semiotics*. Her work on judicial practices in US federal courts has been pathbreaking. Her recent publications appear in *Law and the Humanities: An Introduction* (Cambridge University Press, 2009), *On Philosophy in American Law* (Cambridge University Press, 2009), and journals including the *Stanford Law Review*, *William & Mary Bill of Rights Journal*, and *Washington and Lee Law Review*.

### Andreas Philippopoulos-Mihalopoulos

Andreas Philippopoulos-Mihalopoulos is Professor of Law and Theory at the University of Westminster, England, where he is also co-director of The Westminster International Law and Theory Centre, Director of Doctoral Research Training, and the Staff and Graduate Students Research Seminars Convenor. He is the author of *Absent Environments: Theorising Environmental Law and the City* (Routledge-Cavendish, 2007) and *Niklas Luhmann: Law, Justice, Society* (Routlege, 2009). In 2010, he was awarded the Law Teacher of the Year Award.

### David Saunders

David Saunders is Professor Emeritus, Griffith University, as well as Adjunct Professor Socio-legal Research Centre, Griffith University Law School. He is the author and editor of many books, including *Authorship and Copyright* (Routledge, 1992), *On Pornography: Literature, Sexuality and Obscenity Law* (with I. Hunter and D. Williamson) (Macmillan and St Martin's Press, 1993), and *Anti-lawyers: Religion and the Critics of Law and State* (Routledge, 1997).

### Marc Schuilenburg

Marc Schuilenburg is Lecturer in Law at the Vrije Universiteit Amsterdam, the Netherlands. He is the author, with A. de Jong, of *Mediapolis: Populaire cultuur en de stad* (010-Publishers, 2006); and, *Mediapolis: Popular Culture and the City* (010-Publishers, 2006); and (with J. Blad, M. Hildebrandt, K. Rozemond, K. and P. Van Calster) *Governing Security Under the Rule of Law* (Eleven International Publishing, 2010). He is also one of the editors of the best-seller *Deleuze Compendium* (Boom, 2009).

# Index

actual/virtual see virtual/actual
adjudication, 6, 156, 185–6, 192, 194
adventure, 210–11
advocate, 6, 205–8
affect, 10, 11, 15, 25–8, 35, 39, 61, 97, 115, 134–5, 139–40, 148
Agamben, Giorgio, 33
Albrecht-Crane, Christa, 87
Algerian War, 171
Alliez, Eric, 116
American Revolution, 26
amity, 9, 32
angelology, 40
Ansell-Pearson, Keith, 135
Arendt, Hannah, 56
Aristotle, 38
artisan, 11–12, 141–8
Atiyah, Patrick, 199
Avogadro, Amedeo, 112–13
axiomatic of capital, 6, 17, 27
axiomatic/topical see topical/axiomatic

Badiou, Alain, 4, 8, 51, 131, 203, 204, 208, 210, 212
baroque, 35
Barthes, Roland, 181
Beccaria, Cesare, 111–12, 116, 124
Bellour, Raymond, 3, 17, 20, 202
Bene, Carmelo, 147
Bergen, Véronique, 184
Bergson, Henri, 5, 9, 38, 55–68, 80, 133–4, 141, 158–60, 166–7
Blair, Tony, 146
Blanchot, Maurice, 171, 181–4
body without organs, 94–5, 104–5
Bogue, Ronald, 85
Bourdieu, Pierre, 76, 187
Boutang, Pierre-André, 1
Braidotti, Rosi, 70, 102
Brighouse, Harry, 76

Caenegem, Raoul van, 202
Camus, Albert, 12, 169–84
care, 52–4
Carroll, Lewis, 204

Cartari, Vincenzo, 46
case law, 2, 4, 13, 162–7, 185–203, 205
casuistry see case law
Châtelet, François, 143
Cicero, 3, 5, 7, 9, 202
clinical legal theory, 3, 5, 7, 9, 13, 76, 188–202, 206–7
Cohen, Felix, 201
Coke, Sir Edward, 43, 202
conceptual personae, 6, 39
Connolly, William, 24–5
Conrad, Joseph, 79
Constable, Marianne, 80
constitutionalism, 28, 50, 138, 202
control society, 12, 27, 145–8
Cornier, Henriette, 121, 131
counter-actualisation, 9, 15, 27, 53, 64, 212
counter-effectuation see counter-actualisation
Crawford, Adam, 145
Critchley, Simon, 47
critique, 3, 4, 6, 7, 9, 15, 69–87, 180, 188–203, 206
cruelty, 86–7
Cuban, Larry, 75
Cultural Revolution, 131
Cuvier, Georges, 118

dark precursor, 32, 41, 43
Daryl Slack, Jennifer, 87
Day, Kate Nace, 74–6, 78–80
death, 25, 28, 52, 114, 121, 174, 182, 184
Defoe, Daniel, 92
DeLanda, Manuel, 93–4, 130–1
democracy, 22–4, 26–8, 50, 73, 80–1, 157
Derrida, Jacques, 9, 39, 203
Descartes, René, 4, 35, 127
desire, 7, 18, 22, 28, 31, 40–2, 44, 62–3, 78, 85, 93–4, 103, 116, 123
Detmold, Michael, 155–6, 158
Dewey, John, 73
Dickens, Charles, 52, 54, 62
Donzelot, Jacques, 145
Dorfman, Ariel, 82
Dosse, François, 1, 37, 46
droit/loi see loi/droit

Index 217

Due, Reidar, 171
Dulaure, Antoine, 16
Dumézil, Georges, 139
duration, 11, 134–5, 141
Durkheim, Emile, 11, 57, 113–14, 118–19, 124, 128, 130
Dworkin, Ronald, 203

ecceity *see* haecceity
ecology, 101
Einstein, Albert, 67
*élan vital*, 62–3
empiricism, 69
environmental law, 101
ethics, 35, 39, 49, 73, 75–6, 86, 200, 206–7, 212
Euripides, 77, 79
euthanasia, 25
Ewald, François, 3, 17, 20, 145, 202

falsity, 87, 212
feminine/feminism, 37, 70, 102
Fitzgerald, F. Scott, 115
Foucault, Michel, 17, 30, 38, 44, 49, 71, 117, 125, 131, 169–71, 183–4
freedom, 29, 44, 50, 135, 147, 193–4
French Revolution, 26, 65, 131, 193
friend/friendship, 32–44, 49, 206

Gaber, Paula, 74
Galilei, Galileo, 99
Gandal, Keith, 115
Garland, David, 145
Gatens, Moira, 90–1
genetically modified crops, 102
Geoffroy Saint-Hilaire, Étienne, 118
geography, 10, 90–110
Grosz, Elizabeth, 160
Grua, Gaston, 212
Guantánamo Bay, 10, 70, 77, 80–7
Günther, Klaus, 157

Habermas, Jürgen, 22–3, 28, 157–8
habitus, 76
haecceity, 52, 55, 101
Haraway, Donna, 102
Hart, H. L. A., 199
Hayles, Katherine, 102
Heidegger, Martin, 41
Hobbes, Thomas, 26, 116, 124, 133, 202
Homer, 35, 42
homosexuality, 193
hooks, bell, 70
hope, 93
human rights, 4, 6, 10, 15–19, 28–9, 48–68, 191–2, 196–8, 200, 202
Hume, David, 2, 11, 79–80, 111–12, 116–17
humour, 3, 5, 7, 36, 41, 44, 46
Humphrey, John, 56
Hutchinson, Allen, 73

Iacub, Marcela, 193–6, 203
idiot, 9
Ignatieff, Michael, 56

image, 6, 7, 9, 11, 12, 33–45, 105–6, 134–48
institution, 7, 11, 12, 79, 111–31
institutional theory of law, 12, 161–7
instrumentalism, 1, 5
interpretation, 9, 32–44, 153, 176
irony, 3, 7, 11, 36, 38, 40, 188, 201
*ius/lex see lex/ius*

Jackson, Bernard, 154
Jim Crow laws, 75
*jouissance*, 37, 194
judge, 6, 20, 25, 80, 143–67, 173, 177, 187–8, 202, 206
judgment, 1, 3, 4, 5, 12, 25, 42, 43, 86, 157, 169, 172, 174–83, 185–6, 200, 206, 208
Jung, Carl, 103
jurisprudence, 2–3, 15, 18, 20–3, 26–9, 30–1, 32, 38, 52, 80, 100, 106–10, 111, 128, 185–203, 204–12
justice, 9, 10, 11, 18, 22–3, 26, 28–9, 39, 41, 64–5, 70, 72, 78, 80, 86, 90–110, 174–83, 197–8, 203, 206, 208
Justinian, 47, 191

Kafka, Franz, 2, 6, 7, 12, 33, 46, 71–2, 172–3, 182, 184, 188
Kant, Immanuel, 6, 7, 57, 117, 122, 157, 188–9
Kelsen, Hans, 133, 142, 203
Kierkegaard, Soren, 96
Koh, Harold, 77

Lacan, Jacques, 38, 46, 110
Langdell, Christopher Columbus, 71–2, 201
Lasswell, Harold, 76
Latour, Bruno, 13, 120, 185–203, 208
law and literature, 2, 9, 10, 12, 69–87, 172–84
law and philosophy, 1–14, 33, 38, 42–3, 186
law practice *see* practice of law
League of Nations, 55
legal education, 10, 69–87, 166, 191
legislation, 6, 26, 64–5, 77, 157, 208
Leibniz, G. W., 4, 6, 7, 144, 198, 204–12
Levi, Edward, 162–7
Lévy-Bruhl, Lucien, 59
*lex/ius*, 208–12
Lidner, Richard, 37–8
Locke, John, 26
*logos*, 11, 98–103, 107, 110
*loi/droit*, 3–6, 188–203, 204–12
love, 2, 10, 33, 42, 46, 52–66, 84, 87, 123, 173
Loysel, Antoine, 43
Lucretius, 79–80

MacCormick, Neil, 153–8
Malebranche, Nicolas, 4
Marrati, Paolo, 68
Mascolo, Dionys, 38
McDougal, Myres, 76
Melville, Herman, 2, 6, 7, 184
Merleau-Ponty, Maurice, 170
Mertz, Elizabeth, 74–5
Miller, Flagg, 82
minor literature, 10, 12, 86, 170–1, 181–2

molar/molecular, 9–11, 28, 86–7, 94, 111–31
Morin, Edgar, 103
Murphy, Russell G8, 74–6, 78–80

Negri, Antonio, 20, 39, 46, 80
neoliberalism, 9, 10, 73
Nietzsche, Friedrich, 15, 21–2, 31, 79–80, 96, 117, 135, 148, 170, 188–90, 204–5
*nomos*, 11, 37, 42, 47, 98–103, 107
Nussbaum, Martha, 73, 77

Other-structure, 94–6

paradox, 103–5, 117, 165, 200, 204–6
parallelism, 61
Parnet, Claire, 1, 16, 18, 23, 31, 46, 111, 186, 196, 201
pedagogy *see* legal education
Pentagon, 82–3, 87
percept, 10, 97, 115
Perrière, Guillaume de, 41, 46
perspectivism, 117
philosophy and law *see* law and philosophy
Pignarre, Philippe, 205
Pinochet, Augusto, 82
Plato, 6, 119
poetry, 33, 35, 37, 41–4, 78, 81–7, 174–5, 181
political theology, 12, 133–4
posthumanism, 92, 97, 101–2
power of the false *see* falsity
practice of law, 3–7, 186–203, 204–12
prayer, 37
Prigogine, Ilya, 131
principle, 8
property, 26, 92, 101
Proust, Marcel, 2, 40
Pue, Wesley, 73, 76
punishment, 111–12

Rabinow, Paul, 115
Rancière, Jacques, 182, 184
Rawls, John, 22–3, 26, 31, 56
religion, 43–4, 50, 64, 177, 193, 198
Renault, Emmanuel, 174
rhizome, 12, 98–9, 102, 124, 159–61, 165–7
Ribots, Théodule, 123
Riley, Patrick, 212
Roman law, 6, 7, 190
Rorty, Richard, 60, 73
Rousseau, Jean-Jacques, 26, 133
Russell, Bertrand, 67

Sacher-Masoch, Leopold von, 2, 3, 6, 7, 184, 207
Sade, Marquis de, 6, 7, 110
Said, Edward, 69, 87
Sartre, Jean-Paul, 38, 169–73, 181, 184
satire, 40, 186–7, 197, 201
Schiavone, Aldo, 190–1, 193
Schmitt, Carl, 56, 133, 142
Schopenhauer, Arthur, 117
semiotics, 154
Serres, Michel, 206

Shakespeare, William, 77, 79, 147
Sidney, Sir Philip, 42, 47
Simpson, Brian, 191
slow learning, 35
Smith, Sean, 163–5
smooth space, 99–101, 103, 105–7, 140
society of control *see* control society
Socrates, 6
Sontag, Susan, 51
Soviet Revolution, 26
spatiality, 10, 90–110, 140, 160, 194–5
Spencer, Herbert, 59
Spinoza, Baruch, 61, 68, 79–80, 86, 100–1, 109, 134–6, 138, 148, 202, 209, 212
Stafford Smith, Clive, 80, 83–7
Stengers, Isabelle, 131, 205, 207, 210–11
Stivale, Charles, 40, 46
Stoicism, 4
suicide, 25, 114, 118
Swift, Adam, 76

Tarde, Gabriel, 11, 112, 118–31
terrorism, 77, 178
thermodynamics, 112
Thomas, Brook, 84
Threadgold, Terry, 78
topical/axiomatic, 7, 8, 13, 188–203, 206
*topos*, 93, 105
totalitarianism, 77, 84
Tournier, Michel, 10, 91–110
transcendental empiricism, 8, 205
truth, 43, 87, 117, 137, 159, 177–8, 207–8, 212
Twelve Tables, 43
Twining, William, 73
Tyack, David, 75

*Universal Declaration of Human Rights*, 54, 56
universal jurisprudence, 7, 144, 198, 204–12

Varro, 32
veil of ignorance, 23
Veyne, Paul, 7, 190
Vico, Giambattista, 9, 32–5, 38–43, 47
Virilio, Paul, 145
virtual/actual, 15–16, 27, 100
Vismann, Cornelia, 71
vitalism, 10, 100–3

war, 57–9, 63
Ward, Ian, 71–86
Weber, Max, 123, 202
Wenders, Wim, 148
Whitehead, Alfred North, 210
Wilkes, Gerry, 76, 78
Wilson, Woodrow, 55
Wood, Martin, 158

Yoshino, Kenji, 83

Žižek, Slavoj, 131
Zourabichvili, François, 202, 206

EU Authorised Representative:
Easy Access System Europe Mustamäe tee 50, 10621 Tallinn, Estonia
gpsr.requests@easproject.com


Printed and bound by CPI Group (UK) Ltd, Croydon, CR0 4YY
01/12/2025
02008469-0007